MTV -CYCLO PEDIA

MUSIC TELEVISION ®

MUSIC TELEVISION(R)

THIS IS A CARLTON BOOK

Text and design copyright © Carlton Books
Limited
"MTV: Music Television" and all related titles,
logos and characters are trademarks owned
and licensed for use by MTV Networks, a
division of Viacom International Inc.

MTV logo © 1997 MTV Networks, a division of
Viacom International Inc. All rights reserved.

1 2 3 4 5 6 7 8 9 10

This edition first published in 1997
by Carlton Books Limited

A CIP catalogue record for this book is
available from the British Library.

ISBN 1 85868 336 X

Project Editor: Lucian Randall
MTV Project Consultant: Clare Williams
Copy Editor: Mike Flynn
Project Art Direction: Zoë Maggs, Mark Lloyd
Designer: Steve Wilson
Picture Research: Charlotte Bush
Production: Sarah Schuman

MTV would like to give special thanks to the
following people:

Fleur Sarfaty, Peter Good, Harriett Brand,
Richard Evans, Richard Godfrey,
Geoff Mortimer, Elli Josephs, Jon Critchley,
Julia Sadd, Monique Eban, Tamsin Summers,
Sandra Keenan, Andrew Dell, Lisa Wood,
Graham Swan, Frances Naylor, Kate Copp,
Sophie Bywater, Svenja Geissmar,
Natalie Andre, Silke Super, Bernd Rathjen,
Peter Ruppert, Thierry Thouvenot,
Anna Skelton, George Annan, Jo Noirit,
Stefania Lazzaroni and Christina Beschi.

Printed in Spain

MTV MUSIC TELEVISION ® -CYCLO PEDIA

The Official MTV MUSIC TELEVISION ® Guide to the Hottest Bands, Stars, Events and Music

NICK DUERDEN
MOVERS & SHAKERS

IAN GITTINS
YEAR BY YEAR, DATABASE

SHAUN PHILLIPS
LEGENDS, WORLD OF MTV

CARLTON

Contents

Foreword 6

The Legends of MTV 8

PROFILES OF: Aerosmith, Bon Jovi, Janet Jackson, Michael Jackson, Madonna, George Michael, Nirvana, ♀, R.E.M., U2

Movers and Shakers 30

Who's **Who** in Pop, **A-Z** coverage of over 200 **top bands** and artists

Year by Year 136

The **best** albums, singles, gigs, events
and newcomers as featured on **MTV**

The World of  180

Inside info on MTV, including the legendary **Unplugged** series,
MTV Music Awards, cutting-edge animations, and station idents

Database 188

MTV **Award winners**; MTV's most played videos;
unplugged sessions

Index 191

Foreword

MTV remains something of an oddity in broadcasting: its strength as a global brand, alongside the **Cokes** and **Nikes** of this world, sets it apart from other TV stations.

MTV creates a constantly changing environment for every aspect of youth culture, **24 hours a day**, **seven days a week**. More than the programmes, more than the video clips themselves, it is the channel as a whole which has become a barometer of popular culture. The channel has never been designed to be viewed in the way that other, more traditional channels are, yet it has influenced the pace and presentation of television all over the world. And within that field of influence, MTV must continuously move ahead if it is to retain that **"edge"**.

MTV exists on many levels. It's literal, creative, hip - an integral feature of young **"lifestyles"**. It informs and entertains its viewers by acknowledging their diversity of interests and the changing trends within popular culture as a whole. But ultimately, the channel is all about music. The balance which we always strive to maintain, between Anglo-American and European music, sits comfortably within that overall diversity.

Europe, and indeed the world, has become a very different place since MTV first burst on to TV screens. **Internationalism** has been tempered by national pride and the rising importance of regional identities. If this is the future for **"culture"** - the future for us all - then it is the future for MTV. **Digital technology** has allowed us to programme MTV more selectively and make the channel even more regionally relevant for viewers everywhere. Strangely, that fragmentation actually enhances our international perspective.

However, there's a real danger of over-intellectualizing these issues and MTV's **pivotal position** within popular culture attracts more scrutiny and deconstruction than is really necessary. If you watch MTV then you know what we do - and how we do it. And you probably know how to enjoy yourself too. Just keep moving in that direction - we're right beside you...

Brent Hansen
President, Chief Executive, MTV Europe

OK - let's get this straight. Every boy out there is **Crispian Mills**, **Liam Gallagher**, **David Duchovny**, **Stephen Dorff** or **Leonardo di Caprio** - and every girl out there is a **Spice Girl**, **Juliette Binoch** or **Jenny McCarthy**. You are whoever you want to be. That's what MTV is all about: **you**.

MTV isn't just your favourite music station or TV lifestyle magazine. It isn't your standard fashion mag. And it certainly isn't your usual music magazine. It's all that - and more.

Before I ever joined MTV and was working for other TV channels I was an avid viewer - because I loved the fresh approach and the constant supply of new ideas which MTV always comes up with to inspire its audience. Then, when I joined MTV, I knew that I had to maintain and develop those defining characteristics - irreverence, creativity, innovation and the very best in music.

We've created this book to provide you with an insight into the world of MTV. That world is dominated by **music** but it's also inhabited by fashion, movies, sport and **fun**. And you're a native too. **Enjoy...**

Rachel Purnell
Senior Vice President, Executive Director,
Networks, MTV Europe

Legends of MTV — Music Television ®

Video didn't kill the radio star but it did change the way people think about music forever. If you find it difficult to believe, try humming George Michael's 'Faith' without thinking immediately of that image of the sun-streaked singer wearing jeans, shades and a leather jacket, strumming an acoustic guitar. Now think of a **Madonna** tune and the chances are that it will come with a Technicolor backdrop, be it the ball gown fantasy of 'Material Girl', the spiritual, fundamentalist-baiting 'Like A Prayer' or the slap and tickle of 'Hanky Panky'. When you recall **Duran Duran**, it's likely you'll also be thinking of Simon Le Bon in mid-'80s mode, tied to a windmill in a Mad Max-inspired studio set or running through the jungle in a blind panic and a jacket with rolled-up sleeves.

The superstars of the last two decades embraced the video age and often used the extra dimension it has provided to explore fantastic new avenues. Sometimes the ideas are cyclic: the body builders getting 'Physical' with Olivia Newton-John at the start of the '80s begat Robert Palmer's supermodel backing band in **'Addicted To Love'** begat Tone Loc's pastiche in 'Wild Thing'.

And sometimes videos are just so off the wall that they defy all precedent: **Frankie Goes To Hollywood**'s raging bull presidents fighting it out in 'Two Tribes', Weezer's Zelig-like appearance in a *Happy Days* episode for 'Buddy Holly', the Beastie Boys' TV cop spoof for 'Sabotage', The Cure performing in a wardrobe as it falls off a cliff ('Close To Me'), and passionate Sinead O'Connor's teardrop minimalism on 'Nothing Compares 2 U'.

Then there are the promos that have also been used to promote peace (Dire Straits' epic **'Brothers In Arms'**). Some have been directed toward famine relief (Band Aid's 'Do They Know It's Christmas') and some embrace environmental issues (Michael Jackson's forest-friendly 'Earth Song'). There have even been those which aim to raise awareness of homelessness (Phil Collins's big issue, 'Another Day In Paradise') and of taking precautions against sexually-transmitted diseases (Neneh Cherry's rubber-clad 'I've Got You Under My Skin').

Some stars have been so immersed in the visual opportunities that they find it almost impossible to stop the cameras rolling after the allotted three-and-a-half minutes. If the likes of the Beatles and Elvis used the film medium as an excuse to promote their pop singles years ago, then the stars of the '80s and '90s reversed the principle. They were quick to get hold of the pop promo and turn it around, using it to draw attention to their cinematic interests.

Michael Jackson started the ball rolling to great effect with his theatrical release of the epic **'Thriller'**. The Artist who was then known as Prince picked it up with his feature length *Purple Rain* and then kicked it right into touch with *Under The Cherry Moon*. Meanwhile, David Byrne wove his oddball vignettes with Talking Heads into a bizarre tale of the mid-West, *True Stories*.

Back on the small screen, the very presence of MTV encourages artists and directors to be just that little bit more creative with their visuals, pushing back the boundaries and making jaws drop with each new extravaganza. It's got to be a good thing - where on earth would pop culture be residing without such innovative ideas as 50-foot giants in Rolling Stones videos, Japanese models mouthing REM's songs, **Björk** dancing on a flatbed truck as it drives through New York or U2's tongue-in-cheek **Village People** impression? It'd be somewhere very boring and small with nothing to do on a Friday night, that's where.

So it's time to fasten your seatbelts and hold on tight, as we get ready for a virtual trip through the **MTV Europe**'s A-Z of the most important artists in ten-year history, with a special section devoted to some of the biggest pulls on the planet - Aerosmith, the Artist (that's ♀), Bon Jovi, Jacksons Janet and Michael, Madonna, George Michael, Nirvana, R.E.M. and U2. If this lot don't know how to make it look good, then nobody does.

Aerosmith

Aerosmith: One time Toxic Twins Perry and Tyler

They have the sleaziest **riffs,** the lewdest **lyrics** and their singer has the most **lascivious lips in rock.** Wanna meet with the band that **wouldn't lie down?** Walk this way...

Steven Tyler was the archetypal slacker. Born Steven Tallarico on March 26, 1948, in New York, he was the son of a well-off piano teacher. Tyler was expelled after being arrested for smoking pot in his ceramics class by an undercover narcotics agent. Bitten by the rock'n'roll bug during the first **Britpop** invasion, Tyler formed a string of bands (the Strangeurs, Chain Reaction, William Proud) before meeting Joe Perry (born September 10, 1950, Boston, Mass., USA), in his parents' home town, Sunapee, New Hampshire, in 1969.

Perry, who was working in the ice-cream parlour where Tyler would regularly hang out, asked him to check out his band. Tyler was hooked by the Jam Band's "groove", while Perry and bass player Tom Hamilton (born December 31, 1951, Colorado Springs, Colorado, USA) were impressed by Tyler's worldliness. Relocating to Boston, **Aerosmith's** line-up eventually fell into place with the addition of drummer Joey Kramer (born June 21, 1950, New York) and guitarist Brad Whitford (born February 23, 1952, Winchester, Mass., USA).

Aerosmith signed with Columbia for $125,000 in 1972 and duly unleashed their ragged, rockin' debut album the following January. (In 1991, Sony, by then owners of Columbia, would pay an estimated $33.5 million to get them a second time.) Despite their predilection for the hard-edged blues of Cream and Led Zeppelin, they were soon tarred as **Stones** copyists, not least because of Tyler's looks. At

the time it bugged the hell out of him but come Aerosmith's starring role in **The Simpsons** nearly 20 years later (Homer falls on them), the singer joked on MTV's *Aerosmith Rockumentary II*, "Well, they got the lips down".

Aerosmith's second album, 1974's *Get Your Wings*, was a hit locally but outside of Boston its impact was slight. However, the single 'Same Old Song and Dance' received national radio coverage which, combined with a gruelling tour schedule that included support slots for Deep Purple and Black Sabbath, gradually started the train rollin'.

The follow-up, 1975's *Toys In The Attic*, was a benchmark, and featured 'Walk This Way', a record that would later rejuvenate their career when released in collaboration with rappers **Run DMC**. The song combined an incendiary guitar riff, Tyler's trademark lasciviousness and a chorus line taken from out of the mouth of Igor in the film *Young Frankenstein*. Tyler's dirty mouth spoke the language of America's adolescents (he even got himself arrested for saying "fuck" while on stage in Memphis) and the music kicked proverbial ass. The album sold a million copies before the year was out and Aerosmith suddenly found themselves outselling every other act on the label. *Rocks* (1976) continued the trend, going platinum when it was released.

While Aerosmith epitomized rock'n'roll success, Perry and Tyler became kings of rock'n'roll excess. Rechristened the **Toxic Twins**, their drug-fuelled binges soon became commonplace and a creeping paranoia set in. Tours in Japan and Europe went pear-shaped, while the recording of *Draw The Line* (1977) and *Night In The Ruts* (1979) were beset by self-inflicted problems. As the decade came to an end, Aerosmith looked worn out and out-of-date. Perry went solo, Whitford followed, Tyler nearly killed himself in a motorbike accident and, after one further album – the **Spinal Tap**-spoofed *Rock In A Hard Place* (1982), Aerosmith collapsed. To cap it all, **MTV** had just been launched in America but Aerosmith had shot their videos in unwieldy 3-D! After a two year hiatus,

the band reformed but had still not completely cured themselves of their overly decadent habits. After a lacklustre first album on Geffen, *Done With Mirrors* (1985), the band were thrown a lifeline by Rick Rubin, who came up with the idea of a collaboration with Run DMC. The rap-rock crossover version of 'Walk This Way' literally shook the world. Aerosmith seized the moment, cleaned up and were born again. As the '90s approached, a rejuvenated band recorded two hit albums. *Permanent Vacation* (1987) boasted a genuine international pop hit in 'Dude (Looks Like A Lady)' - which was co-written with **Desmond Child**. *Pump* (1989) featured the typical Tyler raunch of 'Love In An Elevator' and the Grammy winning 'Janie's Got A Gun', a heartfelt tale of child abuse. Aerosmith's sobriety had resulted in a newfound responsibility, and as well as namechecking **Greenpeace** on *Permanent Vacation*, they recorded an anti-drink-drive ad-spot and a *Rock The Vote* video in which Perry warned kids to fight for their right to "wear whipped cream as clothing". On the American leg of the *Pump* tour alone, they played to nearly two million fans and racked up $25 million in ticket sales.

They became one of the most played bands on MTV ('Crazy' was played through 1994 and 1995) and, in 1990, were the first major rock band to perform on **Unplugged**. MTV joined them again in 1993 for a fly-on-the-wall account of their tour in support of *Get A Grip*. "The album is more intimidating, more aggressive," Tyler told MTV. "We were thinking of calling the album *Pitbulls On Crack* and Joe said, 'Get a grip'. And I said, 'That's it!'."

Aerosmith's 12th studio album, released in 1997, was aptly titled - *Nine Lives*.

Tyler: A bad hair day at the first MTV Europe Music Awards, Berlin, November 1994

The Artist

He was the dirty dancing star of the **purple** '80s and became a **symbol** for the '90s. But is the *elusive* Artist Formerly Known As Prince going to be **partying** in 1999?

One of the most prolific and unpredictable stars of the '80s and '90s, Prince (born Prince Roger Nelson, June 7, 1958, Minneapolis, USA) is also one of the most reclusive. Prince's father, a pianist in the Prince Rogers Band, left home and his piano when Prince was a child. The youngster taught himself to play along to TV theme tunes, including **Batman**. (He would later score the soundtrack to the 1989 film.) By the age of 14, Prince had followed in his father's footsteps and later went to live with a high school friend, André Anderson (later known as André Cymone). Together with Morris Day (later of **The Time**) they formed Grand Central (later known as Champagne), ostensibly a covers band although they eventually introduced originals into the set.

In 1977, after learning the ropes at a local studio and getting himself managerial representation in the process, Prince signed a six-figure deal with Warner Brothers - a considerable deal for a new act. After much to-ing and fro-ing, the record company also agreed to let him produce his own material. His first album, *For You* (1978), did little but reveal his virtuosity (the sleeve listed all 27 of the instruments he'd played on the album). The second, *Prince* (1979), included his first R'n'B chart No. 1 in America, 'I Wanna Be Your Lover'. (It reached number 11 on the *Billboard* chart.) Prince's next album, the aptly-titled *Dirty Mind* (1980), was in stark contrast to its soulful predecessors - brash funk-rock, shock lyrics ("My sister never made love to anyone but me/Incest is everything it's said to be") and Prince lauding it in a pair of skimpy black briefs. It did half as well as his previous album but provided a blueprint for Prince's future career as the lord of lascivious pop.

Interestingly, the singer also created an alter-ego project, the Time. Although fronted by **Morris Day** and featuring future production geniuses **Jimmy Jam** and **Terry Lewis**, Prince virtually wrote and produced the band's entire self-titled album under the pseudonym Jamie Starr. One astute journalist guessed as much, theorizing that the Time represented Prince's desire to hold on to his soul roots while pursuing a strategy aimed at winning over a white audience. Whatever, over the next decade Prince's pen went on to underscore a series of careers (mostly women, mostly short-lived) from Vanity 6 to Madhouse, while his prolific workrate means hundreds of songs soon gather dust in the vaults.

Prince's next album, *Controversy* (1981), pretty much followed in the slipstream of *Dirty Mind*, but '1999', the title track from his next album, provided Prince with his first Top 30 hit in Europe in 1983. The following year Prince became a phenomenon.

As an example of cinema verité, the musical *Purple Rain* left a lot to be desired, but as a feature-length promo video it was brilliantly effective. The film spawned four hit records, shifted 17 million albums and gave a fresh lease of life to his previous albums. Prince ploughed the profits into building an empire in the form of a £10 million studio and record label, Paisley Park, which like a **Willy Wonka**-style factory of music, regularly produced new delicacies but kept their creator hidden under wraps. Occasionally, the odd person would slip through the net but usually failed to come away with much. (One journalist reported that Prince hung to the right and had invited him to play on his trampoline, while rapper Monie Love opined, "He was like an uncle," after collaborating with him on her *In A Word Or 2* album.)

MTV did, however, manage to shoot Prince a few questions during a visit to France in October 1995, and the star also partook in a competition that summer whereby the winner would get an exclusive concert in their home town. Unfortunately for Prince, that turned out to be in Sheridan, Wyoming, and the only available place to play was a ballroom at the local Holiday Inn! He would later help out MTV sister channel VH-1, launching it in the UK on 30 September 1994.

The musical arrangements, though, were an acquired taste and other attempts to repeat the film experiment - *Under The Cherry Moon* (1986) and *Graffiti Bridge* (1990) - were largely commercial disasters. Nevertheless, in successive years, Prince released an inspiring canon of work: the marmalade skies of *Around The World In A Day* in 1985; the 'Kiss' and tell *Parade* in 1986; and arguably his greatest album (a double at that), *Sign O' The Times*, in 1987. The latter was accompanied by an impressive tour film. The production line ground to a halt, however, when Prince's next opus, the *Black* album was suddenly put on hold. (Although it eventually emerged in 1994.)

While sales in Europe had been increasing throughout the latter part of the '80s - he played an unprecedented seven nights at **Wembley Arena** in 1988, and 16 in 1990 - Prince's career in America seemed to be in terminal decline. *Lovesexy* (1988) sold a million copies in America, his worst sales since 1981, and at the start of 1989 the media speculated that Prince was having a "cash crisis". He responded with *Batman*, his biggest selling album since *Purple Rain*, and the following year **Sinead O'Connor** added to his coffers with her international No.1 version of 'Nothing Compares 2 U'.

However, the '90s comeback went wobbly in 1992. After releasing a single reminding us that 'My Name Is Prince', he had a change of heart and decided to change his name to ♀ Then, despite announcements that his contract with Warners had been renegotiated, making him a vice-president of the company, he played at the first MTV Europe Music Awards in Berlin with the word "Slave" scrawled on his right cheek.

Promoting the following New Power Generation release, **The Artist Formerly Known As Prince** turned up for performances wearing a sheer red scarf over his face. Finally, after a *Gold* album, a *Black* album and a slew of hits packages, Warners relinquished him and he emerged phoenix-like (but still not called Prince) on EMI in 1996, with a three-CD set, *Emancipation*.

And whatever the future holds in store for him, Prince has certainly secured himself a superb launching pad into the next century: you can be sure of one thing; as the last seconds of the millenium tick away, there will be only one song playing on stereos the world over. He was dreaming when he wrote it, so forgive him if he goes too fast...

Latterday wild west hero, young gun Jon Bon Jovi lived on a prayer and then got shot in his prime during Young Guns II. But everyone knows you can't keep a good cowboy down...

Right: Jon Bon Jovi live and acoustic in Hamburg, 1996

Like Elvis Presley before him, Jon Bon Jovi never let go of his roots. In fact, he still owns a house less than 20 miles from where he was born, as Jonathan Bongiovi on March 2, 1962, the son of a Playboy bunny-girl and a hairdresser-cum-amateur singer. Like fellow New Jersey local **Bruce Springsteen**, Jon's music was grounded in his own backyard, even when he sang about escaping the gravitational pull of blue-collar work for an adventure on the world's freeways.

There's always been a thread linking the two artists' careers: the first album Jon bought was The Boss's *Born To Run* (1975); both artists have dedicated an album to their home state, *Greetings From Asbury Park N.J.* (Springsteen) and *New Jersey* (Bon Jovi); and as a teenager Jon even played support to New Jersey's most celebrated artist. In fact, Jon

Bon Jovi

about everybody who passed through the state, with a succession of no-mark bands, meanwhile working as a gofer at New York's Power Station studio and using downtime to record his demos.

Jon's only commercial recording project at this time was a vocal he recorded for 'R2D2 I Wish You A Merry Christmas' for his cousin's entrepreneurial money spinner, The **Star Wars Christmas Album**, until a local radio station put out a compilation album featuring local acts and included one of his songs, 'Runaway'. The track brought Jon's talents to the attention of several major labels.

A deal with Mercury followed in 1983, and Jon constructed a band of like-minded musicians from New Jersey's pool of bar players. The band was made up of keyboard player David Bryan (born David Rashbaum, February 7, 1962), drummer Hector 'Tico' Torres (born October 7, 1953), bass player Alec John Such (born November 14, 1952), and guitarist Richie Sambora (born July 11, 1959). After six months, the group had honed their melodic, eponymous rock debut (1984), but were still working on their image, a uniform of teased hair, spray-on trousers and slashed T-shirts.

Even before the album's release, Bon Jovi had played the

infamous Madison Square Garden, albeit supporting **ZZ Top**, yet Bon Jovi's meteoric rise was stalled by a relatively tepid second album, 7800° *Fahrenheit*, in 1985. Nevertheless, after playing the Castle Donington **Monsters Of Rock** Festival that autumn, their star was once more in the ascendant. Jon then made perhaps the best decisions of his life, drafting in an outsider, Desmond Child, to help write songs for *Slippery When Wet* under the auspices of producers Bruce Fairbairn and Bob Rock. Child co-wrote 'You Give Love A Bad Name', 'Livin' On A Prayer' and 'Without Love', songs that would take Bon Jovi into the world superstar bracket. The record also included 'Wanted Dead Or Alive', a song that would not only be a massive hit, but would also give Bon Jovi a new identity as latterday cowboys. The album, supported by seemingly round-the-clock - **MTV** airplay, sold 11 million copies in America in 1986, making it the fastest selling album in history at the time. Meanwhile, the steel horse that Bon Jovi rode in on grew wings, and by the time they returned to Castle Donington in 1987 to fulfil their earlier promise of one day headlining the event, it was with the aid of rotor blades.

After a gruelling 16-month tour, Bon Jovi were faced with a mountain to climb if they were going to repeat the success of *Slippery When Wet*. *New Jersey* employed similar tricks (same producer, studio and writing collaborator), but was more expansive as Bon Jovi attempted to display their growing maturity. Again, the band toured the album relentlessly - pausing only to officially switch on MTV in Oslo, Norway - but this time at the conclusion of the tour they split to do their own solo material or, in the case of Tico, to do some painting and flying.

Jon was soon back in the saddle with a solo album, *Blaze Of Glory*, the title track of which was used in **Young Guns II**, but over the next two years there was wide

speculation that Bon Jovi would split. However, all that went were Jon's split ends. He reappeared with a short haircut on MTV Europe's **Headbangers Ball**, in September 1992. The video for 'Keep The Faith' was massive on MTV Europe, and the band were then bigger in Europe than in the States. The album was preceded by an MTV *Unplugged* performance. Between semi-acoustic versions of originals and covers, Jon indulged in a few fond reminiscences, like the early years spent driving over to Richie's house with its "Aluminum foil over the windows, air conditioning up to 10 (even in February), stereo on all night, like know who or what would be in there with him when I opened the door." Jon was hiding something in his own closet. After being blooded in the film *Young Guns II* – 16 seconds, one fatal bullet wound – Jon spent two years training as an actor. While a greatest hits package, 1994's *Cross Road* and another album, *These Days*, kept Bon Jovi going, Jon landed his first major film roles, in **Moonlight And Valentino** (1995) and *The Leading Man* (1996), in which Jon revealed all of his attributes (and we mean all). The cowboy had swapped his silver spurs for the silver screen.

Janet

Janet Jackson: Caught at the 1995 MTV awards

Jackson

In a cut-throat music business that's still **dominated** by the boys, **she took** ***Control*** of her career and got herself a record deal worth **£80 million.** Poetic Justice or **what?**

Giorgio Moroder), a Cliff Richard duet ('Two To The Power') and the help of most of her brothers, the following album, *Dream Street* (1984), actually performed worse than her debut. She later claimed both albums were "way too bubble gummy", even for her own tastes.

During this period her star was so far from the ascendant that the media's main interest in her revolved around her brother Michael's insistence that he'd only do interviews if journalists used Janet as an intermediary. Her love life was equally blighted – her marriage to James DeBarge lasted just eight months.

Then A&M's John McCalin persuaded Janet to relocate to Minneapolis to work with the Jam & Lewis production team. The resulting album, *Control* (1986), was a coming of age, both spiritually and musically, as Jackson explored raw funk grooves and secular topics. She also exerted control over her own body. "I do have to watch what I eat," she later confessed in **MTV's** Janet Jackson **Rockumentary.** "I can't eat sweets. I do like strawberries and whipped cream, and Häagen Dazs..."

J anet Jackson was born to perform (on June 16, 1966, in Gary, Indiana, USA). She was only two years old when her brothers, **The Jackson Five**, signed to Motown. At the age of eight she was wowing audiences with her **Mae West** impression during the Jacksons' performances, and by the time the vocal group made the leap to TV in 1976, she was shoe-horned into a trio with Rebbie and LaToya (imaginatively titled The Jackson Sisters).

Television offered Janet a life that didn't completely rely on association with her brothers, even though it remains unclear how much she jumped for it, and how far she was pushed by her father, Joseph. Janet studied at Valley High Stage Academy and her first role was Penny, an abused child in the sitcom *Good Times*. She later claimed that she got the part because she could cry on cue, a skill that would later be put to good use on her tours supporting the album *janet*. Her next three acting parts were in *A New Kind Of Family*, *Diff'rent Strokes* and the TV version of **Fame**. Although the latter two were both international successes, Janet returned to making music, cutting two unspectacular solo albums. Her lack of experience was transparent on her first album, *Janet Jackson* (1982), and in spite of the assistance of a host of producers (including

Control sold 10 million copies, spawned six hit singles, a remix album and a dance video. For *Rhythm Nation 1814* (1989), Jackson extended her manifesto to include social issues, scored seven hit singles, and racked up the most successful debut tour ever.

However, the dance moves and the militaristic chic were still reminiscent of brother Michael's style. A starring role in **Poetic Justice** alongside Tupac Shakur paved the way for *janet* (1993), her most mature work to date. The album was released on the Virgin label as part of a mammoth £32 million deal that Michael topped nine days later with his £60 million Sony deal, only to see his sister renegotiate an £80 million deal in 1996.

Any memories of the podgy teenager were exorcized by a **Rolling Stone** cover in which a pair of anonymous hands (in reality the property of Janet's boyfriend) reached from behind Janet's back and firmly held her otherwise naked breasts. "I wanted it to be a lot warmer, softer and to be about love," she told MTV later in *Control Through Design*, MTV's celebration of her work from 1986-96. "The record company wanted me to come back with something big, but I wanted to go for mellow and smooth." The video for the opening single 'That's The Way Love Goes', showed Janet at her most confident, relaxing with friends.

When she performed at MTV's 1993 Music Awards in America, dressed like a latterday Native America warrior, she oozed sexuality. (The following world tour saw her simulating oral sex on stage!)

Perhaps the sassiest video of the seven hits was 'You Want This', a homage to Russ Meyer's **Faster Pussycat Kill Kill Kill**, which saw Janet and her sisters tormenting a couple of hitchhikers in the desert. The album also included 'New Agenda', a collaboration with Public Enemy's Chuck D. "I've learned a lot from rap," she told MTV. "I feel in school all we were taught is we were slaves, not kings and queens as well."

No longer just Michael's little sister, but a superstar in her own right, Janet performed a duet, 'Scream', with her brother for his *HIStory* album. Tellingly, Janet had artistic control of its sci-fi video. Later, she offered her support, presenting Michael with an MTV Video Award in 1995 while wearing a T-shirt emblazoned with the slogan, "Pervert 2".

He's sold more records than anyone else in HIStory but during the last few years, the former little Jackson brother had to fight to focus the spotlight away from his private life and back on to the stage.

Whether or not you think of Michael Jackson as the king of pop, there is no disputing the fact that he is the king of pop video. His career, though, began long before the dawning of the age of MTV. Jackson (born August 29, 1958, in Gary, Indiana, USA) started performing with his brothers, **The Jackson Five**, at the age of six. But it was after appearing alongside Diana Ross in **The Wiz** (a version of the Wizard Of Oz featuring a black cast), that Jackson started a partnership with its musical director, Quincy Jones, that would change musical history.

Their first album collaboration, 1979's tireless dance classic Off The Wall, produced a string of hit singles (including the anthem to adolescence 'Don't Stop 'Til You Get Enough') and sold over eight million albums. However, Jackson's follow-up in 1982 would usurp it and all other recordings, eventually selling a staggering 44 million copies worldwide. Thriller was unique. There was an almost military precision to its range of styles and its selection of musical contributors. (Paul McCartney duetted with Jackson on 'The Girl Is Mine', rock star Eddie Van Halen played guitar on the title track.) Equally importantly, and in order to promote Jackson's incredible dancing skills as much as his songs, Epic commissioned a series of ground-breaking videos for the singles 'Billie Jean', 'Beat It' and 'Thriller'.

The nascent **MTV** network didn't start airing the 'Billie Jean' video until a week after it reached No.1 in America. When they did so the response was astonishing. Thriller, which had already sold two million copies, began selling over half-a-million records a week. It was a perfect case of synergy - MTV was spreading rapidly across America - and stocks in both artist and medium rocketed as people rushed to check out Jackson's revolutionary pop promo. One moonstep for a man, one giant leap for MTV.

'Beat It', with its West Side Story-board and rock beat, was even more ambitious. Jackson supplemented his trademark all-too-short trousers with playground bravado.

When Jackson came to release the album's title track, MTV took the unprecedented step of paying for the rights to a documentary, *Making Michael Jackson's 'Thriller'*. The money helped fund John (**An American Werewolf In London**) Landis's 14-minute pop promo-cum-short feature film. Jackson acted, danced and werewolfed his way through the first million-dollar promo video. Jackson was now so important that MTV gave his **Pepsi** adverts a world première!

The launch of MTV Europe three years later couldn't have been better timed. A week after Elton John threw the switch that connected Europe to 24-hour music, Jackson released a new single, a duet with Siedah Garratt entitled 'I Just Can't Stop Loving You', which topped the charts on both sides of the Atlantic and started a run of five successive No.1s in America. It was an amazing return to the spotlight after a hiatus in which his most notable achievements were to partake in the charity recording 'We Are The World' and to purchase the ATV catalogue (which included all of the Beatles' songs).

A month later, MTV was granted a one-week cable and satellite exclusive for the 16-minute promo for 'Bad', in which Jackson paraded his new leather, military chic. The single was followed by the *Bad* album (his last with Jones, which clocked up a respectable 25 million sales), a book (**Moonwalk**), a 17-month, 123-date tour and a film (*Moonwalker*).

Jackson returned after a two-year break with a single, 'Black Or White', and an album, *Dangerous*. The album was built on heavy rhythms and raw energy, and swing guru Teddy Riley produced half the tracks. Although the album nearly matched the sales of its predecessor, cracks were beginning to show in Jackson's status as a global superstar. During the *Dangerous* tour, the world's media seemed more concerned with Jackson's rumoured nose job and skin bleaching than his music. Even his brother Jermaine made his feelings known with the song 'A Word To The Badd!'. Meanwhile, the singer was fainting under the spotlight while on tour. Yet physical exhaustion and gossip about plastic surgery would soon seem small fare indeed.

In 1993 Jackson came under investigation after an allegation was made that he had molested 13-year-old Jordy Chandler. It was the cruellest of ironies for one who seemed to live his life to indulge children's innocent fantasies. Although charges have never been brought (two grand juries questioned nearly 200 witnesses, 30 of them children, but did not find a single corroborating witness), Jackson was eventually to settle a civil lawsuit out of court.

Thereafter, he could have giant statues of himself erected wherever he liked, he could say "Hi" at **Nelson Mandela's** birthday bash if he wanted, but some people could not forget the scandal. Even his marriage to **Lisa Marie Presley**, daughter of Elvis, couldn't help. A new album launched the following year did help. *HIStory* was a 30-song package, split between old hits and new recordings, including the chart-topping 'Earth Song', both of which proved that Jackson could still command his sea of fans. It sold 11 million copies.

In yet another twist to his life, Jackson married again, this time to a nurse, Debbie Rowe, in November 1996. The details surrounding the subsequent birth of Michael Jnr were the subject of media speculation. It seems that whatever Jackson does from now on, there will always be someone touting a conspiracy theory.

Michael Jackson: Playing at statues in Prague back in September 1996

NOŽTE SE

Madonna

In a league of her own, the **material girl** has navigated her career from dancing to singing to **Sex books** to acting. You can look but don't **cry for her** - this is a tough lady with blonde **ambition.**

Madonna's trip to not-so-Lucky Star-dom began in the sixth grade, when she gyrated to The Who's 'Baba O'Reilly' in a dance competition. "I wore a bikini and I had my girlfriend paint fluorescent flowers all over me," Madonna told Kurt Loder in an interview for MTV's *Making Of Evita* in 1996. "My father grounded me for the entire summer... It was well worth it. I got asked on a lot of dates afterwards."

Later, Madonna (born Madonna Louise Ciccone, August 16, 1958, Rochester, Michigan, USA) won a scholarship to the University Of Michigan, where she trained as a dancer. She moved to New York in 1978, and after a stint in Paris on the musical *Born To Be Alive*, began her musical career in earnest back in New York. After drumming in a band called Breakfast Club, she formed Emmy, and eventually began singing under her own name.

Seymour Stein, founder of Sire Records, signed the young Madonna, who debuted with the single 'Everybody'. After approaching Michael Jackson's then-manager Freddie De Mann, and having a minor hit with 'Holiday' and her debut album, *Madonna* (later repackaged as *The First Album*), MTV picked up on 'Borderline' and 'Lucky Star'. Madonna was on the verge of becoming the first female video superstar.

"Three to four years ago dancing was the most important thing - now it's music," she told *Smash Hits* in February, 1984. "That will lead on to something else...acting." The dramatic career didn't start too brightly. After earning $100 in 1983's ***A Certain Sacrifice*** (and a good deal of embarrassment when she couldn't prevent her name being used to promote its video release two years later), Madonna's next role was as a singer in *Vision Quest* (later renamed *Crazy For You*). Meanwhile, after her appearance at the first MTV Video Music Awards in America, in September 1984,

Madonna: Back on the screen in *Evita*

performing the title track of her second album, *Like A Virgin*, Madonna's musical career boomed. In January she appeared on the cover of **The Face**, and confessed that losing her virginity "was a career move". By March, 'Material Girl' was an international hit, while in New York Madonna was receiving her first rave acting reviews for her role in **Desperately Seeking Susan**. April ushered in her first US tour, and a record sixth consecutive Top Ten US single with 'Angel'. In May, 'Crazy For You' became her first British No.1. Even her appearance at Live Aid in July had added extra spice, when she referred to the ongoing battle between *Penthouse* and *Playboy* for some "arty" nude pictures taken of her some years earlier. A month later she married Sean Penn and released 'Into The Groove', another massive hit.

Speculation over Madonna's staying power soon waned. In 1986 Madonna did it again, when 'True Blue' became a best seller in 25 countries, although her Hollywood prospects received a blow when her film, **Shanghai Surprise**, was slated.

The following year, Madonna fared slightly better in *Who's That Girl*, the soundtrack of which charted all over the continent on August 1, 1987, the day MTV Europe went on air. Madonna fever peaked again. Before the month was out, she played to 144,000 people over three nights at Wembley Stadium. As young wannabes struggled to keep up with Madonna's rapidly changing wardrobe, hacks the world over had a field day inventing rumours about her going bald and dieting on popcorn and sardines. The Sean Penn-split story, however, came true two years later.

Soon everything Madonna did courted controversy. A multi-million dollar deal with Pepsi was canned after religious groups complained about their sponsorship of the religiously sensitive 'Like A Prayer' video. Predictably, the album sold millions. Then Madonna admitted she liked a good spanking on **Arsenio Hall's** TV talk show, promoting some more chart action for 'Hanky Panky', the second single from her **Dick Tracy**-related album *I'm Breathless* (she played Breathless Mahoney in the film). And when MTV refused to air 'Justify My Love' (a new song used to promote her greatest hits album, *The Immaculate Collection*) because of its overtly sexual nature, Madonna released the promo as a sell-through video.

To top it off, Madonna turned her **Blonde Ambition** tour into a crusade for freedom of sexual expression, taking her masturbation simulation around the globe (except Italy, where it was banned), then edited it into a nipple-revealing tour film, *In Bed With Madonna* (aka **Truth Or Dare**), in 1991. Madonna spent the following year filming *A League Of Their Own* and negotiating a £60 million-plus deal with Time Warner. This included her own label, Maverick - which made a great signing in **Alanis Morissette**. Madonna also recorded an album, *Erotica*, and worked on a book, *Sex*. The hermetically-sealed fantasy overshadowed the album, and her follow-up, *Bedtime Stories*, suffered as Madonna focused on film. "I had to make a choice," she admitted to MTV, and the film career came first. Madonna even said she got the part in *Evita* after sending a promo video to director **Alan Parker**. 'Take A Bow' was the first pop video CV. As she had used dance to help her become a pop star, so she then used pop to help her become a film star.

He's spent more time in **court** than **Ronnie Biggs**, __and it cost him__ **more money than you'll make** __in a lifetime__ but now he's **Older**, wiser and finally a free man (not a catalogue number).

George Michael: In full voice at the MTV Music Awards

For George Michael (born Georgious Panayiotou, June 25, 1963, London, England), it's been a decade of two halves. At the 1996 MTV Europe Music Awards, the besuited'n'pointy-bearded superstar admitted that the first half of the '90s had been a really bad one but that the success of his third album, *Older* (1996), seemed to suggest that he may have at last turned the corner.

It was certainly an understated way of describing a two-year hiatus during which he spent **three million pounds** trying to extricate himself from his recording contract with Sony. Michael had threatened what amounted to a musical hunger strike during the period, although high profile collaborations with **Elton John** ('Don't Let The Sun Go Down On Me', 1991) and **Queen** (with whom he played a memorial concert in 1992, a single from which topped the UK charts in 1993), plus the inevitable footage of Michael walking briskly in and out of court, ensured that he never really faded from the public's memory.

In fact, in an exclusive and frank interview with MTV last year, George claimed that his side projects had been so well received in some parts of the world that

Older wasn't even perceived as a comeback album at all. Nevertheless, he was realistic about people's perception of him in the States:

"In America, really, *Listen Without Prejudice* didn't have any impact. So, I think to some degree I'm still the boy who did *Faith*... I suppose there are plenty of people that think I'm still wandering around with a cross earring and bleached hair. I had the cross earring surgically removed. And that was where everything went wrong for me in America."

The singer's problems began when he achieved **superstardom** in America with the *Faith* album and tour (1987). At the age of 24, Michael decided that he didn't want to live with the pressure of maintaining his status and would in future focus his attention on making music rather than selling it. Hence his decision to call his next album *Listen Without Prejudice Vol. 1* (1990) and not to do intensive promotional interviews and a **world tour** to support it. Instead, he performed one-off R'n'B revues and started planning an album of songs to coincide with the project, which was to feature guest vocalists, under the name Trojan Souls.

Although *Listen Without Prejudice Vol 1* topped the charts in 15 countries, Michael was disappointed with Sony's efforts to promote the album in America and felt he was being treated like a commodity rather than an artist. He also believed Sony's commitment to the AIDS benefit album *Red Hot & Dance* (1992), to which he'd contributed several new songs, including the chart-topping 'Toofunky', failed to match his own. He then took them to court, claiming that his contract amounted to a restraint of trade. He lost his case but vowed never to record for Sony again. A settlement was later reached between Sony, Michael and Dreamworks/Virgin, which allowed him to leave the label. George opened MTV's first-ever Europe Music Awards (his first appearance in front of a worldwide audience in years) and recorded an *Unplugged* performance in London, which was premi red on December 2, 1996.

A decade had passed since Michael split Wham! to pursue a solo career. His first three solo releases - 'Careless Whisper' (1984), 'A Different Corner' (1986) and 'I Knew You Were Waiting (For Me)', the last a duet with Aretha Franklin in 1987 - topped the UK singles chart, while the subsequent release, 'I Want Your Sex', was almost too raunchy. Michael played another of his controversial singles, 'Father Figure' during the *Unplugged* performance and also included some old Wham! hits - 1984's 'Freedom' and 'Everything She Wants', which was the flipside to 'Last Christmas' and a Top 10 hit in both 1984 and '85.

Wham! - George Michael and Andrew Ridgeley - were the epitome of British pop from the early to mid-'80s. The duo were school friends and formed their first band - Executive - in 1979. As **Wham!**, they released some of the most memorable singles to be sung by men in leg warmers, including 'Wham! Rap', 'Club Tropicana' and 'Wake Me Up Before You Go Go', a Number One on both sides of the Atlantic. In 1985 they became the first western pop band to play in China, an idea devised by then-manager Simon Napier-Bell to capitalize on their success in America.

Right: Nirvana *Unplugged*. Left: Mum, dad and Frances Bean

They were **sub pop** until **they discovered the** teen spirit to take them into orbit. Just as it seemed their **every move** defined the '90s, their career was tragically cut short.

f ever MTV was synonymous with a generation, then it would be the slacker generation. Parodying the slacker stereotype, the station's cartoon couch-potato TV critics, Beavis and Butt-Head, became global anti-heroes. Meantime, in championing one particular Seattle grunge trio, MTV was instrumental in the knighting of Kurt Cobain, the '90s first genuine rock'n'roll icon.

Fame, though, was a double-edged sword with the keenest of blades.

In the biography that accompanied 1989's corrosive debut album, the aptly-titled **Bleach** on Seattle's Sub Pop Records, Cobain (born February 20, 1967, Aberdeen, Washington, USA) foresaw that Nirvana's credibility could prove inversely proportional to their popularity, and joked that his band of backwoods guitar-slingers would "cash in" and "suck butts up to the big wigs" as soon as possible. His real intention was to do anything but.

Arriving in Europe as the '80s exhaled their last desperate grunt, Nirvana revealed not only that they had an incendiary show to match their studio sound, but they also had grunge's biggest star in the making. Amid the carnage of moshing and stagediving, Cobain would appear angelic before proceeding to drop to his knees, or writhe on his back or smash his guitar to death on a nearby amp, drum riser or the occasional bouncer.

After a year of charging up audiences across Europe and America, Nirvana (by now cemented as Cobain on guitars and vocals; Krist Novoselic on bass and bare feet; and Dave Grohl on drums) tapped into the main grid. 'Smells Like Teen Spirit', their first major release (**Geffen Records**, September 1991) proved that anger really was an energy. The subsequent release of an equally splenetic album, *Nevermind*, took grunge from

toilet venues to the tops of charts across Europe. Virtually overnight, Nirvana changed the face of rock'n'roll. *Nevermind* grossed over $50 million. Embarrassed by Nirvana's success, Cobain continually taunted himself and others about the dichotomy of a punk band whose singer sported a holey jumper but whose members carried corporate credit cards. Thus, when Kurt turned up for a **Rolling Stone** cover shoot in 1992, he wore a self-made T-shirt proclaiming "Corporate magazines still suck", as much to mock himself for signing to a corporate label as the magazine for wanting to further itself by putting Nirvana on its cover.

Having given the video of 'Smells Like Teen Spirit' its world premi re in America on **120 Minutes**, and then put it in the high-rotation *Buzz Bin* for nine weeks, MTV had probably done more than anyone to turn Nirvana's small revolution into a global phenomenon. Cobain's natural response was to bite the hand that fed him, whether it be by turning up at *Headbangers Ball* in a dress or by causing consternation at the 1992 MTV Music Video Awards, first by sending a Michael Jackson lookalike to collect Nirvana's first award, and then by slipping a few bars of the then new song 'Rape Me' into the introduction of their live performance of 'Lithium'.

Nevertheless, Cobain recognized that the channel was more than a funnel for pop videos. As he told Michael Azerrad in the biography *Come as You Are – The Story Of Nirvana*: "I've noticed a consciousness that's way more positive, way more intelligent in the younger generation and the proof is in stupid things like **Sassy** magazine and MTV in general. Whether you want to admit that or not, there is a positive consciousness and people are becoming more human."

It's appropriate then, that after the release of **In Utero** in September 1993, an intense,

brooding album obsessed with both birth and sickness - and very possibly inspired by the media witch hunt that followed the revelation in **Vanity Fair** that Cobain's wife, Hole's Courtney Love, had taken heroin during her pregnancy - Nirvana recorded the band's most sensitive performance for MTV.

For their seminal **Unplugged** performance, the band played several songs from their own repertoire, plus a clutch of Meat Puppets numbers with "the brothers Meat Puppet" Cris and Curt Kirkwood, a Vaselines cover and a version of David Bowie's 'The Man Who Sold The World', in which Cobain amended the lyrics to: "I gazed a gazeless stare with multi-millionaires, I must have died alone a long, long time ago." A sense of despair was even more evident in the programme's finale, a version of Leadbelly's haunting murder ballad 'Where Did You Sleep Last Night'. The emotive performance had its first airing on December 14, 1993.

Sadly, the pain evinced in the finale was very much for real. The world was given a clear warning of a forthcoming tragedy when Cobain passed into a coma after an overdose of painkillers and champagne while on tour in Rome in February, 1994. Just six weeks later, on April 8, his body was discovered at his Seattle home by electrician Gary Smith. Cobain had shot himself in the head with a shotgun.

R.E.M.

How this four-piece, uncompromising group from Athens, Georgia, broke out of the college circuit, went supernova, survived stardom and illness and still had time to set off on a new adventure in hi-fi.

Michael Stipe: In a scene from *R.E.M.: The MTV Files*

R.E.M. is an acronym (for Rapid Eye Movement), and acronyms are like the tips of icebergs - you know 90 per cent is out of sight. Likewise, R.E.M.'s appeal comes from their ability to reveal something new about themselves while leaving you with the feeling that you're seeing only a fraction of the picture. Sometimes they can't see it themselves. During the promotion of 1991's *Out Of Time* - an album that saw guitarist Peter Buck (born December 6, 1956, Athens, Georgia, USA) add the words "mandolin" and "baroque" to the rock'n'roll vocabulary - the band seemed convinced that they would follow up with a ballsy guitar record. Yet 1992's *Automatic For The People* proved to be the most poignant of their career. More often than not, R.E.M. are mysterious by design.

Michael Stipe's (born January 4, 1960, Decatur, Georgia, USA) tangled lyrics and unconventional singing style on the band's first, seminal album (1983's *Murmur*) were as oblique as the album's title, while the album's sleeve (also designed by Stipe) was a photograph of weed-strangled woodland. For every song Stipe would later decipher - he once admitted that 'Laughing' from *Murmur* was about a freak mythological figure called **Laocoon**, and that 'Harborcoat' (from 1984's *Reckoning*) was inspired by **Anne Frank's** diaries - a clutch remained encrypted. Even their first hit, 'The One I Love', from 1987's *Document*, was largely misinterpreted as a positive love song.

The R.E.M. enigma has been reinforced by a series of off-centre videos containing images drawn from influences as disparate as the 16th-century Italian artist Caravaggio and the 20th-century king of rock'n'roll Elvis Presley. Throw in cars gridlocked on the freeway and lip-syncing Japanese models and you get some of the most consistently interesting images to have ever graced MTV. Even the channel's fly-on-the-wall documentaries, such as 1995's *R.E.M. Are Dead Boring* (in which a crew shared cabs and changing rooms with the band during a performance at *Saturday Night Live*) seem unable to destroy the myth.

R.E.M. formed in Athens, Georgia, in 1980, a year after the **B-52's** 'Rock Lobster' put the town on the map. They got their first break supporting The Police in Atlanta that Christmas. They subsequently signed to IRS and, after releasing the five-track EP 'Chronic Town', recorded *Murmur*, a beguiling album that married Buck's folk-rock guitar playing and Stipe's incomprehensible vocals with the instinctive rhythms of drummer Bill Berry (born July 31, 1958, Hibbing, Maine, USA) and bass player Mike Mills (born December 17, 1958, Georgia, USA). It was voted ***Rolling Stone's*** Album Of The Year.

Eschewing all the usual rock'n'roll trappings, R.E.M. operated on a shoestring budget and retained control of their output. Their second album, *Reckoning*, saw the culmination of R.E.M.'s first phase and thereafter each album saw significant changes, not least in who was sitting in the producer's chair (up to this point it had been

shared by Don Dixon and Mitch Easter). R.E.M. flew to Britain to record 1985's *Fables Of The Reconstruction*, their "difficult" third album, with **Fairport Convention**. A year later they recorded *Lifes Rich Pageant*

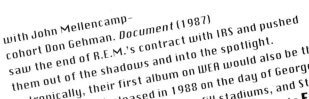

with John Mellencamp-cohort Don Gehman. *Document* (1987) saw the end of R.E.M.'s contract with IRS and pushed them out of the shadows and into the spotlight.

Ironically, their first album on WEA would also be their most overtly political. *Green* (released in 1988 on the day of George Bush's inauguration) was big enough to fill stadiums, and Stipe used the opportunity to promote **Greenpeace** and berate **Exxon** for the oil disaster in Alaska. But they didn't just preach environmental issues. Inspired by the carpets at New York's National Resource Defense Council, which were made out of recycled tyres, R.E.M. turned their Athens office into an eco-friendly operation, from the recycling waste bins upward.

The 11-month *Green* tour sapped the band's strength. R.E.M. stopped touring but put out two albums, the "baroque" *Out Of Time* and the elegiac *Automatic For The People*. "The truth is, the monster had got too big," Berry told **Melody Maker** in 1991. Come 1995, the band were ready to roll again, in support of *Monster*, a frenetic "punk" album of fuzzed guitars and treated vocals. The tour halted in March after Berry suffered a brain haemorrhage while onstage in Switzerland. When the tour resumed in the summer, with a by-now-fit Berry, Stipe joked that they'd renamed the tour **Aneurysm '95**.

Then, in July, Mills underwent a laparatomy to remove an adhesion from his intestine, while in August, Stipe was operated on for a hernia. The tour went on and R.E.M. wrote and recorded as they went. They eventually settled in a Seattle studio owned by the band Heart. Someone in Alice In Chains brought candles, the second engineer hung up a disco ball, and R.E.M. recorded another great album, *New Adventures In Hi-Fi*. Ever the gentleman, Michael Stipe did an exclusive **MTV** interview. "We're making another death record," Michael said with a smile, leaving nine-tenths of the story to the imagination. However, whereas the previous four albums had taken R.E.M. in several new and inspired directions, *New Adventures In Hi-Fi* was undoubtedly a journey back to the source. Majestic, organic, yet still shrouded in mystery, R.E.M. remain one of rock 'n' roll's greatest enigmas, despite their enormous popularity.

U2

Once they were a rather serious bunch of musicians **with a mission in life.** Now they are a **hyper-real** set of **pranksters** for the digital age - and this time **their target is pop.**

On the seventh day, U2 created **Zoo TV**. If video killed the radio star in the '80s, then on February 29, 1992, U2 started a world tour during which video did much the same to the normal conception of the rock'n'roll performance.

This pre-millennium medicine show boasted 32 TV screens that blasted audiences with slogans (including the Edge's favourite, "Everything You Know Is Wrong", and Bono's choice, **"Pig Wife Japan Sucker Bomb Now Pussy"**) and random, decoded transmissions from around the globe. This allowed Bono to download a St Patrick's night celebration to gig goers in Boston or joke about a cricket programme with fans in Sydney. In addition, Bono (born Paul Hewson, May 10, 1960) used mankind's first information superhighway - the phone - to order takeouts (10,000 pizzas to go in Florida), or to bait politicians (funnily enough, George Bush didn't pick up). The tour pushed back the boundaries of entertainment further by including a live broadcast from a war zone (Sarajevo), by having a religious refugee (Salman Rushdie) as a special guest, and by turning one lucky **MTV Most Wanted** winner into a Zoo TV star at a gig in Rome. "We had to get through to the MTV generation," bass player Adam Clayton (born March 13, 1960) told *Details* magazine in September 1992. "From here on in, U2 is an audio-visual idea."

During Bono's transition from **Fly Guy** to cheesy Vegas crooner-cum-anti-Christ, Mister Macphisto, U2 tested their mettle by taking time off to record *Zooropa*, an album inspired by author William Gibson's vision of a cyberpunk future, Dadaist humour and Europe's dislocated geography. It also included a guest appearance by Johnny Cash and perhaps the strangest sample in history, a Nazi Youth drummer boy from the Hitler propaganda movie, **Triumph Of The Will**. "When we were working on *Achtung Baby*, we were looking to discover new sonic terrain," The Edge (born

David Evans, August 8, 1961) told *Q* magazine in September 1993. "On this record that was already established, so we were more confident of what we were doing."

U2 began recording *Achtung Baby* in the autumn of 1990 in the recently reunified Berlin. Ironically, for a while it seemed as though U2 might disintegrate, but they eventually delivered an album that comprised a dozen dark variations on obsession. On its release the following November, *Achtung Baby* proved to be a renaissance for the band, easily eclipsing their previous album. (**Rattle & Hum** was an over-earnest exploration of American heritage, which was tied in with a humourless tour film of the same name.) It also killed off the rock'n'roll leviathan of which drummer Larry Mullen Jr (born October 1, 1961), in particular, had become heartily sick during their tour of Australia at the tail end of 1989.

Formed in 1977, when the four band members were still at school, U2's first release was a three-track EP, 'U2:3', which came out on CBS the following year. In January 1980, they came top of five categories in **Hot Press's** annual readers' poll, and by April were signed to Island Records. Their first three albums - 1980's *Boy*, 1991's *October* and 1983's *War*, all of which were produced by **Steve Lillywhite** - saw a

U2: Take time out to visit Sellafield

paintings made by survivors of the atomic bombs dropped on Japan and which focused on the power of positivism. The second, *The Joshua Tree* (1987), was a bleaker record that focused on the American heartland. It went on to sell 15 million copies, heralding them as the biggest rock band in the world.

Now fast forward ten years to 1997. Having let **Brian Eno** take the U2 collaboration to its logical extreme with *Original Soundtracks Volume 1* under the alias Passengers, the band have moved on, taking Howie B with them. The first single from their collaboration is taken from *Pop* (U2's eleventh album) and is called 'Discothèque'. With customary panache, U2's ensuing tour, Pop Mart, was announced live to the world via MTV. A 62-date sci-fi supermarket spectacular, playing stadia in 20 countries throughout 1997, the stage design would include a golden arch 100-feet high, a 12-foot-wide stuffed olive and a gigantic mirrored lemon! Even when they make Pop music, it seems U2 have a separate agenda.

Bono: Macphisto makes an appearance on the Zoo TV tour

tremendous metamorphosis, as soul searching turned into righteous soldiering. The change was emphasized when Bono appeared in the video *Under A Blood Red Sky*, atop the battlements, waving a white flag. In journalist Bill Flanagan's anthology, *Written In My Soul*, Bono denied the exercise was a device to win over the crowd: "God, I wouldn't want to do that. I think the people understood that it was anger... I was tired of the tri-colour, I was tired of the Union Jack... It was a kind of anti-nationalism stand I was taking."

U2 were increasingly perceived as rock'n'roll's voice of conscience - be it through their contribution to Live Aid in 1985 or the **Amnesty** World Tour in 1986 - and over the following two studio albums their personal and political quests grew ever more global. Under the auspices of producer Brian Eno and his assistant Daniel Lanois, U2 produced two albums, The first was *The Unforgettable Fire* (1984), which was named after an exhibition of

Movers & Shakers

Movers & Shakers

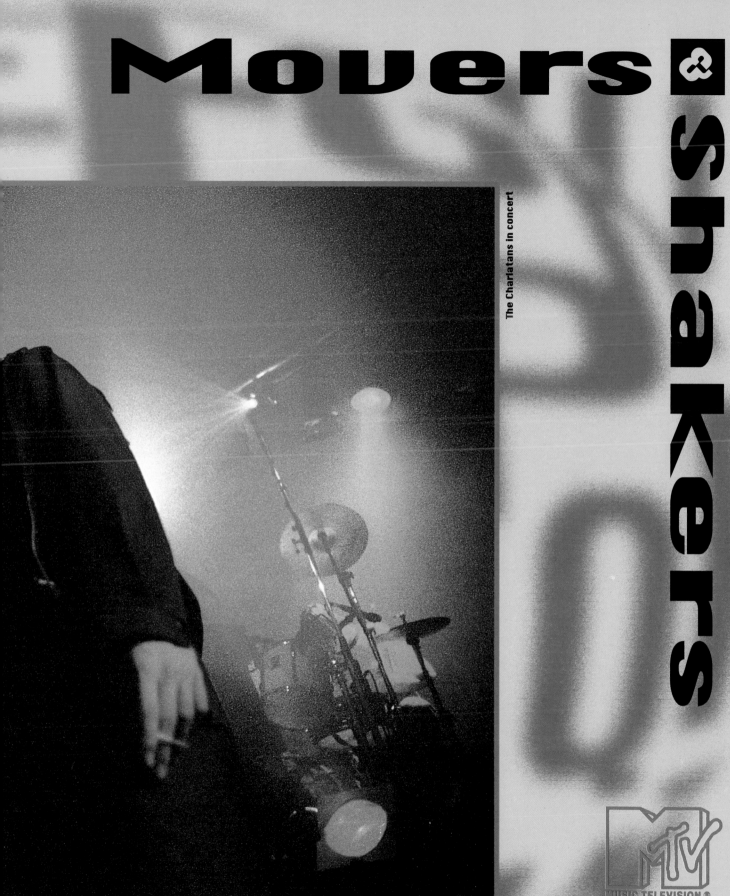

The Charlatans in concert

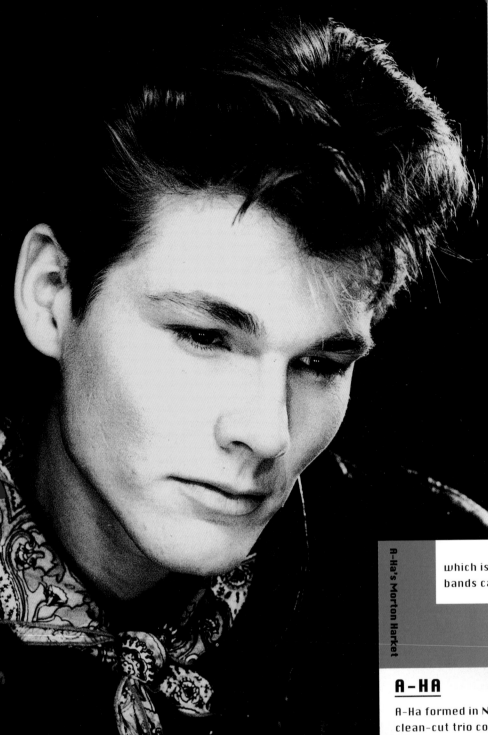

A-Ha's Morton Harket

3T

There are famous relatives and there are **famous relatives**. 3T's relative, an uncle, is more famous than most. Sometimes, that can really help a nascent career. Comprising **Taj**, **Taryll** and **TJ** (hence, presumably, the name), 3T became very successful, very quickly. Taking inspiration from their father's former band, the baby-faced trio proved most adept at singing slushy ballads that beat a direct path to the hearts of lovelorn teenage girls the world over. Unsurprisingly, they also dance rather well, which again is thanks to their uncle, who, incidentally, is the "King of Pop", **Michael Jackson**. In fact, Michael appeared on their biggest hit yet, the treacle-like **'I Need You'**, which is something that very few bands can boast of.

A-HA

A-Ha formed in Norway in 1980, a clean-cut trio comprising **Morton Harket**, **Mags Furuholmen** and **Pal Waaktaar**. Their first single, **'Take On Me'**, flopped on three separate occasions and it wasn't until a year later, after the record company decided to spend $100,000 on an accompanying video, that it finally became a huge international hit. A ground-breaking, semi-animated promo, it went on to win several awards and earn them a place in history for one of the most distinctive videos ever. Thereafter, they proceeded to carve out a successful career, their music a combination of brooding ballads and perfectly-formed pop songs, while singer Harket possessed the kind of looks that could make a teenage girl swoon at 20 paces. In 1993, the band announced that they were calling it a day, with Morton deciding to pursue a solo career.

PAULA ABDUL

Question: What do **Mick Jagger**, **ZZ Top**, **Emilio Estevez** and **Dolly Parton** all have in common? The answer is, believe it or not, Paula Abdul who, with the exception of Emilio Estevez (whom she married, briefly), have all benefited from the singer's dance tuition. Before embarking on a singing career - which led to huge international hits such as **'Straight Up'**, **'Rush Rush'** and **'Opposites Attract'** - Paula Abdul was a dance coordinator extraordinaire. It was she, for example, who guided **Janet Jackson**'s footsteps in the videos for **'When I Think Of You'**, **'Nasty'** and **'What Have You Done For Me Lately'**. Similarly, she also created the **"Velcro Fly"** dance step for **ZZ Top** (no easy task, you'll doubtless agree), although quite how she helped Ms Parton in the foot-shuffle department remains unclear (though famed for many things, Dolly isn't particularly noted for her dancing). Abdul's **transformation** into an all-singing, all-dancing sensation in her own right was an altogether seamless affair, as she became one of the '90s biggest successes.

AC/DC

A peculiar band, AC/DC. As authentic as **heavy metal** can get, they nevertheless possess a guitarist who insists on wearing the school uniform of a six-year-old boy on stage, while the band name itself is a euphemism for bisexuality. Formed in Australia over 24 years ago, they moved to England at the time of punk, turned up the volume to what would become the obligatory "11" and, in the words of their 1977 album, screamed **"LET THERE BE ROCK!"** Their first million seller, **'Highway To Hell'**, came two years later and by the turn of the '80s they were playing to crowds of over 70,000 people, many of whom, scarily enough, had taken to wearing school uniforms themselves. Now veritable old men of rock, their music will never be forgotten, and their overriding influence on every variation of metal cannot be overstated.

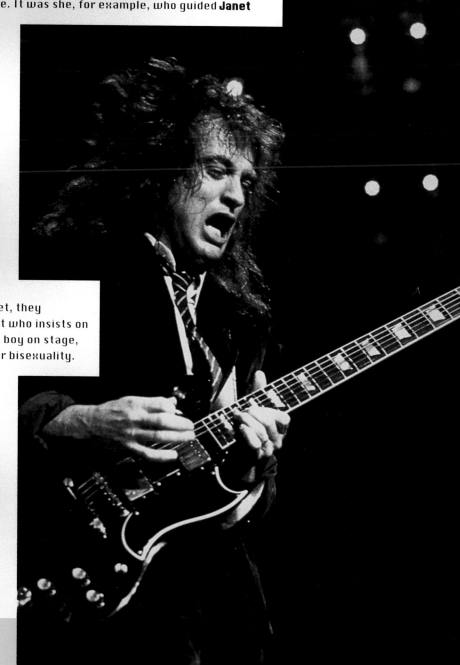

ACE OF BASE

Okay, so there's Denmark and Sweden, Norway and Finland, Germany and America... Sweden's Ace Of Base have enjoyed No.1 status in many, many countries and have, in the 1990s, become one of the most successful bands on planet Earth. Proving that there is more to their native country than just **Abba** and **Volvos**, the four-piece's introductory single, **'All That She Wants'**, became a mega-selling record (its joyful pop melody and universal sentiments transcending all race and language barriers with enviable ease) and they subsequently won several awards, acknowledging the fact that they are indeed the Best Selling Scandinavian Recording Artists anywhere. Their debut album, first entitled *Happy Nation*, then *The Sign* for its full worldwide release, hit the US No.1 spot. Even Abba would have been jealous... And there was more to come: nineteen million worldwide sales later, and *The Sign* was certified as the **best-selling debut album of all time** by the Guinness Book Of Records (who know about this kind of thing). They then experienced the full brunt of fame: singer **Jenny Berggren**, for instance, was stalked by a fan for a time in 1994, but their music remained unspoiled, suggesting that **"Happy Nation"** could well be a motto they live by.

BRYAN ADAMS

Neither particularly tall, nor especially good looking, nor particularly interested in the entire notion of glamour, Bryan Adams is perhaps the very personification of your typical everyman. Not exactly noteworthy in itself, maybe, but take into consideration that here is one of the world's biggest-selling rock stars, and this fact proves almost admirable. In a career now into its 21st year, Adams has reached **the very top of the ladder**. He's packed out stadia the world over, has **broken UK chart records** by spending over four months at No.1 with **'Everything I Do, I Do It For You'** in 1991 (the love theme from the film *Robin Hood: Prince Of Thieves*), and he's sung with everyone from **Tina Turner** to **Barbra Streisand** to **Smokey Robinson**. Much like **Bruce Springsteen**, Adams makes simple and melodic rock music with love-and-dreams lyrics that connect easily with a mass audience. He is without doubt Canada's most famous export ever - **Alanis Morissette**, in comparison, is a mere fledgling - but despite experiencing the kind of fame that suggests he could easily hold a one-to-one conversation with **Michael Jackson** on the subject, he remains unerringly level-headed. Hence his unofficial title as **"The Nicest Man In Rock"**.

ALICE IN CHAINS

Another band to make the crossover from cult to mainstream act in the wake of grungemania in the early 1990s, Alice In Chains, from Seattle, came over like three-dimensional barflies. If anything in this world pleased them, you know, actually made them happy, then it certainly never found its way into their music. Instead, this was music about **drugs** and **death** and **apathy** and **fear** and **loathing** and **hatred**. (Brows were permanently furrowed.) But they still proved hugely successful, with international hit singles such as **'Would?'** and albums such as *Dirt*, and they even made a guest appearance in the movie *Singles*. Various drug problems ensued, they split up, they re-formed, and continued to mine their own personal experiences in order to create suitably dark songs - their own particular forte.

TORI AMOS

Tori Amos is a genuine enigma. Born unto a Methodist minister father and a part-Cherokee mother, she was a musical prodigy by the age of two, a student of classical piano at Baltimore's prestigious **Peabody Conservatory** by the age of five (she was ultimately thrown out for playing by ear - which, if nothing else, must have given her chronic neckache), and was playing dive bars in Washington DC by the age of 13. It wasn't until 1992 that she finally came to international recognition with the beautiful *Little Earthquakes* album, its soporific splendour decidedly

The uncompromising Tori Amos

Bryan Adams

offset by some harrowingly personal lyrics that dealt with subjects such as rape. Then, in true skeletons-in-the-closet style, an earlier Amos album suddenly re-surfaced. Much to her embarrassment, the abysmal *Y Kant Tori Read* (recorded in 1987) cast the otherwise **sensitive singer-songwriter** as a Wonder Bra'd rock chick. Although slightly denting her reputation (it did give cynics ample ammunition), she continued to amaze and intrigue an increasingly loyal fan base, for whom she was a natural extension of **Kate Bush** - with added eccentricities. Her second solo album, *Under The Pink* (1994), was followed by the strange, uncompromising *Boys For Pele* album two years later, which surprisingly spawned a huge club hit with the wildly remixed **'Professional Widow'**; further proof that there really are few more individual than she.

ARRESTED DEVELOPMENT

Arrested Development were no ordinary rap band. Emerging from Mississippi in 1992, they were led by a bewitching frontman, Speech, whose aim was to be, "as influential as **Paul Simon** or **Quincy Jones** and as artistic as **Prince** or **Joni Mitchell**". The seven-piece - who included among their ranks various vocalists, a clothes designer, dancers, DJs, and even a resident spiritual adviser in the form of 60-year-old-plus **Baba Oje** - were together for three years, five months and two days before signing their record contract, and after much logical thought, decided to call their debut album *3 Years, 5 Months And 2 Days In The Life Of...* (1992). On record and in video, the band were pretty much irresistible. "Our mission is to reach people with what we call life music," said Speech. Fittingly, their decidedly earthy take on hip hop, complete with unifying lyrics, found them crossing over into the mainstream with ease, selling upward of four million copies of their first album. After their second album, *Zingalamadun* (Swahili for **"beehive of culture"**), the band went their separate ways, most notably with Speech's eponymous solo album and Dionne Farris's sublime single, **'I Know'**, which enjoyed considerable success and gained a **Grammy** nomination.

Kate Pierson of the B-52's

THE B-52'S

Hard to believe as it may be, The B-52's were actually a real, bonafide band. This needs to be clarified, for they often came across as a deliriously surreal cartoon. Formed back in 1976, an early single, **'Rock Lobster'**, soon became a fraternity party staple throughout the '80s, and after another decade of irreverent leftfield rock'n'pop, they finally hit the big time, in 1989, with the magnificent *Cosmic Thing* album, upon which could be found the singles **'Love Shack'** and **'Roam'**. With a neat sense of continuity, both tracks also went on to become frat party anthems. When, in 1994, film producers were on the look-out for the right band to contribute the theme tune to **The Flintstones**, The B-52's appeared to be tailor-made for the job. They were.

BABYLON ZOO

At the time of writing, it looks likely that Babylon Zoo's future is uncertain. But what a hit to be remembered by! The worldwide No.1 that was **'Spaceman'**, lifted from the Levi's commercial (the one with the girl from outer space), is the jeans company's most successful campaign yet. In Great Britain, it ousted *George Michael* from pole position and quickly became the fastest-selling record since **Band Aid**'s **'Do They Know It's Christmas?'** back in 1984, shifting over 500,000 copies in one week. The bizarre debut album that followed, *The Boy With The X-Ray Eyes*, sounded like someone obsessed with a) **David Bowie**, and b) Bacofoil; a kind of futuristic soundtrack with the year 2000 stamped all over it.

Incidentally, despite the fact that Mr. Babylon Zoo himself sounds like someone straight off the **Starship Enterprise**, it is in fact the showpiece for one **Jas Mann**, a strikingly handsome 24-year-old of Indian and Native American descent (via Wolverhampton, in the British Midlands) who, five years ago, fronted the little-known indie band, **Sandkings**.

BACKSTREET BOYS

The main selling point of the Backstreet Boys is, of course, that they all happen to be rather cute. That, and they can harmonize pretty neatly, too. **Nick**, **Howie**, **AJ**, **Brian** and **Kevin** formed in Orlando, Florida, in 1993. **Fresh** out of school, they named themselves after the local flea market, Backstreet Market. Quickly becoming noted for their ability to sing along to anything *accapella*, they were signed up as the new **New Kids On The Block** and shortly afterward cut their eponymously-titled debut album. Encouraged by loping hits such as **'Quit Playin' Games (With My Heart)'** and **'I'll Never Break Your Heart'** (love songs, their speciality), they soon became No.1 all over Europe. Like the **Spice Girls**, you have to have your favourite. Nick's kinda cute, no?

The Backstreet Boys at the MTV Europe Awards

THE BANGLES

In rock's rich history, Los Angeles's The Bangles hold a very small, but very cherishable, place. In 1986 they released a single that was written for them by somebody called Christopher (a pseudonym, one of too many, for **Prince**). It was **'Manic Monday'**, one of the sweetest pop songs ever. The all-girl four-piece (**Susanna Hoffs**, **Vicki Peterson**, **Debi Peterson** and the curiously-named **Michael Steele**) were never too cute, never too cool, but often a perfect combination of both. To wit, they excelled in elegiac ballads (**'Eternal Flame'**) just as they did in almost comedic pop songs (**'Walk Like An Egyptian'**). General consensus had it that Hoffs, with her doleful eyes and beestung lips, was the band's necessary sex symbol, although, despite earlier efforts, she never quite made it as a **screen siren** (she dabbled in film). The group had split by 1989 and, despite various solo projects, each failed to match their earlier successes.

THE BEASTIE BOYS

Rarely had the warning **"Lock up your daughters"** been so necessary. When the Beastie Boys landed in Europe, in 1987, they arrived with a reputation as America's most unruly and controversial rap act. Incredibly, they also happened to be white and Jewish. Their debut single was called **'Cookie Puss'**, they played live shows alongside naked women in cages and wore Volkswagen-logo medallions around their necks (thus, no VW was safe as their fans followed suit). **'(You Gotta) Fight For Your Right (To Party)'** became the most profound rally cry for teenage anarchy ever, and the band's welding of **Led Zeppelin**-like metal with New York rap hit No.1 everywhere. By 1989, despite still preferring the skateboard as their favoured mode of transport, the trio had grown up (a little) and issued the *Paul's Boutique* album, which would languish for five years before being regarded as a classic. They set up their own magazine and label, both called Grand Royal, and developed a line of skatewear with X-Large. Their third album, *Check Your Head* (1992), received the kind of plaudits usually reserved for bands at the height of their creative powers.

THE BEAUTIFUL SOUTH

While they may well look like extras from, say, *Coronation Street* (only less glitzy), the assorted members of The Beautiful South are in fact homegrown superstars whose records sell in the kind of quantities that keep Liam and Noel in parkas. Formed in Hull in 1989 after **The Housemartins** disbanded, singer **Paul Heaton** continued to write grim, sardonic vignettes, only this time to even greater effect. A celebration of the simplistic,

Beautiful South songs are easily composed: melodies are soft, lilting, sweet and of universal appeal, while lyrics are barbed, cynical, sometimes hateful and always sarcastic. **'Song For Whoever'**, for example, is about the big-money sentimentality of love songs. **'Old Red Eyes Is Back'** is about ravaged alcoholism, while the more recent **'Rotterdam'** manages to criticize every single European citizen while sounding like the most innocent of ditties. It all proved to be a winning, if unlikely, formula. When they released their hits collection, 1994's *Carry On Up The Charts*, it very rapidly became the third-fastest-selling album ever in Britain, eventually selling over two and a half million copies.

The Beautiful South

BECK

Beck Hansen, singer-songwriter and icon-in-the-making, is a glorious mass of contradictions. He possesses the babyface of one who has yet to fully acquaint himself with a razor, and yet his voice sounds like that of a ravaged blues man whose timbre has been affected by years of nicotine and alcohol abuse. His breakthrough single, the magnificent **'Loser'**, had him down as the premier slacker of his generation (the X generation, naturally), but he then followed that up in quick succession with his debut album, *Mellow Gold* (1994), then several independently-released albums. He toured constantly, including a stint on **Lollapalooza**, and then released the fabulous *Odelay* almost immediately afterward (a work rate so prodigious that he could hardly be accused of being someone who slacks off). He is also a bonafide **MTV darling**, and yet one of his most celebrated songs is a track called **'MTV Makes Me Want To Smoke Crack'**. Go figure. And then there's the music itself, which is...what exactly? Well, it's hip hop with a blues influence, it's folk with a country shuffle, it's funky and noisy, slow and fast, occasionally gospel-tinged, acutely tuneful and sounds like no one else around. What better recommendation?

Beck and friends

THE BELOVED

Although they formed back in 1984, London's Beloved had to wait five years before tasting mainstream success when they finally cracked the charts with the wondrous ambient anthem **'The Sun Rising'** single, whose highly sensuous tones had a very similar effect to relaxing in a floatation tank. They followed that with a similarly beguiling song entitled **'Hello'**, which was basically a list of the band's heroes (including **Fred Astaire**, **Little Richard** and cartoon characters **Fred Flintstone** and **Charlie Brown**). In 1991, band-member Steve Waddington left to join ambient band **System 7**, while founder member **Jon Marsh** was joined by his wife **Helena** (as vocalist). Although they never quite managed to parallel their early success, two further albums (*Conscience* and *X*) confirmed that, when it came to pop songs with a vaguely **New Age** otherworldliness, few did it as nicely as The Beloved.

The Beloved

BIG AUDIO DYNAMITE

Being kicked out of punk's most important band, you would imagine, brings with it grave consequences. As in, for example, the end of a career. Not so, however, for **Mick Jones** who, upon being asked to leave **The Clash** promptly formed Big Audio Dynamite, whose welding of rock with techno would become a pioneering influence in British music. The year was 1985, The Clash were already well past their sell-by date, while BAD, on the other hand, were in full bloom. Their hit single, **'E=MC^2'**, which not only possessed a somewhat radical dance beat (for the era) but also a Michael Caine "sample", sounded quite unlike anything that had come before it, and the likes of fledgling bands such as **Happy Mondays**, **Stone Roses** and Jesus Jones quickly started taking notes. Although ultimately a patchy affair, the accompanying album, *This Is Big Audio Dynamite*, provided further proof that Jones's vision was five years ahead of itself, and later represented the band's creative highlight. They disbanded in 1991.

BJÖRK

Ever since Iceland's **The Sugarcubes** emerged in the late-80s, Björk has played the **kooky weirdo** to something approaching perfection. It all started with **'Birthday'**, the strangest single anyone had ever heard, and probably the best souvenir of the entire decade. Then, solo, Björk went mainstream in a big way. Wonderfully, it was all by mistake. *Debut* ('93) was supposed to be a small album with limited appeal (said she), but was instead embraced by everyone for its off-centre sensibilities and its melodies from another planet. Then, two years later, *Post* did more of the same, combining every conceivable style on an album that followed no formula whatsoever. Maybe it's in the eyes, which sparkle as though her soul's on fire; or maybe it's her billowing black hair, which brings with it the air of a French arthouse movie; or maybe it's those weird, wonderful outfits of hers; or maybe it's the "elfin" character she so naturally exudes, one that makes her appear equal parts luminescent and loopy; or maybe it's the single **'It's Oh So Quiet'**, which represents her every emotion, her every nuance, in three minutes. Well, whatever **"it"** is, Björk possesses it in abundance.

BLACK

Generally speaking, pop stars are loud, colourful, self-obsessed, and arrogant; and - if they are doing their job properly - ingratiatingly ubiquitous. They are hungry for the limelight, are often in love with no one as much as they are with themselves, and never miss a photo opportunity. And so to Black. Black, in the world of pop, is, or rather was, something of an anomaly. Black, or rather one-man-band singer-songwriter **Colin Vearncombe**, couldn't have had a lower profile. This much we know: he was from Liverpool; he looked not unlike a pint of Guinness (blonde-haired and perennially dressed in black); and he wrote a song of such gentle wonderment that everyone still remembers it to this day. That song was **'Wonderful Life'** (1987). It made Black a household name throughout Europe and was subsequently used in several TV advertising campaigns. His four albums, however, fared less well and thus he remains known as something of a one-hit wonder.

The man in Black, Colin Verncombe

THE BLACK CROWES

Were this a harsher world than it already is, then surely The Black Crowes would be executed at dawn for their spectacular lack of fashion sense alone. Look at their particularly lurid wardrobe for too long and you might convince yourself that the '70s never actually ended. A godsend to thrift shops everywhere, Atlanta, Georgia's finest also sound like a perfect hybrid of **Free**, **The Faces**, **Lynyrd Skynyrd** and, of course, **The Rolling Stones**. Singer **Chris Robinson** is the very personification of swagger, a frontman every bit as cool as he thinks he is, and the man responsible for one of the finest vocal performances in recent years with his version of Otis Redding's **'Hard To Handle'**. Their debut album, *Shake Your Money Maker* (1990) sold over three million copies in the US alone, while the follow-up, The *Southern Harmony And Musical Companion*, a melting pot of authentic R&B, made them a favourite on the European festival circuit. Their most recent album, *Amorica* (1994) succeeded in getting banned in several American record shops for its cover shot: a close-up of a pair of bikini briefs that were almost too brief to contain their contents.

BLIND MELON

In a world where image is everything, Blind Melon got themselves noticed in a fashion that can only be described as anything but typical. For the front cover of their eponymously-titled debut album (1992), they featured a rather chubby young girl who was wearing glasses and a homemade-looking **bumble bee outfit**, and had a wiry loveheart balancing precariously on her head. It looked simultaneously awful and yet somehow endearing. The very same icon (as she later became) then appeared in the band's breakthrough video, **'No Rain'**. She became something of a celebrity and the band became famous. "We are wholly unconcerned with image," they later said. With a feelgood vibe and a penchant for bluesy electric and acoustic rock, the band quickly got tagged as latter-day hippies and, indeed, when not on the road, they lived together on a commune in North Carolina - tuning in and dropping out in all probability. In 1996, singer **Shannon Hoon** was found dead from an overdose, curtailing the career of a band that appeared to be on the edge of **Grateful Dead**-style success.

Shannon Hoon of Blind Melon

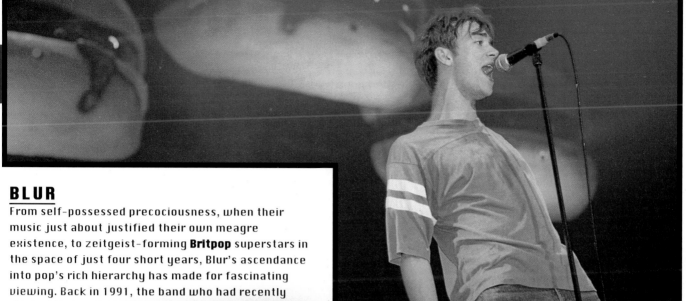

Damon Albarn of Blur

BLUR

From self-possessed precociousness, when their music just about justified their own meagre existence, to zeitgeist-forming **Britpop** superstars in the space of just four short years, Blur's ascendance into pop's rich hierarchy has made for fascinating viewing. Back in 1991, the band who had recently ditched their original name (**Seymour**) in favour of the *de rigeur* monosyllabic moniker were busy cultivating disciples with their *Leisure* album. A mess of guitar feedback, self-consciously slurred vocals, some arresting visuals and a singer with beautiful eyes and cute love beads, Blur were pretty much irresistible. An art-school background and a slight propensity to take themselves a little too seriously then led, in 1993, to the *Modern Life Is Rubbish* album, but it was with the release of *Parklife*, the album that spawned Britpop, that Blur truly arrived. Suddenly, they were everywhere, their arch songs garrulous caricatures of a little England filled with the kind of wide-boy characters usually found in the books of **Damon Albarn**'s favourite novelist, **Martin Amis**. A year later and the UK watched a protracted head-to-head battle between **Oasis** and Blur, each camp declaring, "We're better than you!" It all got deliriously out of hand, climaxing in August '96 when Blur's **'Country House'** and Oasis's **'Roll With It'** fought it out for the UK No.1 spot. The entire media covered the story with surprisingly exhaustive interest (Blur eventually "won"). However, their next album, *The Great Escape*, was considerably overshadowed by Oasis's *(What's The Story) Morning Glory?*, and Damon, tiring of constantly being hounded by the media over his relationship with **Elastica**-singer **Justine Frischman**, slunk out of the limelight for much of '96. Their current, eponymously-titled, album (which was recorded in Iceland) sees the quartet reinvent themselves once more, with music that strikingly resembles the work of American lo-fi exponents, **Pavement**. It is vehemently not a crowd-pleaser, suggesting that they're only too keen to remain masters of their own destiny.

BON JOVI

See Legends of MTV pp. 14-15

DAVID BOWIE

For those too young to remember the '70s without relying on their parents to fill in all the blanks, David Bowie is a distant pop star with a penchant for merging the music of the day (be it dance, rap, drum'n'bass – jungle even) with his own brand of theatrical pop. He's the bloke in the long coat, the sculptured hair, funny teeth, and eyes that you'd just swear were two different colours. In the late '80s, he decided to form a band under the name **Tin Machine**. They "did" rock music. Critics rubbished them and Bowie's own audience nodded in agreement. In 1995, he released the decidedly weird *1.Outside* album (crazy record, crazy name), a collaboration with **Brian Eno** that elicited a huge question mark from all concerned. By 1997, his 50th year, he came out with *Earthling*, an album that embraced the spirit of drum'n'bass. In between such erratic work, he has continued to appear in films, most recently in *Basquiat*, in which he played Andy Warhol. But even those of a young disposition just somehow know that here is someone who deserves a particularly rare kind of respect, the kind that can only come after helping shape modern music for more than 30 years.

BOYZONE

Boyzone: Ronan, Steve, Shane, Keith and Mikey

Imagine the scenario. It is early 1996, and **Take That**, the band who blight Boyzone's very existence, have called a press conference. Boyzone, keeping their fingers crossed, enjoy a discreet shiver of anticipation. Then, as the world's No.1 teen band announce that they are to split, the boys in Boyzone go absolutely mental. They celebrate, for now there is no one to stand in their way. If they were popular before Take That split, they've been increasingly more so since. **Ronan**, **Steve**, **Shane**, **Keith** and **Mikey** are five very good looking Irish boys. They prove most adept in covering old songs by old bands (**Chicago**, **Bee Gees**) that quickly become the soundtrack to a young girl's life. They are rarely out of the **Top Five** and by the end of 1996 their first two albums, *Said & Done* and *A Different Beat*, had hit the UK's top spot. Wherever they go, their voices are drowned out by the schizoid sound of a thousand **teenage girls screaming** at once. From here they have no obstacles in their path. They are unstoppable. And, girls, they're young, free and quite, quite **single**.

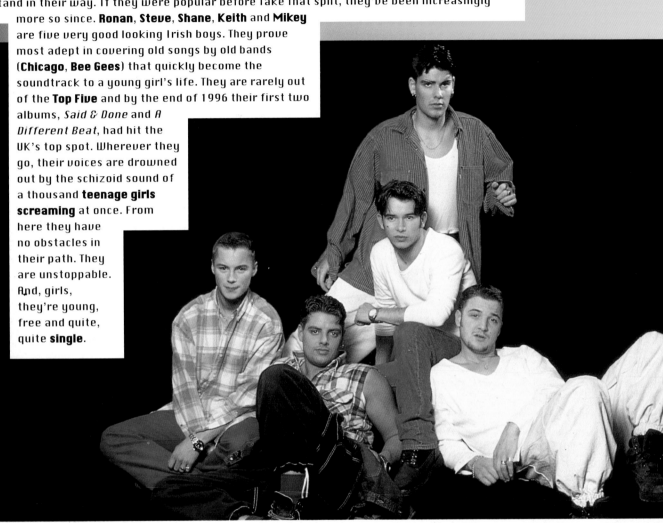

TONI BRAXTON

The impeccably turned out Toni Braxton

If, in Toni Braxton's impeccable turn-out (beautifully corkscrew-curled hair, clothes that look like they've come direct from Rodeo Drive, the subtle employment of high-carat jewellery, etc.), one senses that her purse may well be rather flushed, then it isn't without good reason. She is. Royally so. Having sold ten million copies of her debut album, she is probably the richest swing queen on the block, any block. Not for nothing, then, does she sound rather pleased with herself. Her next album, 1996's *Secrets*, lives its life in the mellifluous lane, with the lights turned low and a whispered directive of sultry seduction. But her songs aren't merely run-of-the-mill romantic yarns. Admittedly, **'Un-Break My Heart'** is a typical, but distinctly beautiful, ballad, but the languorous **'You're Makin Me High'**, for example, is an ode to masturbation, something you could never quite imagine **Whitney Houston** crooning. A refined soul diva, Braxton's voice is fast becoming recognized as the perfect accompaniment to a box of very expensive chocolates.

THE BREEDERS

The Breeders, of course, are responsible for one of the best singles of the 1990s. It is called **'Cannonball'** and there is simply nothing better anywhere. Formed by **Kim Deal** after **The Pixies** went the way of the dodo, the original line-up featured former **Throwing Muses** member and imminent **Belly** founder, **Tanya Donnelly**. An album, *Pod*, emerged at the turn of the decade, and was presently deemed pretty impressive. Its follow-up, The Breeders' *Last Splash*, however, was the real golden nugget, not only because it contained the aforementioned **'Cannonball'**, but also because it combined superlative pop nous with a bizarre leftfield weirdness that could only have come out of the small but perfectly formed New England scene (see aforementioned bands). Things went awry thereafter as guitarist Kelley Deal (sister of Kim) was arrested for possession of drugs and later checked into the Betty Ford clinic. Kim continued with new band **The Amps**, while Kelley eventually re-emerged with her own new project, The Kelley Deal 6000.

BROS

Teenage girls have rarely screamed louder, or been so manic, so fanatic. They camped outside Bros's South-East London home, day and night, rain or shine. Any TV show they happened to appear on was immediately swamped with a territorial-style army of their fans, each clambering over the other to get closer, closer. The band's records, posters and cute embossed T-shirts out-sold everything else in its wake. They were a money-making dream and became more famous than they could ever have imagined. For a spectacularly brief period, Bros were ubiquitous. They were gorgeous and young; two were twins, the other wasn't; they sang in harmony in very high voices; they wore ripped denim and worn leather; they all lived at home, were not married, and were, consequently, "available" (cue a million melting hearts). They had several Top 10s - **'When Will I Be Famous'**, **'Drop The Boy'**, the positively meditative **'Cat Among The Pigeons'**. They became millionaires, seemingly overnight. They were a SENSATION. Twins **Matt** and **Luke Goss** then kicked out guitarist **Craig Logan** (otherwise known as "Ken"). They lost a lot of money. They played Wembley Stadium. They lost even more money. They split up. The twins went on to other projects, "Ken" got a job within a record company. Their fans moved on to **Take That**. All that remained was that brief, incendiary memory.

BOBBY BROWN

Bobby Brown started performing early in life, first toddling out on to a stage (during the intermission of a **James Brown** concert) aged just three. By 11, he was part of pre-teen sensations **New Edition** (**The Jackson 5** updated, essentially), a band so successful that he was forced to forsake his mathematics homework in favour of worldwide stardom. By 1985, at the age of 16, he became a solo act and went on to score several hits, including **'Don't Be Cruel'**, **'Every Little Step'** and the excellent **'My Prerogative'**. Nurturing something of a bad boy image (with the help of a few girls), it came as a surprise to all when, in 1992, he married one of the world's most wholesome singers, **Whitney Houston**. Despite setting up home with the superstar soulstress, he continued to walk on the wild side (a somewhat diplomatic way of saying that he and the police are not exactly strangers to one another). His solo career continues to flourish today and, despite having had several reasons to issue him with his marching orders, Houston continues to stand by her man.

Whitney's other half, Bobby Brown

THE CARDIGANS

Along with **The Wannadies**, The Cardigans are doing great things for Sweden, proving that you don't have to be **Abba** or **Ace Of Base** to take Swedish pop global. Reminiscent of **The Sundays**, The Cardigans make music of almost intense loveliness: if you cast their melodies out to sea, you feel, they would float; if you threw them into the air, they would hover weightlessly. But, as incongruous a vision as it may be, The Cardigans also have "a thing" for **Black Sabbath**. On their 1995 debut album, *Life*, they covered **'Sabbath Bloody Sabbath'**, while on the glittering follow-up, *First Band On The Moon*, they re-interpreted **'Iron Man'**, ditching any satanic overtones in favour of cute, cuddly acoustics. This is but one of their many charms. The Cardigans make wonderful music that comes as close to defining pop-in-excelsis as anyone either before or after them.

MARIAH CAREY

Named after a song from the classic musical *Paint Your Wagon*, Mariah Carey is slightly more successful than your average 27-year-old. Although she started singing at roughly the same time as she started talking (making bath times resemble an MTV *Unplugged* session), she had to wait until 1990, at the grand old age of 20, before scoring her first international hit, **'Vision Of Love'**. Marrying her record company president, Tommy Mottola, along the way, she quickly became as famous as Whitney, with a mellifluous succession of refined, occasionally statuesque, soul songs. (Ballads are her particular forte.) In Europe, she dominated MTV's singles and albums chart; in Japan, her *Merry Christmas* album sold more copies in one week (200,000) than any other before it, and went on to outsell **Whitney Houston**'s *The Bodyguard* to eventually become Japan's best-selling foreign album ever, at 2.7 million copies; while in America she became as celebrated as July 4 when **'One Sweet Day'**, her collaboration with **Boyz II Men**, spent 16 weeks at No.1, the longest run in American chart history. Within just six years, she has hit the US pole position no less than 11 times. Success? Only Mariah knows the true meaning of the word.

They call the wind Mariah

BELINDA CARLISLE

Belinda Carlisle, owner of the finest cheekbones in the entire history of pop, has been making music professionally for 20 years now. Hard to believe, but true. Back in 1978, she formed **The Go Go's** (a prototype **Spice Girls**, if you will), and became very famous indeed. Five girls with the kind of perfect complexions and cute smiles that suggested butter wouldn't melt. However, their image of all-American wholesomeness wasn't as accurate as it seemed. Before long, widely publicized tales of excessive drug-taking hit the headlines and by 1984 the band had split up and checked into the **Betty Ford clinic**. Carlisle's solo career took off shortly afterward as she got into healthy living, streamlined Californian power pop and a clutch of beautifully shot videos that highlighted her magnificent bone structure. By 1987, she was a colossus in pop music. If you watched MTV at all back then and failed to catch her video for **'Heaven Is A Place On Earth'** then, frankly, your television wasn't working properly. Since then, she's campaigned for Greenpeace and briefly reformed The Go Go's, while remaining very successful and extolling the many virtues of clean living.

NICK CAVE AND THE BAD SEEDS

For those acquainted with Nick Cave, it seems entirely befitting that he lifted his band's name from William March's novel *The Bad Seed*, which is about a young girl who comes from a long line of murderers and is therefore rotten to the core. The music of Cave is much like the man himself: gaunt, foreboding, mood-imbued, ragged, aggressive and potentially quite violent. You get the picture, yes? An Australian, he formed The Bad Seeds in London shortly after his previous band, **The Birthday Party**, split in 1983, and has since made as fine a collection of music as you could ever hope to hear. Cave sings about drunks, prostitutes, bad boys and especially about murderers, for whom he has a special place in his heart. To wit, in 1996, he released *Murder Ballads*, an album in which the singer, variously duetting with the likes of **Kylie Minogue** and **Polly Harvey**, covers just about every form of murder known to man, woman or pathologist. (For example, in the sublime **'Where The Wild Roses Grow'**, Cave's character kills Kylie's by smashing her head with rock. Nice.) He is also a novelist and sometime actor and is fast approaching his 40th year.

TRACY CHAPMAN

Long the queen of worthy songs of conscience, Tracy Chapman has sold an incredible **eighteen million albums** in a career that barely spans a decade.

Quietly emerging back in 1988 with an acoustic guitar and dreadlocks, her debut single **'Fast Car'** struck a quiet chord in every heart and, along with her appearance at the **Free Nelson Mandela** concert, made her a worldwide star. A long standing and very public campaigner for **Amnesty International**, she has nevertheless remained something of an enigma who appears never to have consciously sought the limelight or anything even resembling fame. She has recorded four albums (her latest entitled *New Beginning*), each perfect examples of her now trademark **acoustic angst**, proving that image doesn't necessarily have to go hand-in-hand with success.

THE CHARLATANS

Formed in Wolverhampton in 1988, The Charlatans came to public recognition two years later as part of the **Madchester** explosion alongside **Happy Mondays** and **Stone Roses**. Led by the loose-lipped Tim Burgess (Mick Jagger crossed with a street urchin), they created an inspired blend of baggy rhythms and **Rolling Stones**-swagger and immediately landed themselves a UK Top Ten with **'The Only One I Know'**. Thereafter, the band's career remained rooted in the Second Division, alleviated only by the occasional mishap which, if nothing else, kept them newsworthy. In 1991, bassist **Martin Blunt** quit the band, suffering from severe depression. A year later, keyboardist **Rob Collins** was somehow mixed up in an armed robbery and spent eight months in prison. Things started looking up in 1995 when, having outlasted all of their Madchester peers, their eponymously-titled fourth album hit the UK No.1 spot. But a year later, Collins crashed his car, dying instantly. In typically perverse fashion, however, the band immediately hit back with their finest single to date, **'One To Another'**, while their recently released fifth album looks set to be their biggest.

CHER

Cher is very thin indeed. She is also a remarkable looking woman for someone of her "advanced" years (51) and has been a successful singer since the early '60s. She married a man who insisted his name was Sonny and, together, they became a duo. In 1965, they recorded **'I Got You Babe'**, which was fantastic back then and remains so now. By 1971, **Sonny and Cher** had their own US TV show, entitled *The Sonny And Cher Comedy Hour*. The couple divorced three years later. Thereafter, she did further television, sang with **Meat Loaf** and became a fully-fledged actress. For her appearance in the film *Silkwood*, alongside **Meryl Streep**, she received an Oscar nomination. She went on to win an Oscar for her lead role in *Moonstruck*. She also delivered fine performances in *Mask*, *The Witches Of Eastwick* and *Mermaids*. Meanwhile, her music career ticks over nicely, not least with the huge-selling *Cher* (1988) on which she sounded like **Jon Bon Jovi** and Meat Loaf combined. In 1996, she returned with *It's A Man's World*, a strong enough set to suggest she ain't finished yet, not by a long shot.

Madchester's Charlatans

NENEH CHERRY

Had "things" gone according to plan, then by now Neneh Cherry would be a worldwide superstar, a role model for the '90s woman and the thinking man's sex symbol. As it has since transpired, she's managed only to fulfil the last two; that "worldwide superstar" bit having curiously eluded her. Back in the late '80s, however, it looked like a foregone conclusion. Heavily pregnant and bouncing around on expensive sneakers, her twin hits, **'Buffalo Stance'** and **'Manchild'**, were impeccable rally cries for a generation, their author too cool for words. Ditto the debut album, *Raw Like Sushi* (1989). But then, relocation to Sweden, more babies and a slightly disappointing second album (*Homebrew*, 1992) followed and she faded from view. She re-emerged briefly three years later on the No.1 charity single, **'Love Can Build A Bridge'**, with **Cher** and **Chrissie Hynde**, but it was in 1996 that she truly returned triumphant, with an excellent third album,(*Man*), which included 'Seven Seconds', a sublime multilingual duet with Senegal's **Youssou N'Dour**. Finally, in the era of the so-called "It" Girl (young women who, without even trying, personify all that is cool in the oh-so cultural 1990s), Ms Cherry remains the most obvious example.

ERIC CLAPTON

Eric Clapton is a guitarist. He is also "just" a man, a regular human being who happens to be rather handy with a plectrum. His more ardent of fans, however, insist on referring to him as **God**, despite the fact that he had little to do with creation, Jesus, the Bible, Adam and Eve or any of the major world wars. In a career that has spanned over 35 years, Clapton has played his guitar with everyone from **Cream** to **Hendrix** to **Bob Dylan**; he's penned several rock classics, including **'Layla'**, **'Wonderful Tonight'** and **'Lay Down Sally'** (co-written with Marcella Detroit), and plays mammoth tours during which the same set of fans return night after night after night (their devotion being the main reason he is referred to as God). A legendary blues guitarist, he was rumoured to be passing all his skills (instrument-wise and otherwise) to his current companion, who was claimed to be **Sheryl Crow**.

Eric "Slow hand" Clapton

PHIL COLLINS

Now one of the world's better selling **artists**, the kind of man who needs only click his fingers to receive anything he so wishes (he's that rich, that famous), Phil Collins's inauguration into the world of showbiz was altogether more humble. A jobbing child actor, Master Collins appeared on the London stage, age 14, as the Artful Dodger in a production of Lionel Bart's *Oliver*. From there, he undertook his first UK tour (promoting crisps, believe it or not), before deciding that his true future lay behind a drum kit - as the drummer in **Genesis**. When frontman **Peter Gabriel** flew the nest in 1975, a slightly nervous Collins took sole responsibility for all vocals, a role in which he was later to excel. In 1981 he began a highly lucrative career as a solo singer, basing much of his first three albums on the emotional fallout caused by the breakup of his marriage. His lead role in the film *Buster* (1988), based on the true story of the **Great Train Robbery**, reaped considerable praise, suggesting a possible future in movies, but Collins later decided to leave acting to the actors, while he later left Genesis for good, deciding that a solo career was all he really wanted.

COOLIO

These days, life for Coolio is not what it was. Back then, before major success, life for Coolio was heading for just that: life. Behind bars. A former gang-banger and **crack addict** in his native Compton, LA, he eventually woke one morning and decided that this kind of lifestyle was no longer for him. He turned wise and he turned to rap. Today, he has a **platinum-selling** debut album (*It Takes A Thief*) behind him; he's in major demand on both sides of the Atlantic; and with his 1995 single, **'Gangsta's Paradise'**, he created UK chart history as the first rap star ever to enter the charts at No.1. The album of the same name, his second, eschewed the guns'n'violence stance typical of the LA rap scene for a far more reflective style. Equally at home rapping as he is crooning, and sampling heavily from acts such as **Kool & The Gang**, Billy Paul and **Stevie Wonder**, much of this album was impressively graceful, sleek of funk and smouldering of soul. Which is something you could never say for Ice T. To call him a reformed character, therefore, is to understate matters considerably.

THE CRANBERRIES

The Cranberries story is, simply, the stuff of legend. Born unto simple folk in Limerick, Ireland, not very long ago at all, **Dolores O'Riordan** is asked to join the nascent band in 1989, then called The Cranberry Saw Us, because rumour had it that she sang very well in church. Seven years and several hairstyles later, The Cranberries have shifted over 20 million records globally. Their recipe is simple: winsome, seductive songs about love and dreams, presided over by a set of vocals that sound like they are dipped in fresh honey. *Everybody Else Is Doing It...So Why Can't We?* and its follow-up, *No Need To Argue* were albums that existed on their own merits; there was no discernible image here, just overtly beautiful songs. Only **'Zombie'** (a song about the IRA), from their second album, suggested a possible interest in polemic. As their success grew, so Dolores began her transformation from shy country girl to unabashed rock'n'roller, shaving her head, wearing fewer clothes and eventually getting married to **Duran Duran**'s tour manager. Their third album, *To The Faithful Departed*, built upon 'Zombie', with Dolores singing about war and injustice with all the passion of early **Bono**, and revealing a hitherto unknown fighting spirit.

The far from dumb Crash Test Dummies

CRASH TEST DUMMIES

It is probably fair to assert that Canada's Crash Test Dummies are a DJ's worst nightmare. The reason being their first major hit single: **'Mmm Mmm Mmm Mmm'**, a title that is impossible to introduce without looking a fool. Laden with irony and a wonderfully twisted sense of storytelling, the Crash Test Dummies formed in the mid-80s, but didn't receive any kind of recognition until nearly a decade later. Unsurprisingly, singer-songwriter **Brad Roberts** possesses an enormous knowledge of English literature and philosophy, and his songs are imbued with strange, lyrical tales about, among other things, chest X-rays, embarrassing birthmarks and intelligent ducks. They entitled their debut album *God Shuffled His Feet*. It was very warmly received indeed, being compared to the recorded works of **R.E.M.** and **Talking Heads**, and immediately established the band as consummate purveyors of all things wry.

SHERYL CROW

Putting a pretty face to AOR, the genre in which her cinematic cruising music nestles so snugly, Sheryl Crow clawed her way to the top the hard way. A stint of school-teaching was later replaced by singing on TV adverts, a job she, unsurprisingly, found somewhat unfulfilling although, she says, the money was very good. Then she moved to LA and landed a gig providing backing vocals for **Michael Jackson**'s world tour. From there she sang backing vocals on many artists' records, including **Sinead O'Connor**, **Stevie Wonder** and **Don Henley**, while honing her own songwriting talents at the so-called Tuesday Night Music Club, presided over by

friend and Jacko-collaborator Bill Bottrell. She later borrowed the name for her debut album in 1993, which, powered by the single **'All I Wanna Do'**, finally broke her as an artist in her own right. Now living what can safely be described as the high life, Crow is currently consolidating her initial bout of success with her eponymously-titled second album, and is rumoured to be playing happy families with AOR's own crown prince, **Eric Clapton**. Additional note: Sheryl Crow has very lovely hair.

CROWDED HOUSE

The following statement may not sound particularly impressive. But it is, it is. Crowded House is New Zealand's best ever band. Their swansong album, *Recurring Dream*, is as fine a greatest hits collection as you could ever hope to come across, and its author as skilful a melody maker as either **Lennon** or **McCartney**. Its release, however, saddened many a fanatical fan for it meant the end of their favourite group, who had decided go their separate ways. Formed Down Under in 1985 following the demise of **Split Enz**, Crowded House found instantly the worldwide recognition that curiously eluded the Finn brothers former band. **'Don't Dream It's Over'** made US No.2, and they looked all set to go global. It was not quite to be, however, because thereafter Crowded House became something of a cult band, always receiving fanatical critiques and gaining a very loyal following, while only ever selling their eminently delightful albums in modest quantities. Their services to music were nevertheless not unnoticed and in 1993 both **Neil Finn** and brother **Tim** were awarded OBEs from the Queen for their services to New Zealand.

MTV
MUSIC TELEVISION

THE CURE

One of the world's more enduring acts, The Cure are led by **Robert Smith**, a man who seems not to have aged a day since their inception 21 years ago. This suggests one of two things: 1) he is, in fact, immortal; or 2) his foundation covers his wrinkles quite magnificently. An entire generation of twentysomethings discovered the Cure at around the age of 16. It was a rainy Saturday night and the band were singing songs about **despair** and **dislocation** in despondent tones that were addressed directly to them. In other words, Smith's lyrics described perfectly your average teenager's all-pervading sense of angst. Through such classic albums as *The Head On The Door* and *Disintegration*, their music struck a chord the world over, and gigs were populated with Smith clones: young people, of either sex, with electric-shock hair, smudged lipstick, plenty of foundation, big, shapeless jumpers, drainpipe jeans and oversized sneakers - this was worship on a major scale. While there were many line-up changes along the way, some of them quite acrimonious, the band's music remained unerringly consistent and, thus, they remain as essential as ever. The music world wouldn't feel quite the same without them.

Robert Smith of The Cure

CURIOSITY KILLED THE CAT

Although tagged as a teen band, largely because singer **Ben Volpeliere-Pierrot** was somewhat photogenic, Curiosity Killed The Cat actually made music that could quite easily exist outside of the pages of pop magazines. Their debut album, 1987's *Keep Your Distance*, contained several excellent, even mildly funky, pop singles such as **'Down To Earth'** and **'Misfit'**. In 1986, the band met **Andy Warhol** at a London art exhibition. He was so taken with these young whippersnappers that he decided to publicly endorse them (which could have proved fatal, as Warhol had a thing for attaching his name to anyone who could keep him in the public eye). He later appeared in the 'Misfit' video, looking very white and very frail indeed. A year later, the pop-art connoisseur was dead, but the Cats continued to eke out a rather profitable existence until 1989, when the light kind of fizzled out.

Cypress Hill at the
Brixton Academy

CYPRESS HILL

Touched by the hand of cool, Cypress Hill were often regarded as **The Grateful Dead** of rap, not because they toured incessantly, nor because they boasted a fan base of Generation X-ers for whom "tune in, turn on, drop out" was a veritable religion, but because their (seemingly sole) purpose in life was the promotion of weed. Without marijuana, Cypress Hill wouldn't even exist. Their most celebrated anthem was **'I Wanna Get High'**, while sleevenotes outlined the case for legalizing the soft drug. On a more musical trip, Cypress Hill are more than just your average rap act. A trio of Cuban-Americans (Sen Dog, B-Real and DJ Muggs), their production is swamped in an overload of murky sound and atypical samples (anything from **Black Sabbath** to **Dusty Springfield**), while B-Real's squeaky, high-pitched vocals makes Minnie Mouse sound like Louis Armstrong. By 1993, with *Black Sunday*, they were on the way to becoming megastars, and with collaborations with the likes of **Pearl Jam** and **Sonic Youth** they continued to make inroads into the mainstream, not least with their huge hit single, 'Insane In The Brain'.

DE LA SOUL

The difficulty De La Soul have experienced in attempting to follow up their classic 1989 debut album has not gone unnoticed. *3 Feet High And Rising* introduced the world to **Daisy-Age Rap**, which, at the time, seemed like the best place on Earth to cool your boots. Including the classic cut, **'Me, Myself And I'**, De La Soul practically reinvented rap, replacing the typical West Coast gangsta-isms that dominated the genre with something more peaceful and positive. Their second album, however, pronounced that *De La Soul Is Dead*, and sounded like it. Seemingly tired of what they had created, they developed a harder, more typical mainstream rap sound that subsequently proved not quite as popular. Their third album, *Buhloone Mindstate*, was a dark, brooding affair, while their fourth, *Stakes Is High*, went some way to revisiting former glories. Whatever their position in rap now, De La Soul are one of the genre's most important exponents.

The delightful De La Soul

DEEE-LITE

Three minutes is all it took. Three minutes to announce their arrival, cement the foundings of a career (which had actually begun almost a decade earlier), create a day-glo image that would influence millions and put a skip into the world's step. If 1990 had a zeitgeist, then it really was that groove is in the heart. And responsible for that particular zeitgeist was, of course, Deee-Lite, whose single **'Groove Is In The Heart'** (from the album *World Clique*) will be regarded as a classic dance track for all eternity. Sadly, it'll also probably be the only thing they'll be remembered for, because since then the New York trio (of **Lady Miss Kier**, Super DJ **Dmitry Brill** and Jungle DJ **Towa Towa**) have never managed to match its incredible effervescence. After three subsequent albums, the band tottered off in different directions, leaving one truly great hit behind them.

DEEP FOREST

Deep Forest are two French record producers, **Michel Sanchez** and **Eric Mouquet**, who, in 1994, had the rather clever idea of marrying soporific ambient music with an African influence. The result was **'Sweet Lullaby'**, a bewitching song that sold millions across the world. Their eponymous debut album, which offered more of the same, was also a massive success and the duo donated some of the proceeds to environmental charities, which helped them receive an official endorsement from UNESCO. For their next album, 1995's *Boheme*, they turned their attentions to the music of Eastern Europe and Asia, stitched it all together with those same soporific ambient tones, and duly repeated their earlier success. Currently, the pair are studying the atlas carefully, attempting to decide which nation's music they should unearth next.

DEF LEPPARD

Def Leppard are the biggest rock band to have ever come out of **Sheffield**. Admittedly, this isn't a particularly spectacular fact, because Sheffield is hardly England's answer to America's **Seattle**. Nevertheless, the band who emerged from such humble surroundings grew into a multi-million selling act - and helped to make long, shaggy hair fashionable again (for which they should never be forgiven). Formed in 1977, they were an instant hit with fans of **heavy metal**. They successfully crossed over into the mainstream in 1983 with the *Pyromania* album, which sold over seven million copies in America alone. Its successor, the fabulous rock beast that was *Hysteria*, sold double that amount and suddenly the "Lep" straddled the rock world like a colossus. Their success, however, was beset by tragedy. Drummer **Rick Allen** lost an arm in a car accident in 1985, but miraculously continued to fulfil his role with a specially-adapted kit, while guitarist **Steve Clark** was found dead six years later after mixing alcohol with anti-depressants and painkillers. But still they bounced back, and their last album, 1996's *Slang*, saw something of a reinvention, proving that the band's legs are as strong as they ever were.

Def Leppard in concert

DEPECHE MODE

When Depeche Mode started, back in suburban Britain in 1980, no one could have predicted the career path they would subsequently follow. (The band - who began as a fluffy, synthesizer-led pop group - would end up as rock monsters with a lead singer who appeared desperate to attain legendary status by killing himself.) Between their inaugural year and 1995, Depeche Mode sold over 30 million records, making them one of the UK's most successful ever bands. Their music has changed down several gears from uptempo pop songs (**'Just Can't Get Enough'**, **'See You'**) to brooding, foreboding anthems (**'I Feel You'**, **'Personal Jesus'**) and, like **The Cure** before them, they have graced the world's stadia with the kind of midnight malevolence normally to be found only in horror films. But with their increasing success came a decreasing grip on reality for singer **Dave Gahan**. In 1995, Gahan was rushed to a Los Angeles hospital. An official statement from the band later explained that this was not a suicide attempt, rather an accident during a party. But Gahan appears to be a survivor and the band continues to create beguiling soundtracks for the disaffected, such as their latest, *Ultra*, one of the biggest records in Europe this year.

Depeche Mode gracing one of the world's stadia

DEUS

Proof, if proof were needed, that Belgium isn't as **dull** as some people would like to believe. dEUS are Belgian, all five of them, and they write their name dEUS because typographically it looks rather arresting. And Deus - okay then, dEUS - are responsible for the greatest, downright weirdest, debut single of the decade, 1994's **'Suds 'N' Soda'**. Starting with some terrifyingly violent violins - violins that not only sound like the music from the shower scene in Hitchcock's *Psycho*, but like they actually committed the murder themselves - it proceeds to mix in elements of Tom Waits, Captain Beefheart and **The Doors**. This is jarring, jagged, psychotic, insanity-inducing pop-rock, which spirals down into some very murky musical waters. Yes, it's that good. Local heroes in their native country, the band have extended their propensity for the bizarre through two excellent albums, *Worst Case Scenario* and *My Sister Is A Clock*.

Mark Knopfler of Dire Straits

DIRE STRAITS

Until **'Money For Nothing'** came along in 1985, with a video that trailblazed computer-graphics with the kind of hype one is unable to ignore, Dire Straits were indeed in dire straits, image-wise. A solid, some say stolid, adult rock band, **they formed in 1977** and made a series of brooding guitar rock albums, characterized by singer **Mark Knopfler**'s gruff, detached tones. The most celebrated of their singles was **'Romeo And Juliet'**, which soon became unavoidable on jukeboxes across Europe. While the aforementioned 'Money For Nothing' finally brought them huge international recognition, the accompanying album, *Brothers In Arms*, went on to be a massive seller, not least in their native UK, where an estimated one in ten British households owns a copy. Their last studio album, *On Every Street*, came out in 1991, but it met with a muted response. While various members have busied themselves elsewhere (notably Knopfler, who has pursued a solo career), the band have never actually split, and currently show no signs of doing so.

DISPOSABLE HEROES
OF HIPHOPRISY

One of the most arresting rap crews to have emerged from the genre to date, the Disposable Heroes of Hiphoprisy formed in San Francisco in 1990 and appeared to offer a wholly necessary flipside to the endless macho posturing and gangsta-isms of **NWA** and **Ice T**. An offshoot of **The Beatnigs**, and led by the pencil-thin **Michael Franti**, they were quickly tagged as **"avant-garde"** due to their mixture of industrial jazz, funk and lyrical poetry. Indeed, Franti remains one of the most articulate lyricists of recent times, either from rap or any other area of music, a factor that makes the band's debut album *Hiphoprisy Is The Luxury* (1992) something of a classic. An incredible live spectacle - percussionist **Rono Tse** is part musician, part mechanic (and in this case, seeing really was believing) - the band proved very influential, and helped pave the way for the likes of **Arrested Development**. Upon their demise, Franti went on to front the excellent **Spearhead**.

DR. DRE

Dr. Dre has his fingers in many different pies. He is probably rap's prime mover, having been involved with everyone from **Ice Cube** to **NWA** to the **D.O.C.** to **Snoop Doggy Dog**. A rapper, writer, performer and producer, when Dre finally got around to fronting his own solo project in 1992 with the ferocious *The Chronic* album, eight million people went straight out and bought it. This was the first record to introduce the world to the aforementioned Snoop, whose loquacious vocals were all over it. He later produced the canine one's *Doggy Style* album, and went on to work on the soundtracks for the films *Above The Rim* and *Friday*, as well as directing his own movie, *Murder Was The Case*. Further collaborations came: **'Natural Born Killaz'**, with his former sparring partner, Cube, while alongside **Tupac Shakur**, he scored a major international hit with **'California Love'**. Each year, he acquires a few more "pies". Thus, within the next decade, the man will be a veritable media empire in himself.

Dr. Dre (PhD)

DURAN DURAN

Although justifiably famous for the great pop music they made, Duran Duran will forever be regarded as a band who could spend money. One hell of a lot of money. As the video age was coming into full effect in the early 1980s, Duran Duran - five very pretty young men from Birmingham, England - decided to not so much make promos for their singles as actual mini movies. Hence, for **'Girls On Film'** (1981), they hired a bloody great yacht, which sped up and down a very blue ocean while the band lounged luxuriously on board with lots of girls (on film). For **'Wild Boys'** (1984), meanwhile, they cavorted - often upside down on giant hamster wheels - on a set that looked like it had been borrowed from *Alien*. The band's very existence made girls scream very loudly indeed, not only because **John Taylor** had exquisite cheekbones, not only because **Simon Le Bon** possessed much cuteness (and, it must be said, an expanding beer belly that proved him to be human, if nothing else), but also because for the under-18s, Duran Duran were rock'n'roll, each of them living rock'n'roll lifestyles (boats, cars, big houses and, sadly for some of the fans, beautiful, supermodel girlfriends). They still exist today, having enjoyed huge success, considerable failure, several bad ideas (a cover of **Public Enemy**'s **'911 Is A Joke'**, for one) and innumerable line-up changes.

Brian Harvey
with East 17

EAST 17

While **Take That** were busy cultivating a particularly wholesome image at the turn of the 1990s, East 17 were boldly walking on the wild side. Here was a band whose audience consisted largely of young girls, and yet they were clearly a bit of rough. For instance, **Tony Mortimer**, the band's songwriter and co-singer, admitted to losing his virginity just before his 16th birthday to a prostitute, which is hardly a good example, now is it? In many ways, East London's premier "teen" band were the **Oasis** for under 18s. Forever courting controversy, one of the group's greatest songs, **'Deep'**, may have sounded like a lovely slushy ballad, but was in fact a celebration of cunnilingus, which was a very sly slice of subversion, not least when they sang the song on a Saturday morning kids' TV show. Pretty soon, **Brian Harvey** (the band's squat singer) took centrestage as his relationship with a television soap star was practically serialized in the tabloid newspapers, while in January 1997, he was somewhat sensationally sacked from the band after a radio interview in which he claimed that he had not only taken 12 tablets of **Ecstasy** in one night, but also deemed the controversial drug to be "safe". This resulted in widespread condemnation for his reckless comments, leaving the remaining three members of the band with no other option but to "let him go".

EMF

Consensus had it that EMF were the best thing to happen to pop music since The Sex Pistols two decades earlier. Arriving at the beginning of the '90s, they launched a full-on assault of punk-meets-teenage testosterone pop that took them, with shocking haste, to the top of the charts for a brief but cataclysmic burst of fame. Their first two singles, **'I Believe'** and **'Unbelievable'** typified their style, while live shows combined the muscular funk-rock power of **Faith No More** with the frenzied wild abandon of the **Beastie Boys**. With all the logic in the world, *Schubert Dip*, their debut album, became 1991's ultimate party soundtrack. They quickly became notorious for their hedonistic lifestyle (especially while on tour in America, where they were huge), which not only

included the typical rock'n'roll vices of sex and drugs, but also a curious fascination with their own genitalia. Specifically, bassist **Zac Foley** became obsessed with squeezing small fruits underneath his foreskin, often demonstrating this particular "talent" to anyone who expressed an interest. Predictably, their success didn't last, the parties dwindled and after a disappointing third album (1995's *Cha Cha Cha*), they split up and went their separate ways.

EN VOGUE

In a genre where soulful, four-part, all-girl vocals are ten-a-penny, En Vogue stand out a mile. Why, exactly? Well, they are more sassy and more sexy than the others, they look great and they sing even better, and where most US girl groups on a soul trip are all too preoccupied with singing about the power of love and the wonderment of men ad infinitum, En Vogue are more likely to stand tall and sing about female empowerment. Frankly, they take shit from no one - as is obvious from such gargantuan anthems as **'Free Your Mind'**. Stand Ice T and Cube alongside **Dawn Robinson**, **Cindy Herron**, **Terry Ellis** and **Maxine Jones**, and the rappers come across like mere pussycats in comparison. En Vogue came together in 1988; they became the world's funkiest divas two years later with the very wonderful **'Hold On'** single; they celebrated "Man" with the raunchfest that was **'Whatta Man'**; and after a three-year hiatus (in which babies were made and private lives led), they returned triumphant with their most accomplished album to date. They are America's spiciest spice girls.

ENIGMA

As is only entirely befitting, Enigma is something of an enigma. No really, it's true. Enigma is in fact **Michael Cretu**, a Romanian who hides under the aforementioned disguise. He first appeared back in 1990 with a bewitching song called **'Sadeness'**, which mixed a soporific melody with the sound of Gregorian monks chanting. The result was a sublime slice of languorous ambience that gave him a **worldwide No.1 hit**. He continued in a similar vein with three more albums, and has since become one of the few "rock stars" to sell over 17 million albums without anyone really knowing what he looks like. If his music sounds like the perfect background soundtrack to, say, an evening with a few bottles of good wine, then the ideas behind them are actually quite philosophical. Titles such as **'Prism Of Life'** and **'Odyssey Of The Mind'** suggest that Cretu spends much of his time in The Thinker's position, constantly scratching at that mental itch.

ERASURE

Like football, Erasure is a band of two halves. In the one half, there is **Andy Bell**, a twirling, pirouetting frontman for whom the word subtlety holds no meaning whatsoever. He is the very personification of camp, he has OTT imprinted on to his very soul and has far more in common with a pantomime dame than, say, **Liam Gallagher**. He is very pretty, is in possession of a lovely singing voice and he dresses like a punk flamingo. He is the heart, soul and voice of Erasure. And in the other half, there is **Vince Clarke**. Vince Clarke is Erasure's musical mastermind, ever to be found hiding behind a bank of keyboards and computer screens. He is from Essex and is practically bald. A smile has never knowingly settled upon his constantly frowning features. He is the straight man of the duo, the serious one. Together, they are a winning combination and something of an institution. A duo for 12 years, they've notched up over **22 UK Top 20 singles**, have reached the top of the UK album charts on four separate occasions and have taken their flamboyant live show to huge audiences across the world.

While most bands live for rock'n'roll excess, Erasure live for entertainment overdose, and few do it quite as wonderfully as they.

Vince and Andy of Erasure

Eternal minus Louise Nurding

ETERNAL

Eternal are Britain's foremost soul sensation. Back in 1993, Eternal were **Kelle Bryan**, **Easther** and **Vernie Bennett**, and **Louise Nurding**, four young women with stars in their eyes. Having been enrolled by a pop svengali type two years before, Eternal quickly grew in stature, and scored six Top 20 UK hits from their debut album, *Always And Forever*. Success stretched as far as South East Asia and Australia, the masterplan having paid off very nicely, so it came as something of a surprise when, just before the release of their second album, *Power Of A Woman*, Louise left the group. It later transpired that she wanted to set her sights on becoming the new **Madonna**, while the remaining three-piece followed a more spiritual path, mixing only the purest of soul and gospel. It worked a treat, because Eternal, with their proviso of **"music with substance"**, quickly became a ubiquitous presence throughout the European music scene. They were later invited to meet and perform for the **Pope** (as high a seal of approval as anyone of a religious disposition could wish to earn) and also contributed the sublime ballad **'Someday'** to the Disney film *The Hunchback Of Notre Dame*.

EURYTHMICS

Two people, one male, the other female. Two very different haircuts, a lot of makeup. Very specifically, **AN IMAGE**. The advent of the Eurythmics was the best thing to happen to the world of music video in the early 1980s. They were forever playing with gender, androgyny and sexual ambiguity - and Duracell-bright ginger hair. After four years as a couple, then another four as **The Tourists**, Eurythmics was born in 1981 and, through such startlingly individual songs (coupling the voice of an angel with the production wizardry of a studio genius), they went on to become one of the world's biggest draws. There were some singles: **'Sweet Dreams'**, **'There Must Be An Angel'**. There were some albums: *Touch, Be Yourself Tonight*. There were some collaborations: **Aretha Franklin**, on **'Sisters Are Doing It For Themselves'**, **Al Green**, on **'Put A Little Love In Your Heart'**. By the end of the 1980s, Eurythmics had achieved pretty much everything a band could ever hope for (worldwide No.1s, stadium-status, more awards than they knew what to do with). Thus, in 1990, one went one way, the other another. **Annie Lennox** became a solo artist of no little repute, while **Dave Stewart** became a guitarist-for-hire and a producer. He made records with ex-**Specials** vocalist **Terry Hall**, he dabbled in photography and film-making, he built a state-of-the-art studio (which he rents out to stars from all over the world), he married **Siobhan Fahey (Shakespears Sister)**, he set up his own record label (Anxious), he discovered **Alisha's Attic**, he continues to do a vast array of other things beside and inexplicably suffers from a form of depression called Paradise Syndrome. Strange, that.

EVERYTHING BUT THE GIRL

The endurance of Everything But The Girl proves without doubt that no other genre is as revitalizing as dance. For, after 13 years of making introspective bedsit music that inevitably led, by 1994, to a creative dearth, along came trip hop pioneers **Massive Attack** to help them back to credibility via a few good bpms. **Tracey Thorn** and **Ben Watt** met at university in 1982. They became friends, then lovers, then formed a band. Over the ensuing ten years, they wrote and released a series of quietly wondrous albums; music inspired by jazz and folk, while oozing the kind of atmosphere you'd find in Parisian cafés in the 1960s. In 1992, Watt was in hospital suffering from Churg-Strauss Syndrome, a rare and life-threatening disease. The band's future appeared anything but certain. Massive Attack asked Thorn to contribute vocals to two tracks on their *Protection* album, and the union proved so perfect, so natural, that after Watt's recovery, EBTG adopted a drum'n'bass "vibe" to their *Walking Wounded* album in 1996, which featured contributions from jungle producers Spring Heel Jack and Todd Terry. The result was magnificent, the response overwhelming and EBTG enjoyed the greatest comeback in years. Subsequently, a number of washed-up bands followed their lead, later insisting that there was always a dance element to their music.

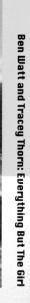

EXTREME

Signed after winning an MTV video contest in 1988, Extreme are best known for their acoustic paean to love, **'More Than Words'**, which topped the American charts in 1991 and gave them considerable international recognition. The sultry black-and-white video confirmed that not only could **Nuno Bettencourt** play a fine guitar, but that the band's torsos were well acquainted with the inside of a gym and that, judging by the magnificent sheen, they washed their hair regularly. (Bettencourt's fingers were later insured for $5 million.) After eight years together, and ten million album sales, the band split up, the guitarist going solo (his debut effort, *Schizophrenic*, appeared early in '97), while frontman **Gary Cherone** went on to front **Van Halen**.

FAITH NO MORE

The very existence of Faith No More illustrates perfectly the dangerous corruptive powers of a heavy rock band. After original vocalist **Chuck Mosely** was dismissed from the line-up in 1988, the Los Angeles band recruited the young **Mike Patton**, an attractive, well-bred young man whose greatest claim was that no illegal substances had ever passed his lips. He was the kind of guy you could quite happily take home to meet mother, and thus distinctly at odds with the usual requirements of a singer in a rock'n'roll band. However, fast-forward to 1992 and Patton had transmogrified into a depraved young man whose lyrics suggested that he was quite possibly sick to his soul, while his extra-curricular activities left little to be admired. He once bragged about defecating into hotel hair dryers before checking out, a "joke" which left a very nasty surprise indeed for the room's next occupant. Meanwhile, the band's music was corrosive and quite brilliant. Between them, their two biggest albums, *The Real Thing* and *Angel Dust*, represent a large chunk of classic American heavy rock. Here was a band who were at once demonic (**'Be Aggressive'**) and sublimely romantic (their superlative cover of **The Commodores**' **'Easy'**), making them no ordinary rock band. Their latest album is modestly entitled *Album Of The Year*.

Extreme (see entry on facing page)

DIE FANTASTICHEN VIER

In Germany, Die Fantastichen Vier have been breaking musical barriers since their inception back in 1986. The quartet - **Ypsilon**, **Smudo**, **Dee Jot Hausmarke** and **Thomas D** - started out rapping in English, which, at that time, was unprecedented for a German band. In 1988 they spent six months in America on a fact-finding mission, where they slowly began to develop their unique style. They then returned to Germany with a mixture of American rap and hip hop sensibilities and a distinctly European attitude. The reaction was instantaneous: DFV quickly became one of the country's most admired bands, scoring several No.1 singles and albums. They supported **Run DMC** on tour, released records in America, and have since paved the way for a myriad of young German bands, all of whom are eager to follow their lead. Now elder statesmen of the German hip hop scene, Die Fantastichen Vier are rightly respected as genuine pioneers.

FINE YOUNG CANNIBALS

For starters, there was that voice. The vocals of **Roland Gift** were not like those of other male singers. It appeared as if he was singing from his nostrils, which flared appropriately to reach the high points. If before the description "nasal whine" was usually critical (and usually attributed to **Bob Dylan**), then Gift single-handedly turned it around to make it a compliment. He was one of the '80s most distinctive singers, and his band one of the most proficient. Fine Young Cannibals were born in 1980. Musicians **Andy Cox** and **David Steele**, who used to be in **The Beat**, enrolled the rather beautiful Gift (his physical features as atypical as his voice) and by 1985 they were enjoying huge success with the single **'Johnny Come Home'**. Their career, however, proved a faltering one because Gift increasingly moonlighted as an actor, appearing in films such as *Sammy And Rosie Get Laid* and *Scandal*. By 1989, their second album, *The Raw And The Cooked*, had made them international superstars (in America, for example, it toppled **Madonna**'s *Like A Prayer* from the top spot). Thereafter, things went very quiet and it wasn't until a greatest hits collection in 1996 that the group, as was, finally admitted that they were history, with Cox and Steele continuing under the same name, while Gift set out on his own.

FOO FIGHTERS

The odds were stacked against him, but somehow he triumphantly confounded every expectation. After **Kurt Cobain**'s suicide, it seemed highly unlikely that anything would be heard from the remaining two **Nirvana** members, especially sticksman **Dave Grohl**, for rarely does a drummer go on to become a convincing front man in his own right, not least when he's the ex-drummer of **The Coolest Band On Earth** (1991-94). But with Foo Fighters, Grohl has done just that. The most significant thing about their eponymously-titled debut album is that it sounds nothing like his former band, and there's no reference to Cobain whatsoever. Instead, it's a sharp, acute rock record, harnessing the melodies of **The Beatles** and **The Beach Boys** and wrapping them around some Seattle aggression, all delivered in Grohl's appealing nasal whine. Ridiculously commercial (the single **'This Is A Call'** is only the tip of the iceberg), this is fabulous stuff. Their new album is *The Colour And The Shape*.

FRANKIE GOES TO HOLLYWOOD

Perhaps one of the most memorable bands of the '80s, Frankie Goes To Hollywood enjoyed phenomenal success, controversy, tears, acrimony, failure and an eventual split - all within the space of four very hyperactive years. Having graduated from the gay scene of the early '80s, they came to the attention of genius producer **Trevor Horn** in 1983, who moulded their debut single **'Relax'** into a magnificent throbbing disco epic. After the song was banned by the UK's Radio One for its *risqué* lyric, "Relax, don't do it/When you want to come", it instantly shot to UK No.1 and stayed there for a month. The follow up, **'Two Tribes'** spent nine entire weeks in the UK pole position, helped by an incredibly entertaining video featuring two Reagan and Chernenko lookalikes fighting in a wrestling ring. From there came the wonderfully overblown debut album *Welcome To The Pleasure Dome*, which was impressive, ambitious and probably their last cohesive step as a band. The eventual second album, *Liverpool*, was poorly received, the No.1s stopped coming and they fell apart. While four-fifths of the band promptly sunk into oblivion, singer **Holly Johnson** went on to mild success as a solo singer and painter. In 1993, he was diagnosed HIV positive.

The Fugees
In concert

THE FUGEES

Without contention, The Fugees were the greatest chart phenomenon of 1996. Formed two years earlier, their debut album, *Blunted On Reality*, revealed their particular skill for merging languid, laidback rap (and endless lyrical positivity) with classic samples from the likes of **Earth, Wind & Fire** and **Kool And The Gang**. After a break, during which singer **Lauryn Hill** pursued her burgeoning acting career (including a small role in *Sister Act II*), the band returned in '96 with *The Score*, which spawned three huge international hits: 'Killing Me Softly' (a re-working of the **Roberta Flack** classic), **'Ready Or Not'** and a souped-up version of Bob Marley's **'No Woman, No Cry'**. Their entire reason for being, they explained, was to "bring musicality back to hip hop". By the end of the year, as their album's total worldwide sales went into the many millions (the best-selling hip hop album of all time, actually), they could well afford to sit back and think, "Yeah, good job".

PETER GABRIEL

Unlike the band he once fronted (the nothing-if-not-dependable **Genesis**), Peter Gabriel is one of rock's most fascinating characters. By 1975, he was already married with children, and had guided Genesis (**Phil Collins**, at this stage, was simply the drummer) to huge success and seven complex albums. But suddenly he had had enough and promptly quit the band. Thereafter, he simply did as he pleased, gradually releasing four titleless albums that took him to the beginning of the '80s, launching **WOMAD** (World of Music and Dance), building up his own sprawling studio complex (Real World) and penning soundtracks to various films, including **Martin Scorsese**'s controversial *The Last Temptation Of Christ*. Meanwhile, his love of African music began to have an influence on his own, but it wasn't until 1986 that he made a conscious effort to get back into the charts, which he did so magnificently.

The album actually had a title - albeit a small one: *So* - and the single made video history. **'Sledgehammer'**, which had a claymation promo that used highly advanced stop-motion techniques, remains one of the most distinctive videos ever made. Since then, Gabriel has explored multimedia, producing several CD-ROMs, and his vision remains permanently focused on tomorrow.

Shirley Manson of Garbage

GARBAGE

Imagine **Nine Inch Nails** with the lights down low, a back-of-the-throat vocal growl and dark, dysfunctional music that lurks threateningly somewhere in the background. Imagine the spirit of techno melting into the ghost of goth, all dressed up in rock's shoddy overcoat. Yes? Then offer a tentative hello to Garbage. Formed by drummer **Butch Vig**, the man who produced **Smashing Pumpkins**' *Siamese Dream* and **Nirvana**'s *Nevermind*, Garbage are an industrial-grunge, pseudo-goth outfit who, in just one short year, have become one of the best new bands of the 1990s. Their self-titled debut album, which came out in the autumn of '95, was awash with synthesizers, serrated guitars, the dry-ice vocals of **Shirley Manson** (formerly of little-known Scottish band **Goodbye Mr. MacKenzie**) and the most bewitchingly strange songs (**'Queer'**, **'Stupid Girl'**) this side of a **David Lynch** movie. It won them Best New Band in 1996's **MTV Music Awards** and the kind of following for whom total devotion is the only kind of worship.

GENESIS

Genesis met at school. A posh school. They found success in the '70s with what people with beards were calling "progressive rock". A chap called **Peter Gabriel** was their singer. He had a propensity to dress up as a flower, suggesting that somewhere in his adolescence something had gone drastically wrong. When they were particularly famous, Gabriel left to do his own thing - in a very real sense. A smaller man who used only to play the drums, one **Phil Collins**, became the replacement singer, a role in which he rather excelled. They made a selection of peculiarly titled albums, including *Selling England By The Pound* and *Abacab*. Whenever they played live, a lot of people turned up and proceeded to get quite excited. In the '80s, Genesis were positively huge. Splinter groups emerged, with **Mike Rutherford** forming **Mike & The Mechanics**, Collins becoming Phil Collins, "solo artist", and **Tony Banks** doing...his own thing. *Invisible Touch* ruled the world in 1986, but a decade later the band were no more, each member deciding to exist apart from the monster they had so successfully created. The end.

GOLDIE

As jungle became an increasingly important underground force in early '90s British clubland, Goldie was the man responsible for bringing it to public recognition. Born to a Scottish mother and a Jamaican father, he spent much of his childhood in foster care, dabbled in petty crime and developed his skill for graffiti art before becoming fully embroiled within the tight-knit jungle scene. After attaining the kind of hardcore street credibility that rendered him practically an icon, he released his debut album *Timeless* in 1995 and scored a major hit single with **'Inner City Life'**. This was no small achievement, because jungle's fanatical rhythm and racing bpms are hardly easy listening fare. But, with his cool sagacity and cheeky humour, Goldie provided jungle with an identifiable public face (i.e. his own), and via several highly profitable collaborations (including **Björk**, with whom he enjoyed a brief but intense relationship), jungle filtered through to the mainstream until its influence was pretty much ubiquitous. Meanwhile, he's developed his own label, Metalheadz, with the express aim of propelling this "new" music to as wide an audience as possible.

The cheeky Mr Goldie

GREEN DAY

The emergence of Green Day in 1994 was an entirely necessary antidote to the permanently furrowed brow of grunge. In America, and therefore the world, grunge's influence was all-pervading. The music was loud, it was harsh and its overtones undeniably depressing. "I Hate Myself And I Want To Die" could well have been its motto. And then its guiding light, **Kurt Cobain**, did die. Clearly, something had to be done. Enter Green Day, a raucous American trio not long out of their teens, whose spirit-lifting, speed-limit-testing tunes and lyrics had you questioning their IQs. Officially, this was grunge with a stupid smile painted on its lips. Their 1994 album, *Dookie* (actually their third), proved to be a perfect combination of *Wayne's World*-meets-*Beavis And Butt-Head*-meets-The Spirit Of British Punk. Indeed, as incongruous a vision as it may have been - one imagines John Lydon (nee, **Johnny Rotten**) would have something to say about Green Day calling themselves **"punk"** - their album went on to sell eight million copies in America alone, bestowing it with the following title: America's biggest-selling punk album of all time.

Billie Joe Armstrong of Green Day

G.U.N.

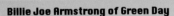

Named after the small, hand-held firearm (for reasons known only to themselves), Glasgow's G.u.n. are one of the more authentic rock acts of the '90s. With entirely appropriate self-confidence, the Glasgow quartet entitled their 1989 debut offering **Taking On The World**. It was an album that impressed not only fellow Scots **Simple Minds** (whom they supported at Wembley Stadium), but also the **Rolling Stones**, who hand-picked them to accompany them on their Urban Jungle World Tour. Consolidating their position as a band worthy of wearing leather jeans, they later released *Gallus* and the assured *Swagger*, on which they re-interpreted Cameo's funk classic **'Word Up'** with impressive bravado. Both albums led to a healthy international reputation, which their eponymous fourth album, looks all set to build upon.

GUNS N'ROSES

For those too young to remember **Led Zeppelin** the first time around, Guns N'Roses are the biggest, and probably the best, heavy rock act the world has ever seen. It is 1987 and the band's debut album, *Appetite For Destruction*, is released. A record of bruising malevolence, intense volume, and the kind of frenzied passion a drunk puts into projectile vomiting, *Appetite...* doesn't go ignored. Enormous tours are embarked upon, from which innumerable rock'n'roll rumours flow, keeping both the music press and the tabloid newspapers happy for months at a time. Singer **Axl Rose** is cited as problematical at best, intolerable at worse, and rarely sees eye-to-eye with guitarist **Slash**. Hence, the band are in a permanent state of war with each other, resulting in them often taking to the stage two hours late. Predictably, the situation worsens. Their second full album, the double *Use Your Illusion I & II* (1991) illustrates perfectly their capacity for overblown gestures, and rarely does a day go by without rumours of a split. Finally, after years of inactivity, Slash does indeed go his own way. The band say they'll continue nevertheless. Whether they actually do or not, however, remains to be seen.

HAPPY MONDAYS

There is ample evidence to suggest that Happy Mondays were the greatest rock'n'roll band ever. Or at least, they were pretty damn close. Led by the streetwise poet laureate, **Shaun Ryder**, the band formed in 1984, but didn't come to public recognition until 1990, when they and fellow Mancunians **The Stone Roses** spearheaded the triumphant **Madchester** scene. *Pills 'n' Thrills And Bellyache* proved to be the era's most narcotic-fuelled party album, and with the ensuing success came a huge amount of money, which the band promptly spent on drugs. They then appeared in a British pornographic magazine as "guest editors" (translation: they got to lounge in a Jacuzzi with lots of naked women) and continued to court controversy the way Romeo did Juliet. Deciding to record their next album in The Bahamas was a patently ridiculous idea because they were all far more interested in pursuing extracurricular activities than making music. When it finally emerged, in 1993, *...Yes Please!* was a total mess. The band split amid terrific acrimony and all that appeared left for Ryder was the almost obligatory overdose. Somehow, he managed to bounce back with his new band, **Black Grape**, a collective with an even greater propensity to party than the Mondays. For this reason alone he deserves our respect.

HOLE

When someone finally gets around to making the film version of the life and times of **Courtney Love**, it will probably be regarded as the greatest rock'n'roll story ever told. After several years in which she dabbled in punk rock, exotic dancing (translation: stripping), photography, acting (she appeared in *Straight To Hell* and *Sid And Nancy*) and had a brief stint as lead singer of **Faith No More**, Love formed Hole in Los Angeles in 1989. The spirit of punk meets the angst of Generation X grunge, Hole quickly became local heroes. Local became global in 1992, when the singer married **Nirvana**'s **Kurt Cobain**, whose child (**Francis Bean Cobain**) she was carrying. Interviews around the time gave weight to the rumour that despite her pregnancy, Love had continued to take drugs, making her arguably the most controversial American figure of the day. The baby was born healthy. On the eve of the band's second album release (*Live Through This*), Cobain put a gun to his head and thereafter Love's life spiralled out of control. Love came through, her redemption taking the form of films. After encouraging responses to her cameo in *Basquiat*, she delivered an incredible performance alongside **Woody Harrelson** in *The People vs Larry Flynt*, for which she received a **Golden Globe nomination** and, in turn, a new lease of life. Hole are working on an album with Smashing Pumpkins' Billy Corgan as producer.

Ireland's own
Hothouse Flowers

HOTHOUSE FLOWERS

Hothouse Flowers had it easy, very easy. Basically, everyone loved them. Back in the late '80s, when no one outside of immediate family had ever heard of them, US music bible *Rolling Stone* called them "The best unsigned band in the world". Shortly after, **U2**'s **Bono** saw them on Irish TV and invited them to record for his Mother label. The result, **'Love Don't Work This Way'**, made them the most sought after new band of their era and, shortly after signing a major record deal, they appeared during an interval in the 1988 **Eurovision Song Contest** before a worldwide audience of several hundred million viewers. Their debut single proper, **'Don't Go'**, went very far indeed, and the band became the biggest Irish act since U2, with their introductory album, *People*, being fresh, real and universally admired. The band's popularity wavered thereafter, however, and after two more albums they went their separate ways, each continuing to make music wherever they happened to end up.

HOUSE OF PAIN

Despite being born and bred within New York, House Of Pain were nevertheless very proud of their Irish heritage. They drank in New York Irish pubs, professed a fondness for the old shamrock and, boy, did they like their Guinness. Their chosen music, however, was not a fresh take on the entire recorded works of **Van Morrison** and **U2**, but wide-boy, streetwise rap. Although never the most original of rappers, the trio will remain eternally celebrated for their excellent 1992 single **'Jump Around'**, which instantly usurped the **Beastie Boys'** **'(You Gotta) Fight For Your Right (To Party)'** as the greatest fraternity party record ever recorded. It has since proved surprisingly enduring, having appeared in several Hollywood films and at least one television advert extolling the many wonders of Irish beer, which must please the boys no end.

WHITNEY HOUSTON

Whitney Houston's got a lovely singing voice. Born in church, grown up gospel, and given to displaying a considerable breadth of emotion, it's a fine instrument indeed. And it has made her arguably the world's most famous singer. Or at least one of them. In a career spanning just 14 years, the soul singer has sold over 96 million records, a feat that is staggering by anyone's standards. Her best-selling album to date is the soundtrack to *The Bodyguard*, the movie in which she starred alongside Kevin Costner and his very dodgy haircut. From the movie came the single **'I Will Always Love You'**, a truly almighty ballad, that sold almost **400,000 copies in one week** in America alone (something no one else had ever achieved), before becoming the second biggest selling single in America of all-time (behind USA For Africa's **'We Are The World'**), and No.1 in practically every other territory on Earth. (There were also unconfirmed reports that it went down very well with the Martians.) Enough statistics, however. Elsewhere, Ms Houston is an increasingly famous actress (she has starred in *Waiting To Exhale* and *The Preacher's Wife* alongside **Denzel Washington**), and is married to singer, and occasional hellraiser, **Bobby Brown**.

The very wholesome
Whitney Houston

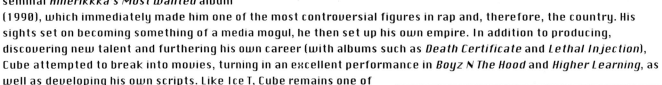

ICE CUBE

After a brief but highly memorable stint in **NWA**, Los Angeles's Ice Cube broke away to pursue a solo career. The result was the seminal *Amerikkka's Most Wanted* album (1990), which immediately made him one of the most controversial figures in rap and, therefore, the country. His sights set on becoming something of a media mogul, he then set up his own empire. In addition to producing, discovering new talent and furthering his own career (with albums such as *Death Certificate* and *Lethal Injection*), Cube attempted to break into movies, turning in an excellent performance in *Boyz N The Hood* and *Higher Learning*, as well as developing his own scripts. Like Ice T, Cube remains one of rap's most influential leaders, but unlike the thirtysomething **T**, Cube is only 27 years old. His work has only just begun.

ICE T

The most famous rapper in the world? Well, the man himself will dare you to suggest otherwise. Ice T is recognized the world over not for his music, but for the (carefully orchestrated) controversy that dogs his every move. Growing up in the ghettos of Los Angeles, the young "T" (improbably, his real name is **Tracy Morrow**) has certainly earned the controversy tag. His adolescent activities included burglaries, robberies and drive-bys but, as his friends either ended up in prison or dead, he realized quickly the need to break out. With impressive alacrity, his cool West Coast rap soon landed him a record deal, growing fame and even acting roles (*New Jack City, Trespass*). But it was with his speed metal band, **Body Count**, and their single **'Cop Killer'**, that Ice T became "the most feared black man in America". Moral America was in uproar, and **President George Bush** pegged him as a major threat to society. As a result, his record label dropped him and he became not so much famous as infamous. The gangsta image, however, is something of a misnomer. The real Tracy Morrow, despite his fixation on guns, is an intelligent, entertaining man who now straddles all areas of the media with such consummate ease that were he white, his fellow countrymen would regard his achievements as the American Dream made real.

Ice T: don't call him Tracy

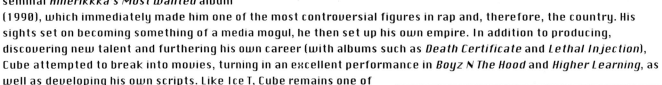

BILLY IDOL

Permit us, if we may, to take this time to come over a little religious. Billy Idol is lucky to be alive. The now 42-year-old punk rocker has come off his motorbike more than enough times to become a fully paid-up resident of the hereafter. But somehow (the miracle of science, in all probability), he is still up and about, breathing oxygen and enjoying the splendours of nature like the rest of us. These days, when the man with the most famous curled lip this side of Graceland takes his **Harley Davidson** for a short ride, he does so with all the due care and attention of someone who truly values his life. (He even wears a helmet.) Well, thank God for that. While he has apparently slunk into retirement over these past few years, Billy Idol has nevertheless had the kind of past that proves him worthy of inclusion in any music compendium. He began his career during the punk era with the splenetic **Generation X**, before decamping to America and churning out an admirable selection of camp, teenage angst anthems (**'Rebel Yell'**, **'White Wedding'**, **'Eyes Without A Face'** and the particularly memorable **'Hot In The City'**). Caricatures don't come much better.

INXS

Seventeen years ago, INXS started playing pubs in and around Australia. They didn't stop. A few years later, after earning a reputation as a rather incendiary live act, they started to scale the national charts, soon becoming one of the biggest acts their country had ever seen. Come 1985 they released *Listen Like Thieves*, the album that successfully broke them in America, selling over a million copies. And then came **Live Aid**, which brought the band to a worldwide audience. Since then, they've sold over 15 million records, collected armfuls of awards and toured the globe umpteen times over. They've gone from playing pubs in the Outback to Wembley Stadium in England and - intentionally - back again. They've released 11 albums, and have seen their six-man line-up remain unchanged. They also have a singer who dates supermodels and who fulfils every requirement of a legendary rock band frontman. For many, they're the ultimate stadium band - probably one of the very best - and for many others they're the greatest thing to have ever come out of Australia (*Neighbours* excepted). Occasionally, they are really quite exceptional. And more recently? More recently, **Michael Hutchence** has set up home with British TV presenter **Paula Yates** (previously married to **Bob Geldof**) and had a child. And, in support of their latest album, they plan to tour again. Some things never change.

Michael Hutchence of INXS

CHRIS ISAAK

As his rather crooked nose may suggest, singing was not Chris Isaak's first choice of career. Throughout his teens, he pursued boxing, with dreams of turning professional. But, as strumming the guitar proved far less painful than being punched in the face, he became a singer, songwriter, sometime actor and major sex symbol instead. Few would question his decision. Although he began back in 1984, he didn't find true success until six years later when his song, **'Wicked Game'**, was used in the **David Lynch** film, **Wild At Heart**, and became his first international hit. Thanks to cheekbones that most male models would envy, he appeared as much in magazine fashion spreads as music titles, and by year end America's *People 15* magazine listed him as one of the most beautiful men in the world. The country-tinged albums continued (Isaak's voice is most often compared to *Roy Orbison*'s), as did his interest in acting, and he has since appeared in *Silence Of The Lambs*, *Married To The Mob*, *Twin Peaks: Fire Walk With Me*, and *Little Buddha*.

JANET JACKSON

See Legends of MTV pp. 16-17

MICHAEL JACKSON

See Legends of MTV pp. 18-19

Neneh Cherry and Jason Kay (wearing hat) at the MTV Europe Music Awards

JAMIROQUAI

When **Jason Kay** talks, there is no room for punctuation. This is because the man who became a 24-carat star overnight has so much to say and so much to do and so much to achieve and so much to prove that when he begins, there's really no stopping him. He catches a thought and immediately he's off up and running with it, giving it some serious hyperbole: about the quality of his music and the finery of his threads and the genius of his dance steps and the loquacious wonderment of his vocals and the fact that Jamiroquai are a legendary force in the making. We should, he informs us, be glad he's around. Incredibly, he's only been around for four years, in which time he's already unleashed **three platinum-selling albums** that not only confirm the fact that he's rather familiar with the entire back catalogue of **Stevie Wonder**, but that his style (eco-funk, with extra streetwise suss) is currently unrivalled. Jason Kay wears a very large hat. Well, he would, wouldn't he?

JANE'S ADDICTION

Jane's Addiction were no ordinary American rock act. Formed in Los Angeles in 1986 by **Perry Farrell**, a man for whom the word "enigmatic" tells only half the story, JA went on to create an incendiary blend of art rock that would leave an indelible influence on America's more mainstream rock pool. Psychotic, nightmarish and almost preposterously "artistic", their music merged scorching guitars with loose-limbed rhythms and lyrics that suggested that drug-taking was a major influence. The cover of their breakthrough album, 1988's *Nothing's Shocking*, featured a set of naked Siamese twins with their heads on fire. The follow-up, 1990's *Ritual De Lo Habitual*, meanwhile, featured a sculpture of Farrell (and two women) naked on a bed, surrounded by voodoo paraphernalia. As if this didn't incense the Moral Majority enough, live performances were part gig and part freak show, featuring transsexual strippers, fire-eaters, snake-dancers and porn films. Inevitably, such intensity and round-the-clock hedonism led to friction, and the band imploded in 1991. Guitarist **Dave Navarro** later joined **Red Hot Chili Peppers**, while Farrell continued to develop the American touring festival, **Lollapalooza**, and formed his new band, **Porno For Pyros**.

The brothers Reid of Jesus And Mary Chain

JESUS AND MARY CHAIN

Back in 1985, Scotland's Jesus And Mary Chain were receiving a huge amount of press coverage for making one hell of a racket and sparking off riots after playing live sets that lasted just 15 minutes (with, of course, no encore). Their "style" (or lack of it) whiffed distinctly of ageing punk, while any musical expertise they may have laid claim to was, to say the least, questionable. When he signed them to his then-fledgling Creation label, **Alan McGee** commented that, "I had to sign them. They were either the best or the worst band I'd ever seen." They went on to become a seminal '80s band, their debut album, *Psychocandy*, a veritable classic. In 1986, JAMC slimmed down to just two permanent members, brothers **Jim** and **William Reid**, as their allegedly inept drummer, **Bobby Gillespie**, went off to form **Primal Scream**. While no one would ever dare accuse them of attempting musical maturity, later releases did suggest that they had at least toned down the pure white noise in favour of fulsome, albeit determinedly grizzly, pop melodies. In 1995, they returned briefly with the magnificently splenetic **'I Hate Rock'n'Roll'** single, confirming that their antagonistic streak hadn't entirely dissipated.

ELTON JOHN

Reginald Kenneth Dwight. Famous for: being Elton John; for wearing glasses; for spending the '70s wearing the most ridiculous clothes ever known to man, woman or **Vivienne Westwood**; for playing the piano, very well; for being rather fond of **Watford Football Club** (where he is chairman); for having an awful lot of money; for "coming out"; for donating all proceeds of his singles sales to AIDS charities; for hosting, annually, the most glamorous post–**Oscar** bash; for being great friends with **George Michael**; for living in a very big house in the country; for becoming the unofficial **Voice of Disney**; for being awarded the CBE by the Queen in 1996... and then there's the music: 'Candle In The Wind', 'I'm Still Standing', 'Crocodile Rock', 'Your Song', 'Nikita', 'Song For Guy', 'Don't Go Breaking My Heart' (with Kiki Dee), 'Pinball Wizard', playing piano on 'He Ain't Heavy He's My Brother', 'Goodbye Yellow Brick Road', doing a song for Disney in 'Circle of Life'... (cut to fade)

Singer and DJ Jovanotti

JOVANOTTI

It's not his real name, of course. But under the guise of Jovanotti, **Lorenzo Cherubini**, who was born in Rome in 1966, became something of a teen sensation in his native Italy. Starting out as a DJ on both radio and television when aged just 19, Jovanotti then got increasingly ambitious. He decided that instead of introducing songs, he should be the one making them, and so the not entirely subtly-titled *Jovanotti For President* album was released in 1988. "The Kids", as they shall henceforth be called, loved him and it, buying over half a million copies of the record between them, while "The Critics" publicly derided his style as the kind of simplistic pop rap that blasted out of under-18 nightclubs throughout the country every Friday and Saturday night. He became a runaway success, and that same summer he had **three singles in the Italian Top 10**, a feat never before accomplished by anyone. From here, he later released *La Mia Moto*, an album that had very little trouble in quickly notching up 600,000 sales to "The Kids", and he even enjoyed a brief stint as a **DJ** for **MTV**. It was here that he came to more international recognition, if only for his televisual skills, and on the strength of his MTV appearance, the singer was asked to present a youth programme, *Gimme Eight*, for BBC2. Inevitably, Jovanotti was leaving the eternal boy behind and becoming a man, and this growing maturity was reflected on *Giovani Jovanotti*, an album that didn't sell quite as well as its predecessors. For later releases, however, it was business as usual, the boy-child proving a remarkably enduring teen idol, whose walls now creak under the collective weight of all those **platinum discs**.

KLF

In its very essence, rock'n'roll is all about subversion. In reality, however, rock'n'roll is about as well-behaved as little **Prince William** (excepting, of course, the occasional weekend binge). KLF, however, took subversion to its very apex and, therefore, have gone down in history as one of the most fascinating bands ever. At first they were **The Justified Ancients Of Mu Mu** (1987), formed by **Bill Drummond** and **Jimmy Cauty** who, between them, had spent over a decade in the music business. Their first album was entitled *What The Fuck Is Going On?*. A year later, they became **The Timelords** and had a UK No.1 with **'Doctorin' The Tardis'**, which sampled the *Doctor Who* theme tune along with the music of **Gary Glitter**. They then self-published a book entitled *The Manual (Or How To Have A Number One Without Really Trying)*. Shortly after Cauty founded **The Orb**, the duo became KLF. Then came their "Stadium House Trilogy" - **'What Time Is Love'**, **'3am Eternal'** and **'Last Train To Transcentral'**, all of which were huge international sellers. Next, they duetted with **Tammy Wynette**, set fire to one million pounds (and filmed the stunt for posterity), deposited a dead sheep into the foyer of the 1992 Brit Awards party, quit the music business, awarded Turner Prize winner **Rachel Whitbread** £40,000 for the year's worst work of art, and recorded a song that won't be released until world peace is established. (It has yet to see the light of day.)

The former Justified Ancients Of Mu Mu

LENNY KRAVITZ

For those whose vision requires the aid of glasses, Lenny Kravitz is a confusing proposition. Is it **Jimi Hendrix**? Well, sure sounds like him, hair looks similar, as does the bone structure, and as for the dress sense...it is him, isn't it? Despite appearances to the contrary, Lenny Kravitz is emphatically **NOT** Jimi Hendrix - he just sounds rather a lot like him. Half Jewish, half Bahamian, all rock'n'roll, Kravitz started out as a teen actor until he discovered the music of 1967, which he has since attempted to recreate to often spectacular effect. For many, he embodies **sex**; for many others, his particularly psychedelic wardrobe suggests a prevalent influence of illegal substances. All would appear to agree on the quality of the man's music, however, which is staggering, swaggering, blues-drenched

rock'n'roll, of which the 1989 album, *Let Love Rule*, represents the pinnacle. Married to, then divorced from, *The Cosby Show*'s **Lisa Bonet**, Kravitz next hooked up with French pop starlet **Vanessa Paradis**, for whom he wrote an entire album in 1992. Another highlight is **'Justify My Love'**, the song he wrote for **Madonna**, who had never sounded sexier.

KULA SHAKER

When *How To Make It In The World Of Pop* is finally published, Kula Shaker will command an entire chapter to themselves. After a few unproductive years as **The Kays**, they decided to forego any more years of anonymity and instead get famous. Singer **Crispian Mills** (son of actress **Hayley**, and grandson of British cinema legend **Sir John**) went to India, got into spirituality and re-christened the band Kula Shaker. Under the spiritual guidance of an ancient Indian emperor (it says here), they started to make a highly entertaining blend of '70s prog rock and '90s worldly psychobabble. They sang in the ancient language of Sanskrit (**'Tattva'**), wore spectacularly ridiculous clothes and spouted deeply profound philosophical musings to anyone who'd listen. The result? They got famous, quickly. The release of their debut album, *K*, proved, even to their detractors, that the band certainly could play, while the sly twinkle in Mills's baby blue eyes suggested that their "plan" was paying off very nicely. Within the space of 12 months, they'd gone from obscurity to the top of the British charts. Armageddon notwithstanding, Kula Shaker could well go global.

k.d. lang

The transition from country crooner to torch song megastar was a slow, but nevertheless, seamless one. k.d. lang, who favours lower case over capital letters, began singing in the early '80s. Her voice was a most impassioned instrument, which she unfurled slowly atop the kind of schmaltzy country ballads that had couples dancing very romantically in converted barns right across middle America. But as the 1990s approached, then settled in, lang transformed into a openly lesbian singer-songwriter par excellence, about whom **Madonna** famously said, "Elvis is alive - and she's beautiful". In 1992, she released *Ingenue*, the most mellifluous album of her career. It made her internationally famous and garnered her several awards, including a **Grammy**. From there, she became something of a celebrity and later appeared on the cover of US magazine *Vanity Fair*, sitting in a barber's chair, being wet-shaved by a noticeably under-dressed **Cindy Crawford**. The supposed "controversy" this sparked made her more celebrated still and film roles followed (including *Salmonberries*), as did almost iconic status.

CYNDI LAUPER

Like something that magician **David Copperfield** might produce from a hat (a rabbit, say, or maybe a supermodel), Cyndi Lauper appeared as if out of nowhere. It was 1984, and suddenly the singer with the peculiar dress sense, the day-glo hair and the really rather remarkable voice was all over MTV with an unforgettable debut single entitled **'Girls Just Wanna Have Fun'**. An overnight success, yes? Actually, no. Rather, a fitting conclusion to ten years of hard graft spent paying her dues in anonymous clubs and bars across her native America. But it did prove to be the beginning of a lengthy and varied career. There were the hits: **'Time After Time'**, **'I Drove All Night'**; and the occasional scandal - the track **'She Bop'** came under fire from right-wing American pressure groups for its alleged "promotion" of female masturbation. In between, she became a born-again Christian and a female wrestling manager (!), while in the early '90s she dabbled in a little acting. But it is within music that she is most cherished, as her compilation album, *12 Deadly Cyns...And Then Some*, will testify. She's a cross between the classic cartoon character **Betty Boop**, a canister of helium and a lot of New York streetwise suss. She released *Sisters Of Avalon* in 1997.

"Elvis is alive - and she's beautiful."
k.d. lang in concert

MUSIC TELEVISION®

THE LEMONHEADS

At the height of his fame to date (1993-94), **Evan Dando** was the world's favourite slacker. Here was someone who made wonderful music without even trying, for Dando's entire demeanour was one of a **narcoleptic**. Whether on stage, on video or in person, he appeared permanently sleepy-eyed, his speech slurred. He dealt with any problems that came his way with a simple shrug of the shoulders. With his hair long and his shirt checked, he personified Generation X and people started to wonder whether he was, in fact, merely an invention of novelist **Douglas Coupland**. But Dando was real enough. *Come On Feel The Lemonheads* was an album of sublime acoustic wonder that made him a star. Predictably, he didn't take too well to this sudden fame. He took to wearing dresses and, as he later freely admitted, to taking as many drugs as he could lay his hands on. Scarily, he even messed with crack and for a worrying time it looked likely that Dando wouldn't live to see his 30th birthday. Since then, he's thankfully cleaned up his act and got his head together. In 1996 he released the warmly-received *Car Button Cloth* album and, for now at least, has packed the dresses away.

Evan Dando of
The Lemonheads

LL COOL J

LL Cool J's overwhelming (some might say overbearing) love for himself even puts Narcissus himself to shame. For those who don't know, his moniker stands for **Ladies Love Cool James**, and it is probably safe to assume that James's favourite pastime is to stare deep into his mirror at the handsome image staring right back. For this reason, and a few more, he is a total star. He is also rap's most enduring icon, for in a world of one-hit wonders and fly-by-nights (anyone remember **Vanilla Ice**?), "J" has remained on the scene for over thirteen years. Ever since his seminal single, **'I Can't Live Without My Radio'**, "J" has understood the true meaning of popularity. It hasn't all been easy: his biggest hit, 1987's **'I Need Love'** (an unashamedly schmaltzy ballad) was roundly ridiculed by the hip hop fraternity, and whenever he attempted to play it live he'd was met with derisive boos. In 1991, he turned his hand to acting, appearing in *The Hard Way*, and later appeared with **Robin Williams** in *Toys*. Music remains his main occupation, however, and his 1996 *Mr. Smith* album showed that he's lost little of his style and even less of his charm. He enjoyed a huge hit single (including a UK No.1) early in 1997 with 'Ain't Nobody'.

LOS DEL RIO

For most of the people on this planet, Los Del Rio mean just one thing: **'Macarena'**. Despite enjoying success in their native Spain for over 30 years, they have only very recently come to worldwide attention. An old song (it was first released earlier in the decade), 'Macarena' was re-jigged and remixed, and in came a chorus sung in English by some long-legged girls with very high voices. Clearly it was designed for the 18-30 set (i.e. young people on holiday with too much sun, too much alcohol and an awful lot of sexual temptation), and despite the fact that **Antonio Romero Monge** and **Rafael Ruiz** insisted on appearing in their own video (two old men in suits cavorting with plenty of scantily-clad women made for a particularly uneasy sight), the song became first a hit single, then a veritable phenomenon. Huge the world over, it also came with its own dance, which even the **Pope** attempted and, like it or not, it is now probably the most recognizable summer beach anthem ever recorded.

MADNESS

In the 1980s, no other band had a more vice-like grip on Britain's Top 20 than Madness. Formed in London in 1978, Madness, like **The Beat** and **The Selecter** before them, married ska and pop with irreverent humour, and before long became the decade's definitive singles band. Between their debut, *The Prince* in 1979, and their lacklustre cover of **Scritti Politti**'s **'The Sweetest Girl'** in 1986, they scored 21 UK Top 20 hits, including **'One Step Beyond'**,

Suggs indulging in a little Madness

'Cardiac Arrest' and - their only No.1 - **'House Of Fun'**, an hysterical tale about a teenager attempting to summon up the courage to purchase condoms at the local pharmacy. They also became stars of the video age, each single accompanied by a promo that looked like a terrific Saturday night out. By 1986, things had run their course, so they disbanded. A splinter group emerged briefly in 1988 - imaginatively called **The Madness** - but it wasn't until the early 1990s that the full line-up reassembled for a series of gigs and, curiously, several TV advertising campaigns. Frontman Suggs went on to carve out a successful solo career for himself.

MADONNA

See Legends of MTV pp. 20-21

MANIC STREET PREACHERS

Despite a career spent courting controversy, daubing polemic slogans on to the mindset of the nation's youth and living a hedonistic, "Search And Destroy" lifestyle, nothing could ever have prepared the Manic Street Preachers for recent tragic events. Since February 1, 1995, the date **Richey Edwards** (full name Richey James Edwards), co-lyricist, fledgling guitarist and, for many, chief motivator, went missing, the remaining three members of the band have lived under an excruciating limelight of questions, doubts, accusations and even ridicule. Against expectation, however, the band continued as a three-piece and, with no little irony, have since enjoyed their most successful period to date. Their magnificent fourth album, *Everything Must Go*, has sold over half a million copies in the UK alone, and scooped two 1997 Brit Awards (Best British Band and Best British Album). Back in 1990, however, it was a very different story. The Welsh quartet were trash punk updated and existed on anarchy and subversive intelligence. With songs such as **'Motown Junk'** and **'You Love Us'** acting as war cries for the disaffected (i.e., confused teenagers), they were celebrated and reviled in equal measures. However, over the course of their three subsequent albums - *Generation Terrorists*, *Gold Against The Soul* and *The Holy Bible* - they gradually reaped universal respect, attaining the kind of status that every other band is now forced to worship. In the late 1990s, there is no more relevant band than they.

The Manic Street Preachers in sombre mood

M.A.R.R.S.

Widely acknowledged as the first house No.1, M.a.r.r.s .was a one-off collaboration between **Colourbox** and **AR Kane** - two influential yet ultimately obscure bands - in the autumn of 1987. The track was called **'Pump Up The Volume'**, its creators hoped that the track would make a small but significant impact on UK clubland. So excellent was it, however, that it soon found its way on to daytime radio and, shortly afterward, on to MTV, who placed its memorable video (lots of space rockets taking off) on heavy rotation. The result was a landmark UK No.1. Its splenetic rhythm and visionary use of a **James Brown** sample remain a major influence today. While one half of the alliance, **CJ Mackintosh**, went on to become a respected dance DJ, the other half, **Dave Dorrell**, has since gone on to manage British grunge act **Bush**, now one of the biggest rock acts in the world.

MASSIVE ATTACK

If trip hop is one of the major forces in '90s
music (and anyone who suggests otherwise is a fool), then Massive Attack are its chief pioneers. Emanating, in one or
other form, from Bristol as far back as 1983, the constantly fluctuating line-up finally settled in 1991, making slow,
soporific music that lived for the midnight hour. Core members **Daddy G**, **Mushroom** and **3-D** would create the moody
backing tracks (each of them heavy on dub and vibe), while various vocalists (among them **Horace Andy**, **Shara Nelson**,
Tricky and Everything But The Girl's **Tracy Thorn**), donated lyrics and vocals. The combination proved spectacularly
bewitching, and the band's two albums to date, *Blue Lines* ('91) and *Protection* ('94), are little short of being
masterpieces. The debut, which included the magnificent singles 'Safe From Harm' and 'Unfinished Sympathy',
launched the solo careers of not only Shara Nelson and Tricky, but also überproducer **Nellee Hooper** (**Björk**, **Soul II
Soul**), and a certain **Geoff Barrow**, who graduated from tea boy and co-engineer into the brains behind **Portishead**.
(Barrow latter got Massive Attack noticed by **Madonna**, with whom
they later collaborated on her *Something To Remember* album.)

MC SOLAAR

The young, impressionable MC Solaar, who spent his early teens
tuning into every rap station his portable radio could find, was a
big admirer of the **Beastie Boys**, **Public Enemy**, **NWA** and **X-Clan**.
American rap, he decided at the time, was definitely all that
mattered. But Solaar soon realized that the influences he grew up
with were too valuable to ignore. Born in Senegal to parents who
came from Chad, he grew up in Paris, listening to a combination of
African music and American jazz. His formative years were spent
checking out everyone from **Serge Gainsbourg** to **Bob Marley** and
Jimi Hendrix, and a year spent in Egypt, aged 12, opened his ears to
an even more exotic mix of music - traditional and otherwise. By
the age of 14, Solaar knew that his destiny lay within rap, his own
highly specific blend. In 1989 he teamed up with **Jimmy Jay**, a
Parisian DJ, singer **Melaaz** and rapper **Soon EMC** to form **The 501
Special Source**, and before long clinched a record deal. His debut
album, the highly lyrical *Qui Seme Le Vent Recolte Le Tempo* (He Who
Sows The Wind Shall Reap The Tempo), quickly established him as an
atypical rap artist, someone who was more likely to expound on
philosophy than his libido. He also proved a fairly peerless rapper,
whose mellifluous tones and liquid-gold rap attacks remained
unrivalled anywhere. Comparing himself to a journalist, someone
who believed he had a very serious message to impart, Solaar
quickly became one of France's most celebrated exports, and he
toured throughout Russia, Poland, Austria, Japan, the UK and 15
African countries. By the time his second album came out, 1994's
Prose Combat, the fledgling rapper had become a major star,
selling over 100,000 copies in just ten days in his
native country. Again, his lyrics had more in
common with literature than tales from the 'hood.
Thus, by now, MC Solaar is as much a French
diplomat as he is pop star, and one of rap's most
eloquent voices worldwide.

Senegal's MC Solaar

Mr Loaf in concert

MEAT LOAF

If there is one thing that Meat Loaf hates more than being questioned about his weight - and he hates being questioned about his weight - it's people spelling his name "Meatloaf". Drives him insane. Two words, people: "Meat" and "Loaf". There. So now you know. Onward, then. Meat Loaf is to rock histrionics what **Andrew Lloyd Webber** is to musicals - The King. Along with regular collaborator **Jim Steinman**, he created the seminal *Bat Out Of Hell* album, which exuded over-exaggerated passion from every orifice. Subtlety was conspicuous by its absence, a factor which sat well with his over-zealous fans, who made it one of the best-selling albums of all time. Fast-forward through the lean years (the 1980s), and Meat Loaf returned triumphant with - wait for it - *Bat Out Of Hell II* (1993), yes, a sequel to *Bat I*. Cue more rock histrionics, as well as one of the most expensive videos ever shot - for the No.1 single **'I'd Do Anything For Love (But I Won't Do That)'**, a song so full of swooning that **Celine Dion**, in comparison, resembled **Suzanne Vega**. Whatever his excesses, Meatloaf (only joking) remains one of rock's most entertaining leading men.

METALLICA

Let's survey the evidence. Long hair. Gruff voices. Poor skin. Amplifiers that go up to 11. A live album delectably entitled *Live Shit: Binge And Purge*. Tattoos. It seems safe to assert, therefore, that Metallica are heavy metal, possibly the heaviest of them all. Part Danish (in singer **Lars Ulrich**), part American, Metallica formed in 1991. They quickly developed a reputation as consummate rockers and became a staple of the live metal circuit for the next decade. The album that finally catapulted them into the super league was the so-called *Black Album* in 1991 (it was actually titleless). Its sales were boosted by the huge hit single, **'Enter Sandman'**, and the band's ubiquitous presence at every heavy rock festival in Europe, including the Monsters Of Rock tour alongside **Mötley Crüe**, **The Black Crowes** and **Queensryche**. Their very existence, however, could well be blamed for the "invention" of *Beavis And Butt-Head*, for which they deserve no forgiveness whatsoever.

MIDNIGHT OIL

Put simply, Australia's Midnight Oil are the world's most **politically correct** band of all time. But far from just a gimmick to give the band an all-important "caring" tag at a time when these things count, the Oil are phenomenally committed to the cause. Just about every cause you'd care to mention. In their 20-year history, they have lent their support to **Greenpeace**, the Tibet Council, nuclear disarmament, miners, apartheid and the Aborigines. When singer Peter Garrett stood for the Australian Senate on behalf of the **Nuclear Disarmament Party** in 1984, he received 200,000 votes and was only very narrowly defeated. A loyal worldwide following eventually saw them enjoy significant mainstream success in 1987 with the *Diesel And Dust* album, which spawned the **'Beds Are Burning'** single. As a band who truly exist outside of all fads and fashions, Midnight Oil could well carry on forever, as long as there's a worthy cause to fight for and as long as people still want them around. Both seem inevitable.

ROBERT MILES

Despite growing up amid piano lessons, and dissecting the work of soul legends **Marvin Gaye** and **Howard Melvin & The Bluenotes**, Italian-born Robert Miles had his heart set on becoming a DJ. By the age of 18, he was a local face around the clubs of Venice, playing hardcore trance, but after his father, a military man, returned from war-ravaged (former) Yugoslavia with photographs of wounded children whose lives were senselessly destroyed by the conflict, Miles then decided that his music needed a message. That message was **'Children'**, a mellifluous, synth-driven track that went on to sell over three million copies worldwide, reaching the No.1 position in Holland, Germany, France, Belgium, and an amazing three-month residency at the top spot in his native Italy. The single then went on to provide the musical backdrop for TV shows everywhere, confirming that if 1996 had one particular anthem, then this was it. The following album, *Dreamland*, which has already spawned another huge single, **'One And One'**, suggests that Miles could also define the sound for '97.

Metallica looking very smart

The not-exactly-beautiful New Kids On The Block

ALANIS MORISSETTE

Alanis Morissette is a genuine phenomenon. Although she seemed to appear out of nowhere in 1995 with what would become one of the biggest selling albums of all time (just behind **The Eagles**' *Greatest Hits* and **Michael Jackson**'s *Thriller*), she was in fact something of a child star, appearing on television at the age of ten. Her debut album, Alanis (1988), sold over 100,000 copies in her native Canada, and she once opened for white "rap" star **Vanilla Ice**, although this is something she may prefer to forget. In 1994, she left home for Los Angeles, teamed up with producer **Glen Ballard** and began work on an album. A year later, after signing to **Madonna**'s Maverick label, the 21-year-old released *Jagged Little Pill*, a record of assertive straight-talking and shockingly emasculating sentiments, not least on the single **'You Oughta Know'**, which featured the memorable line: "Are you thinking of me when you fuck her?"

Unsurprisingly, lyrics such as this made sure that she wouldn't remain unknown for long. Over the next two years she became a ubiquitous presence, selling over 15 million copies of her album in the process. Whereas before her, female singer-songwriters were often pigeonholed as kooky individuals, Alanis Morissette represents **strength through determination**. There is nothing even mildly eccentric about her, rather she is someone who is capable of achieving anything she sets her heart on. No wonder she's already approaching iconic status.

YOUSSOU N'DOUR

Youssou N'Dour is Africa's biggest singing star. Born and brought up in Senegal, he began singing professionally at the age of 12 as part of the groundbreaking group **Etoile De Dakar** (which would later influence the likes of **Paul Simon**), where he developed the "mbalax" sound, a combination of traditional Wolof percussion, cyclical guitar patterns and the music of Cuba and the Congo. Over the next 15 years, he recorded perhaps hundreds of albums (many of which were cassette-only African releases), which eventually brought him to the attention of an international audience. In 1986, N'Dour collaborated with **Peter Gabriel** on the latter's *So* album, and accompanied him on a world tour, after which he appeared alongside Gabriel, **Bruce Springsteen**, **Sting** and **Tracy Chapman** on the **Human Rights Now!** tour. Doing for African music what **Bob Marley** did for reggae, N'Dour continued to reach worldwide audiences through various collaborations including, in 1995, the huge international hit **'Seven Seconds'** with **Neneh Cherry**.

NEW KIDS ON THE BLOCK

New Kids On The Block were more than a sensation, they were an absolute phenomenon. Five teenagers from New England, they actually came together in 1984, but it wasn't until five years later that they were able to exercise an incredible control over the world's young female population. Quite how they did this remains unclear (for, let's face it, outside perhaps of main vocalist **Jordan Knight**, they weren't exactly beautiful), but their excitable five-part harmonies - in songs that were either uptempo, dance-routine pop ditties or slushy soul ballads - hypnotized an enormous audience, who suddenly began to wonder how they ever survived without them. By 1991, *Forbes* magazine had the band listed as the top-earning entertainment act of the year, with earnings of $115 million. But, perhaps predictably, their fame was to be short-lived. The band were often in trouble with the police (alleged arson, alleged violence), and soon started to renege on a number of commitments, actions that lost them many fans. By 1994, they appeared to be a spent force, their last album *Face The Music* faring poorly, and a year later they officially split up, slightly bruised from their experiences, but considerably wealthier.

NEW ORDER

New Order formed from the remains of Joy Division - after the death of singer **Ian Curtis**. Their faltering start in early 1981 belied the status they would later attain. By the end of the decade, New Order were a genuinely seminal band whose image, sleeve designs and use of dance music would influence many other bands. Inspired by **Kraftwerk** and New York's electro scene, New Order began to experiment with computer technology years before any of their peers, and early singles **'Temptation'** and **'Everything's Gone Green'** sound like nothing else that was around at the time. **'Blue Monday'** went on to become the biggest selling 12-inch single of all time, cementing the band's position at the forefront of indie-dance fusion. 1989 saw the release of one of their most celebrated singles, **'True Faith'**, which had an incredible accompanying video directed by **Jean Baptiste Mondino**. The following year, they penned England's official **World Cup** theme, **'World In Motion'**, which, in reaching the UK No.1 position, fared even better than the team (who didn't make it quite as far). In the early '90s, the group pursued other projects - **Peter Hook** formed **Revenge** and **Monaco**, **Bernard Sumner** collaborated with **Johnny Marr** in **Electronic**, while **Stephen Morris** and **Gillian Gilbert** became **The Other Two**. By 1994, the band were rumoured to have split up, but confirmation either way has yet to come.

New Order on their holidays

NINE INCH NAILS

Despite the existence of established and respected bands such as **Ministry** and **Pigface**, industrial metal was ultimately a sub-genre which, although incredibly popular among its hardcore fans, remained something of a cult. But, with his band Nine Inch Nails, **Trent Reznor** brought it up into the mainstream and proceeded to give the American moral majority enough nightmares to last an eternity. To undergo the Nine Inch Nails live experience, for example, was to finally comprehend just how **Linda Blair** felt when her head did that whole 360 degree "thing" in *The Exorcist*. In other words, pure white fear. This is because Nine Inch Nails' take on industrial metal is unrelentingly feral; music that sounds like a sharp descent into hell, its monochrome riffs heavier than a lead weight. Unquestionably deserving of an 18 certificate, it is nevertheless also quite magnificent music. *Pretty Hate Machine* (1990) remains an astonishing album, with a classic lead single, **'Head Like A Hole'**, that is possessed of an aural ferocity that can melt metal. After an even darker album, 1994's *The Downward Spiral*, Reznor was asked to produce the soundtrack for **Oliver Stone**'s highly controversial film, *Natural Born Killers*, and it remains one of the greatest soundtracks ever compiled - an opinion held by everyone except the faint of heart.

Gwen Stafani and "friend", no doubt

NIRVANA

See Legends of MTV pp. 24-25

NO DOUBT

"They" are calling No Doubt's album, *Tragic Kingdom*, the *Nevermind* of the late 1990s, a zeitgeist-forming phenomenon. What this means is that this mega-selling album (last count: five million) has tapped into the global conscience in a fashion not seen since the grunge meisterwork six years earlier. But where *Nevermind* wore its angst and confusion on its sleeve, No Doubt has day-glo positivity scrawled across its forehead. Coming out of Anaheim, California, the quartet formed in 1987 out of a love of **ska**, particularly that of British exponents **Madness** and **The Specials**. Initially, they seemed doomed to obscurity. Their first singer, **John Spence**, committed suicide in their inaugural year, while for the next six years their every musical effort went all but ignored by everyone except immediate family. In 1995, however, *Tragic Kingdom* emerged, the tide turned and **Madonna** lookalike/soundalike **Gwen Stefani** became something of an icon. While the album made the US No.1 spot, over in Europe the single **'Don't Speak'** was fast becoming the decade's most elegant ballad, debuting right at the top of the UK singles chart. They have since become further celebrated for the fact that Stefani is currently stepping out with **Bush**'s frontman, **Gavin Rossdale**, which will keep them in column inches for some time to come, no doubt.

NWA

NWA (Niggers With Attitude) formed in Compton, California, in 1986. By 1991, they would be regarded as possibly the most influential, certainly the most explosive, rap act yet, although their career was beset by conflict, federal investigation and tragedy. With the nucleus of **Eazy-E**, **Dr. Dre** and **Ice Cube**, they scored instant notoriety in 1988 with their *Straight Outta Compton* album, which, via songs with titles such as **'Gangsta Gangsta'** and the highly inflammable **'Fuck Tha Police'**, led to multi-platinum sales and an investigation by the FBI. But success led to conflict and Ice Cube soon decided to quit the crew after his constant warring with Eazy-E. The band's natural way with controversy continued apace, right up to their last album, in 1991. *Efil4zaggin*, with tracks such as **'Findum Fuckum And Flee'**, put an entirely predictable frown upon the faces of the moral majority. After the band split, Dr. Dre went on to produce **Snoop Doggy Dog** and his half-brother **Warren G**. Eazy-E continued to work until his death (from AIDS) in 1995.

Niggers With Attitude

SINEAD O'CONNOR

In a career now into its tenth year, Sinead O'Connor has courted success and controversy in equal measures. To wit: she is responsible for one of the most startling debut albums of recent times with 1987's *The Lion And The Cobra*; **Frank Sinatra**, meanwhile, has publicly stated that he wanted to "kick her ass" for refusing to take the stage after the American national anthem was performed; she has scored a worldwide No.1 hit, in 1990, with her exquisite rendition of a little-known **Prince** song, **'Nothing Compares 2 U'**; the **Pope** couldn't possibly disprove of her any more than he already does (she's not exactly supportive of Catholicism); her second album, *I Do Not Want What I Haven't Got* (1990), sold over six million copies worldwide; a house she bought in Los Angeles was later sold, the money donated to the Sarajevo war fund; a year later she released her most personal, most haunting single yet in **'My Special Child'**, which was rumoured to be about three recent abortions she had had; she was booed at a **Bob Dylan** tribute event - held at New York's Madison Square Garden - following an earlier US TV appearance in which she ripped up a photograph of the aforementioned Papal figure, telling a stunned audience to "fight the real enemy"; while her 1994 *Universal Mother* album revealed that here was a woman whose emotive power remains unrivalled in the 1990s.

OASIS

(Deep breath now.) A young man with just the one eyebrow quits his job as a roadie for the Inspiral Carpets to join his younger brother's band, where he takes over all songwriting duties and a few short months later **'Supersonic'** is released, which marks the beginning of the band Oasis, who within the incredibly short space of two years become Britain's biggest band since **The Beatles** and one of the world's most notorious acts. (Still with us? Good. Onward.) After three singles, each of which are delivered with an overwhelming self-confidence, the band released their first album, *Definitely Maybe*, which was regarded instantly as one of the key debuts of all time. Oasis's spectacular rise increased with each passing day and before long they were playing to live crowds of over 30,000. (Keep up, will you?) By 1995 the band were already on to their second album *(What's The Story) Morning Glory?*, which housed two of the most wondrous songs ever written - **'Don't Look Back In Anger'**, **'Champagne Supernova'** - and not only shamed **Blur** into submission, but also quickly became one of the UK's best selling albums of all time, causing an impossible tension within the band that prompted them to split up at least twice a day and led to singer **Liam** becoming an unpredictable and utterly fascinating frontman. Meanwhile, they won innumerable awards worldwide, which they accepted without even the slightest hint of appreciation. They broke UK concert records by headlining **Knebworth** in front of half a million people before heading off to America, which they conquered with ease (before almost breaking up again) and then Liam got engaged and married to British actress **Patsy Kensit** and they were never out of the papers, and while the band work on their third album, which is due in autumn '97, the world waits with the kind of baited breath that is reserved only for true legends. Oasis, in a class of their own.

THE OFFSPRING

The Offspring offered further proof - as if it were needed - that in America in 1994, teenagers were reawakening to the strains of day-glo punk, a "scene" that appeared as the last nail in grunge's coffin was being diligently hammered in. The Offspring appeared to be the kind of band who cherished their skateboards more than their relatives. They wore their skate shorts long, their hair even longer, while musically they diluted the essence of **Nirvana** into the lingering legacy of British punk. The result was *Smash*, a noisy, effervescent album that startled even the band themselves by selling an incredible **eight million copies**, making them the most successful independently-signed band in history. After gracing various European music festivals with their hyper-energetic presence, they retreated into the studio, emerging in 1997 with their follow-up album, *Ixnay On The Hombre*. The album is a virtual facsimile of its predecessor, and has clearly been produced in the hope of repeat success.

THE ORB

The ambient Orb

For two men of nondescript features who, on stage, hide behind a bank of synthesizers and computer screens and who, in person, hide permanently behind sunglasses, The Orb are nevertheless a fascinating proposition. While ambient house music may, like a bad rash, be everywhere these days, back in the dim and distant past (1989, actually), The Orb were the genre's only real exponents, and can proudly lay claim to the fact that they created the first ever ambient house record. That was **'A Huge Ever Growing Pulsating Brain That Rules From The Centre Of The Ultraworld'** and, predictably for ambient house, the song's title possessed more words than did the song's lyrics. A year later and they released the seminal *Little Fluffy Clouds*, paving the way for a myriad of other bands to follow. This was music for floatation tanks, aural hypnosis for a blissed-out generation. In '92, they issued the longest single ever released, short on words (**'Blue Room'**), but very long on minutes (39). Pioneers of the scene, and leaders of their generation, The Orb's importance, therefore, cannot be overstated. Additionally, their music also provides the perfect soundtrack to grow plants to.

ORBITAL

Few people know what Orbital look like. Even fewer care. Just for the record, however, Orbital (who are brothers **Phil** and **Paul Hartnoll**) look like police photo-fit pictures before they've been made up (i.e., both are bald and of largely nondescript features). For reasons all their own, they named themselves after the stretch of road that encircles London, and have spent the last eight years making innovative electronic music for the masses (and **Jean Michel Jarre**, who admires them greatly). They've made a habit of releasing albums without titles or any cohesive images, but have nevertheless come to the attention of everyone within the music world, who clamber for their remixing skills. (They remixed **Madonna**'s *Bedtime Stories* album to great effect.) Mainstream acceptance came in a rather major way after **Glastonbury 1994**, when they played the coveted final slot on the Saturday evening. In 1996 they even released a properly titled album, *In Sides*, while early in 1997 they recorded the theme tune to *The Saint*, the movie starring **Val Kilmer**, and appeared alongside heroes **Kraftwerk** at **Tribal Gathering**.

ROBERT PALMER

He's one smooth operator, is Robert Palmer. The kind of guy who'll treat a girl right, show her a good time, then show her his fabulous double bed (king-sized, naturally). He'll even make breakfast the following morning. So screams his image, anyway. Despite claims of being a shy performer, Palmer has manipulated the video era quite magnificently. A caricature of class, impeccably dressed, beautifully manicured, Palmer is able to swagger in a suit the way **Pamela Anderson** does in a bikini, without even breaking into a sweat. Let's rewind to 1986 and the video to his biggest hit yet, **'Addicted To Love'**. Palmer up front, looking like a cross between **James Bond** and **Jack Nicholson**, while behind him are his "band" members who, for this performance only, are a group of leggy ladies, their fulsome figures poured into too-tight dresses. Hair scraped back, lots of lipstick, lots of close-ups. Decidedly un-PC, deliciously sexy, the result is all too obvious. A huge international hit, with the video on endless rotation, and Palmer becomes an inspiration to middle-aged men the world over. Robert Palmer is now into his 48th year. He still looks great and still puts your own father to shame, which is quite a feat.

Robert Palmer and friends

PEARL JAM

Along with **Nirvana**, Pearl Jam re-moulded American rock music for the '90s. But while they were often portrayed as corporate rockers to Nirvana's more **live-fast-die-young** ethos, the Seattle band were in fact stubbornly awkward. For example, their response to the unprecedented success of their 1992 debut album, *Ten*, which outsold Nirvana's *Nevermind* and scooped just about every award at that year's MTV bash, was to shun the limelight almost entirely. The follow up, *Vs*, arrived with minimal publicity and a single only after the record company begged them to release one. And 1994's *Vitalogy* showed all the signs of a band with little time for conformity. They appeared dissatisfied with everything that came their way, from fan worship to their relationship with their record company, to agents and promoters who, they claimed, were overcharging on concert ticket prices. In fact, the only event they appeared to take pleasure from was providing their hero, **Neil Young**, with a backing band when the legendary rocker toured in 1995. While dedication to their music was never in question, it quickly became clear that Pearl Jam wouldn't play the corporate game for anyone. In a very real sense then, this rock five-piece are genuine **mavericks**.

PET SHOP BOYS

Arch ironists of pop, the Pet Shop Boys have exercised an impressive dominance over the charts for over 13 years. Possessed of poise, stature and an intentionally contrived sense of cool, they lend new depth to the word wry and prove that, yes, it is indeed possible to pursue a career in music without ever once having to break into a smile. A former assistant editor on the British pop magazine *Smash Hits*, 27-year-old **Neil Tennant** met **Chris Lowe** in a hi-fi shop in 1981 and immediately decided to jack in their day jobs and start a band. By 1985, their debut single **'West End Girls'** had made them hugely popular in France, Belgium, the UK and the US, after which much of the rest of the world followed suit. Unusually clever for pop stars, the Pet Shop Boys combined sardonic lyrics with disco, techno and an entire bank of synthesizers, making music that is often deceptively beautiful (**'Rent'**, their collaboration with **Dusty Springfield** on *What Have I Done To Deserve This?*, for example) and some peculiar cover versions (U2's **'Where The Streets Have No Name'**, which they blended wondrously with **Frankie Valli**'s **'Can't Take My Eyes Off You'**). They are the musical equivalent of a very fine wine and had a vintage year in 1997 with the hit album *Bi-Lingual*.

TOM PETTY

Along with his band, **The Heartbreakers,** Tom Petty has been making cinematic American road music for the

Tom Petty: the new Bob Dylan

better part of the last 25 years. Becoming huge in Germany and France before the rest of the world took notice, Petty was tagged as **"the new Bob Dylan"**, while his band remain worthy successors to **The Byrds**. In the mid-80s, they came to MTV recognition with a series of highly inventive videos, especially with their **Lewis Carroll**-inspired promo for **'Don't Come Around Here No More'** (1985). Many of their greatest hits, including **'American Girl'** and the wonderful **'Free Falling'**, have since featured in innumerable films, including soundtracks to key scenes in *Silence Of The Lambs* and *Jerry Maguire*.

Pink Floyd: who left
the lights on?

PINK FLOYD

Ask any of them. They'd all give you the same answer, without doubt. Were Pink Floyd asked
to name the greatest single invention on Earth, all of them would tell you, probably in unison,
that it was the light bulb. Back in 1965, the Floyd were experimenting with long, rambling
instrumental music while their audience were experimenting with **acid**. As your typical acid
user is prone to see lots of colours anyway, the Floyd decided to overload their senses with incredible multicoloured
lightshows, for which they quickly became famed. As their success grew, through albums such as *Dark Side Of The
Moon* (1973) and *Wish You Were Here* (1975), so too did their lightshows, which grew to such an extent that in 1990,
founder member **Roger Waters** (who had gone solo after splitting
acrimoniously with the band) lit up all of Germany with his
extravagant live spectacular, The Wall. Recently, ambient kings The
Orb have cited Pink Floyd as a major influence, assuring that the '70s
progressive rock act continues to attract a new, younger fanbase
with the passing of each year. (Further proof of their light bulb
obsession: their recent live CD release, *P.U.L.S.E.*, comes with its
own flashing light box.)

THE PIXIES

Possibly the most influential band ever to
be led by a singer with the name of **Charles Michael Kitteridge Thompson IV**, The Pixies formed in Boston in 1986 and
disbanded seven years later, leaving a body of work that, in part, was responsible for making **grunge** so damned
melodic. **Black Francis**, as he later re-named himself, was obsessed with two things in life: 1) the music of the **Beach
Boys**; and 2) UFOs, and all things extraterrestrial. These, combined with his own buzz-saw guitar
and the delectable bass work and purring harmonies of **Kim Deal** (later of *The Breeders*), made
for some of the most entertaining albums of the era, particularly the inspirational *Doolittle*
(1989) and *Bossanova* (1990). In early 1992, the band, who were long courted by the media,
looked all set to crack the big time when U2 took them out on their world tour. Less than a year
later, then, when Francis decided to split the band up, the surprise was considerable. Since then, his solo work has
continued to mine similar themes, but with less success.

PJ HARVEY

In terms of originality, Polly Jean Harvey remains unrivalled in modern music. Here was someone who emerged in 1991 with two startling singles (**'Dress'** and **'Sheela Na Gig'**) that simultaneously sounded rubbed red raw and wholly invigorating, and whose debut album, 1992's *Dry*, was a dark, twisted, arresting work that immediately established her as a genuine individual. Harvey was just 22 years old at the time, a seemingly depressive, sullen loner from whose eyes emerged only grave sadness and confusion. While the limelight clearly didn't suit her, she nevertheless freely posed naked (and bound) for her CD sleeves, an action that led to considerable over-exposure (if you will) in the media, who dubbed her **"The Indie Madonna"**. Unhappy with such frenzied attention, she retreated to her family home where, it was later revealed, she suffered two nervous breakdowns. In 1995, however, she underwent a radical reinvention, transforming herself, on the wry *To Bring You My Love* album, into a heavily lipsticked glamour puss in a catsuit, with an evil glint and a poisoned-irony tongue. For the first time, she appeared to be genuinely enjoying herself, and when she later guested on **Nick Cave**'s *Murder Ballads* collection, it appeared to be a match made in heaven.

Polly Jean Harvey

PM DAWN

PM Dawn, rap's own answer to **Laurel & Hardy** (i.e., one's fat, the other thin), have rarely been pigeon-holed as hip hop because they make music that shamelessly flits between a whole variety of styles. One moment they're rapping languidly like **The Jungle Brothers**, the next funking in true X-rated fashion like **Prince** under the duvet, while next again, they're harnessing an old **Spandau Ballet** song and taking it all the way to No.1. **'Set Adrift On Memory Bliss'**, which memorably sampled the aforementioned New Romantic's classic ballad **'True'**, took them to the top of the charts on both sides of the Atlantic in 1991, while the accompanying album, *Of The Heart, Of The Soul And Of The Cross: The Utopian Experience*, beautifully represented their otherworldly state of mind. In other words, **Prince Be** and **J.C.** (real names Attrell and Jarrett Cordes) were not your typical rappers. Their songs were high on melody, low on gangsta-isms and were filled with muse and philosophy. Consequently, they found far more fans from a mainstream audience rather than a rap one, where they tended to be derided. Regardless, they remain a blissful proposition.

THE POGUES

Perhaps the greatest pub-rock band of all time, The Pogues (originally **Pogue Mahone** - "kiss me arse" in Gaelic) were born out of a love for punk and good drinking. If before their existence the whole idea of Irish folk sounded as unpleasant as a lesson in line-dancing, then The Pogues soon changed the image entirely. Essentially, they were **The Clash** with a few fiddles, and you only qualified as a fan if you could hold your drink. As, indeed, could the now-legendary but almost toothless **Shane MacGowan**, one-time lead singer and possessor of a quite triumphant addiction to alcohol. In addition to such classic albums as *Rum, Sodomy And The Lash* (1985) and *If I Should Fall From Grace With God* (1988), The Pogues also created possibly the finest Christmas single ever in **'Fairytale Of New York'**, a duet with **Kirsty MacColl**, which boasted about as much goodwill to all men as a Bowery bum. As his alcoholism reeled out of all control, MacGowan was asked to leave the band, who replaced him - on occasion, anyway - with The Clash's **Joe Strummer**, while the exiled singer formed a new band, The Popes.

IGGY POP

Iggy Pop is rock'n'roll incarnate and is currently enjoying something of a renaissance due to the fact that: 1) his remarkable back catalogue deserves it, and 2) one of his greatest hits, **'Lust For Life'**, provides the soundtrack to one of the best scenes in the film *Trainspotting*. A man as proud of his vocals as he is of his penis, Iggy often appeared on stage partially dressed, smearing food, among other things, all over his body, and he was busted more than once for indecent exposure. By the mid '70s, Iggy had taken to cutting himself (usually his wiry torso) on stage - with either razor blades or broken bottles - and breaking his teeth after seemingly attempting to fellate the microphone, which, if nothing else, suggested that a vast intake of drugs can make you do rather strange things. In the late '70s, he became honorary **Godfather of punk**, worked considerably with **David Bowie** and enjoyed healthy sales for the albums that followed. His 1996 offering, *Naughty Little Doggy*, showed the Igg had lost none of his spirit. He also turned his hand to films such as *The Crow*, *City Of Angels* and **Jim Jarmusch**'s *Dead Man*.

PORTISHEAD

Slow and seductive, soulful and so very sad, interspersed with hip hop beats and positively awash with cinematic atmospherics, Portishead's *Dummy* is quite possibly the most distinctive album release of the entire decade. Coming in third after **Massive Attack** and **Tricky** in Bristol's emergent trip hop scene, Portishead soon stole the limelight from both, selling over a million copies of the album worldwide, and finding themselves in the peculiar position of suddenly having everyone wanting to work with them. **Geoff Barrow** and **Beth Gibbons** met in 1991 on an Enterprise Training Scheme. He was a film buff and fan of the music of **John Barry** (who composed the original **James Bond** theme, among others) and **Bernard Herrmann** (who composed the soundtracks to **Hitchcock**'s finest films). She was in awe of **Janis Joplin**, the **Cocteau Twins' Elizabeth Fraser**, and **Astrud Gilberto**. Barrow, who had previously worked on Massive Attack's first album, is a peerless musical composer. In *Dummy*'s grainy black-and-white texture, its seedy '60s subculture and its staccato melancholy, he's created an incredible work that has not only won endless plaudits (and, in 1995, the **Mercury Music Prize**), but has also set in motion innumerable soundalike bands who are desperate to emulate his success. Their next step could not be more eagerly anticipated.

Beth Gibbons of Portishead

THE PRESIDENTS OF THE UNITED STATES OF AMERICA

Like **Green Day**, Seattle's Presidents Of The United States Of America (or **PUSA**, if you're pushed for time) capitalized on grunge overkill by injecting a much-needed dose of humour. With an image that had more in common with a cartoon than a rock band, PUSA's music was questionably tagged "punk", while their lyrics suggested a sense of humour that bore more than a passing resemblance to that of **Bart Simpson**'s. Take their biggest hit, **'Lump'**, for example. Depending on your source, 'Lump' was either about a fat lady sitting in a swamp, or a peculiarly upbeat ditty about cancer. Their next single, **'Peaches'**, contained the memorable line, "Movin' to the country, gonna eat a lot of peaches", while their self-titled album (1995) continued the surreal theme. All of which subsequently proved a winner with the record-buying public, who snapped up over two million copies of the album in America alone, suggesting that despite the lingering legacy of **Nirvana**, American rock audiences still know how to **laugh**.

MUSIC TELEVISION®

Bobby Gillespie
with Primal Scream

PRIMAL SCREAM

From humble Scottish beginnings - vocalist **Bobby Gillespie** used to drum with **Jesus And Mary Chain** - Primal Scream have developed into a great rock'n'roll band with a heart full of spliffed-out dance, funk and classic rhythm and blues. When they were a jangly indie band in the mid-80s, few even bothered to acknowledge their existence, but come 1990, and the Scream were being credited with delivering the first dance anthem of the new decade in **'Loaded'**, possibly the most beautiful paean to getting wasted ever recorded. They practically defined the whole indie-dance era with the blissed-out, drugged-up *Screamadelica* album (containing the spirit of the **Rolling Stones** combined with the rhythms of **George Clinton** and **Parliament**), which remains one of the most important albums of the '90s. Equally famous for their propensity to party, the band practically attained legendary status, with their singer - who, incidentally, is so thin that **Kate Moss** looks like **Roseanne** in comparison - becoming an icon to weekenders everywhere. In 1994, the band delivered the swaggeringly soulful *Give Out But Don't Give Up* album, containing 'Rocks', which almost did **Mick Jagger** out of a job. They followed that with *Vanishing Point*.

THE ARTIST/PRINCE/ TAFKAP/

See Legends of MTV pp. 12-13

THE PRODIGY

Formed in 1991 by **Liam Howlett**, The Prodigy became an instant underground hit. Hardcore dance for the hardcore dancers. But any band that boasted someone like **Keith Flint** in their line-up was always going to be more than just a cult act. Thus, in 1997, The Prodigy are well on course to becoming the biggest dance act on the planet. How, exactly? Well, unlike other dance acts (chief complaint by inhabitants of mainstream culture: "They're all too faceless"), The Prodigy had an image, an angle. Boffin Howlett remained happy behind a bank of keyboards and computer monitors, while two highly aggressive frontmen wrestled for the limelight. On the left was **MC Maxim**, a tall black man with tiger contact lenses, a prowling predator who stalked the stage as if contemplating murderous acts; while on the right stood a diminutive lunatic, Keith Flint, his hair erect, dyed either blood red or electric green, a stake through his nose, his mouth full of heavy metal, and a style of dancing that could easily be mistaken for epilepsy. Combined, they made an electrifying spectacle. And then, of course, there was the music. *Music For The Jilted Generation* (1994) mixed techno with the crunching riffs of Sepultura, the result being strangely spectacular. In '96, they released **'Firestarter'**, the technohead's **'Common People'**, and signed to **Madonna**'s label, Maverick, their sole purpose: world domination. *Fat Of The Land*, due in mid-1997, may do it for them.

PUBLIC ENEMY

Perhaps the most celebrated rap act of them all, Public Enemy formed in New York in 1992 around the nucleus of **Chuck D**, **Hank Shocklee**, **Terminator X**, **Professor Griff** and the decidedly wayward "vibes" master **Flavor Flav**, who always knew what time it was. Two of their albums, *It Takes A Nation Of Millions To Hold Us Back* (1988) and *Fear Of A Black Planet* (1990), remain intensely powerful tomes, with Chuck D proving as important an educator through music as **Spike Lee** is through films. While the band succeeded in bringing their music to an increasingly white audience (touring, for example, with thrash metal outfit **Anthrax** in 1991), Flavor Flav kept the band in the headlines for less salubrious reasons. He was arrested on charges of assaulting his girlfriend, the mother of his three children, in 1991 and arrested again a year later for non-payment of child support and for driving without a licence. In 1995 he was sentenced to prison for 90 days for a gun-firing incident and later broke both his arms in a motorcycle accident in Italy. Chuck D, meanwhile, when not fronting the band, would undertake university lecture tours, and recently presided over his own talk show.

PULP

Before they became known the world over for antics which we will come to presently, Pulp were merely the best band in Britain. While, in 1995, the UK was fighting over who was best, **Blur** or **Oasis**, along came Pulp on the outside and stole everybody's hearts. This was what pop music was all about, and Pulp did it perfectly. What seemed like an overnight success was in fact the result of 15 years hard work, starting out in the mind of a dangerously thin **Jarvis Cocker** back at a time when everyone was still going ga-ga over a nascent **Duran Duran**. Cocker, a man seemingly obsessed with sex and voyeurism, soon realized that these were the perfect ingredients for great pop and duly set his many, shall we say, sexual themes, to exultant melody. Magic was made. By 1994, the wheels were finally in motion, and four subsequent events made them first local, then international, heroes. These were: 1) the *His 'n' Hers* album in 1994; 2) their triumphant headlining slot at **Glastonbury** in 1995, specifically the closing song, **'Common People'**; 3) *Different Class*, the album of 1995; and 4) the **Jarvis vs Jacko** incident at the 1996 **Brit Awards**. Midway through Jackson's performance of **'Earth Song'**, Jarvis ran on stage as "a form of protest at the way Michael Jackson sees himself as some Christ-like figure with the power of healing". Jackson was severely insulted, the news was reported across the world, and Jarvis instantly became very famous indeed. As he should be.

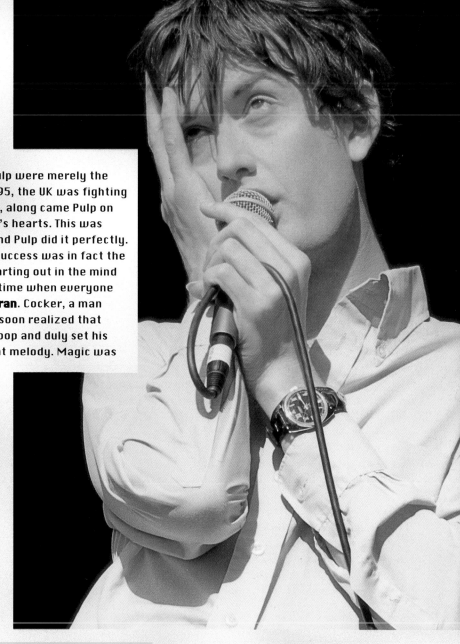

Jarvis Cocker bemoaning his bad-hair day

QUEEN

Despite, or perhaps because of, **Freddie Mercury**'s death in 1991, the legacy of Queen remains as great as it ever was. Queen's contribution to British rock music could never be overstated. Put simply, they are one of the country's biggest bands ever. They transformed stadium rock from something to be ashamed of - indeed, something to run away from - into something to be celebrated and richly enjoyed. Mercury was part **rock'n'roll front man** and part Christmas **pantomime dame**. To wit: "We're the Cecil B. de Mille of rock'n'roll, always wanting to do things bigger and better." There never was a more striking-looking frontman. With those teeth, that moustache and that horrendous collection of *Lycra* bodysuits, he could hardly have been mistaken for, say, **Led Zeppelin**'s **Robert Plant**, now could he? (Then again...) While their albums were admittedly often patchy (rock histrionic overkill, etc.), their singles were consistently fabulous. From **'Bohemian Rhapsody'** to **'Radio Ga Ga'** to **'The Show Must Go On'**, your average Queen seven-inch (before the days of CD, mind) represented high kitsch, sound-surround flamboyance and total enjoyment. Singalong-a-Queen has since become a pastime in bars everywhere, and only Abba are more popular in the karaoke stakes.

Queen: the kings of stadium rock

R. KELLY

Sex sells. This is something of which R. Kelly is only too well aware. Hence, one of his biggest hit singles lives under the title **'Bump N'Grind'**. Furthermore, Chicago's R. Kelly makes music for Saturday night couples who have dimmer facilities in the bedroom. Born 25 years ago, Kelly, like so many before him, started singing on street corners before the big break came along. In his case, the big break came when he appeared on a national TV talent contest - hosted by **Natalie Cole** - and won. From there, he wrote songs for **Janet Jackson**, **Gladys Knight**, **Toni Braxton** and heroes **Quincy Jones** and **The Isley Brothers**, as well as penning the worldwide No.1, **'You Are Not Alone'**, for **Michael Jackson**. A major player by this stage, when he finally got around to releasing his second major album, the statuesque *12 Play*, he shifted five million copies of it, and was later proclaimed "The New King of R&B". Unquestionably the smoothest sex god on the block, he only lowers his guard these days in the company of his mother, who still calls him **Robert**.

RADIOHEAD

Radiohead are five unlikely looking rock stars from Oxford, England. They are shorter and less attractive than most musicians. They are uncomfortable with the limelight, hate interviews and detest being photographed. None of them has a famous girlfriend. Their drummer is balding and happily married. On paper, then, Radiohead sound like an anomaly in the world of rock'n'roll. Fact is that Radiohead are one of the five best bands on the planet today. Take **'Creep'** for example. A dour tale of self-loathing, it paradoxically became an uplifting anthem for a generation and had everyone from **Blur** to **Bon Jovi** wishing they'd written it. In 1993, they became unexpectedly huge in America with their debut album, *Pablo Honey*. Two years later, with *The Bends*, they learned what it felt like to be truly successful, not only in England, but also in territories as unlikely as South Africa and Israel. Widespread acclaim became a given and *The Bends* was acknowledged as an album so good it didn't even have to stand on tiptoes to kiss the sky - which is some achievement, considering that singer Thom Yorke is barely 5 feet 5 inches tall. In 1997, *OK Computer* was preceded by the single 'Paranoid Android', which came with an epic six-and-a-half minute animation video by Magnus Carlsson, creator of cartoon character Robin.

Thom from Radiohead: he's got *The Bends*

RAGE AGAINST THE MACHINE

Back in 1992, Rage Against The Machine were a ravishing proposition: a fiercely polemical, acutely political band of hyper-intelligent musical activists whose marriage of rock and rap - with singer **Zack de la Rocha**'s trademark "shouty" vocals - was wondrously appropriate in a post-Rodney King world. Rarely had anger been articulated so expertly. In the still-awesome **'Killing In The Name'**, they offered us the perfect revolt-line with, "Fuck you, I won't do what you tell me", which was not only a successful call to arms for your average Joe, but also the perfect retort in any unpleasant situation Joe may have happened to find himself in. In 1996, after considerable worldwide success, the band returned with their *Evil Empire* album, in which they revealed themselves as pissed off as ever in their now-trademark musical style, which is so incendiary that if you struck a match in its vicinity, it would explode into flames. The most annoyed band in the world, and also the most **passionate**.

EROS RAMAZZOTTI

Eros Ramazzotti was born in Rome on October 28, 1963. At the age of 18, he entered a **New Voices** competition in Castrocaro, convinced that his future lay in music. From there, he moved to Milan, and three years later achieved his first chart success with **'Terra Promessa'**. A young writer with a penchant for lyrics of a polemic bent rather than the more typical lovelorn sentiments of his peers, Ramazzotti quickly received critical respect, as well as a burgeoning, and increasingly fanatical, fanbase, due in no small part to the fact that he was also a rather attractive young man. By 1985, he had become one of Italy's most successful singers, his single **'Una Storia Importante'**, having topped the charts not only at home, but also in Switzerland, Australia and France, where it sold over 700,000 copies. From here, his every utterance appeared to garner him a platinum disc. His third album, for example, 1987's *In Certi Momenti*, became a huge European seller, shifting over 2 million copies; its successor, *Musicae*, beat that figure by a further 500,000, and broke him in South America, where he recorded a Spanish version. He played to over three million people on the ensuing tour. Such success, of course, brought with it several comparisons, among them "Italy's answer to **George Michael** and **Elton John**". The most telling, however, was **"the James Dean of music"**, a direct reference to his abject shyness and reclusiveness. Despite his celebrity, he remains a very private man, who lives with his family in his sprawling villa in Brianza, outside Milan, where he has his own recording studio, along with several horses, dogs and a selection of top-of-the-range sports cars - one of his many passions. In 1996, *Dove c'e Musica* was Top 10 all over Europe (and Number 1 in Germany). His main ambition now is to break into the markets of America and England, and his ever-present determination suggests he won't stop until he's successful.

RED HOT CHILI PEPPERS

Of course, they have only their penises to thank. Without their particularly large appendages, Red Hot Chili Peppers would be nowhere today. Well, probably not, anyway. Appearing on stage, naked but for socks on their cocks, ensured that the Chilis weren't going to languish unnoticed for long. But in addition to possessing godly forms, the band's music was also something to behold. An unholy welding of classic rock with awesome funk (and, of course, lyrics that obsessed over sex), Red Hot Chili Peppers instantly became America's perfect bachelor party band. The legendary **George Clinton** produced, **Flea** played a particularly loose bass, while **Anthony Kiedis** stood upfront, his vocals half rock's mighty roar, half languorous rapping. If you could bottle the energy that this heady combination produced, you could sell it as an aphrodisiac. By the early 1990s, the band had hit their stride, and 1991's *Blood Sugar Sex Magik* proved a classic record, not least for its two genius singles, the ballad **'Under The Bridge'** and the funk epic, **'Give It Away'**, whose accompanying video won several awards. Despite several line-up changes (including the death of Hillel Slovak in 1988 from a heroin overdose), the band nucleus of Kiedis and Flea (who, incidentally, are good friends with **Alanis Morissette**) remains as cohesive as ever.

Eros Ramazzotti: the James Dean of music

Lou Reed: contemplates a walk on the wild side

LOU REED

Lou Reed is an icon for the following reasons: 1) for being an integral member of seminal '60s band **Velvet Underground**, who made the unlistenable listenable; 2) for singing about drugs in a manner that had drug users everywhere lifting a limp arm - almost defiantly - into the air in celebration; 3) for becoming one of the most influential exponents of, for want of a more appropriate term, "rock'n'roll" without ever selling out, or becoming truly successful, or particularly famous; 4) for the *Transformer* album; 5) for abusing his body with all manner of illegal substances without dying; 6) for, 24 years into his career, delivering the sublime *New York* album in 1989, a record of sweet and sour sentiments that confirmed him as much a poet as he is a lyricist; 7) for another superlative album three years later, *Magic & Loss*; 8) for allowing his song, **'Perfect Day'**, to be used in the best bit of the movie *Trainspotting* (the OD scene); 9) for appearing in the **Wayne Wang/Paul Auster** film, *Blue In The Face*, extolling the many virtues of smoking cigarettes with all the passion of someone in the grip of love; 10) for, at the age of 54, still possessing all his own, very curly, hair.

R.E.M.

See Legends of MTV pp. 26-27

THE ROLLING STONES

Where to begin? The Rolling Stones are an institution, more legendary than any British band outside of **The Beatles**. Despite extra-curricular activities that could have led more than one of them to an early grave (original member **Brian Jones** drowned while under the influence of drugs and alcohol in 1969), **Mick Jagger**, **Keith Richard**, **Ronnie Wood**, **Charlie Watts**, and the recently departed **Bill Wyman** - all remain surprisingly... well, alive. After over 20 years in the business, the band remained an active proposition throughout the '80s, a time in which they also pursued successful solo careers. By the 1990s, they became genuine rock dinosaurs, whose world tours were gigantic events that lumbered across the globe, regularly grossing over **$300 million** - this despite the fact that the ever pencil-thin Jagger (now over 50) continued to squeeze into ludicrously tight leggings that made him about as desirable as a lamppost. Today, they remain a favourite tabloid target, they are rarely out of the limelight and, yes, rarely manage to get into bed before the midnight hour. An inspiration to **elderly gentlemen** everywhere.

Henry Rollins, renaissance man

HENRY ROLLINS

A singer, actor, writer, publisher and editor, Henry Rollins is a renaissance man for the '90s. But it wasn't always this way. Back in the early '80s, Henry Rollins sang in **Black Flag**, America's ultimate hardcore punk band who were noted for their fearsome live performances and feral record releases. From there he set up his own **Rollins Band** in 1987, who toured relentlessly for the next five years, becoming one of the country's most respected groups. But this was just one of the heavily-tattooed, self-confessed workaholic frontman's many talents. He was also cultivating a following for his spoken word performances, as well as writing several books, which he published under his own **2.13.63** imprint. By the mid-1990s, Rollins was viewed as something of a god for the X Generation, a status he was far from comfortable with. He appeared in films (*Johnny Mnemonic*, *Heat*, *Lost Highway*), he published books, not only his own but books by the likes of **Nick Cave**, wrote for several high-profile US magazines and became America's No.1 youth hero. Currently, he is pursuing his band duties with the Rollins Band's latest album, *Come In And Burn*, but tomorrow he could be doing, well, anything and everything.

ROXETTE

Like fellow Swedes **Ace Of Base**, Roxette's mission in life is to bring toothpaste-bright pop music to the world, and in this they are phenomenally successful. With a strict diet of MTV-friendly songs, **Per Gessle** and **Marie Fredriksson** are these days only slightly less famous than **Coca-Cola**. Since their formation ten years ago, they've sold 21 million albums and 12 million singles worldwide (which presumably means that it is entirely possible that even the hill tribes of Northern Thailand are acquainted with a selection of Roxette's songs). A pretty impressive statistic, when you consider it. Appropriately, they are tagged as **"The World's No.1 Duo!"** and continue to churn out hit after hit with nonsensical titles such as **'Crash! Boom! Bang!'**, and a greatest hits collection entitled *Don't Bore Us, Get To The Chorus*. Which is almost funny.

The almost-funny Roxette

RUN DMC

In almost every sense, New York rappers Run DMC were there first. By 1984, a year after they formed, their debut album, *Run DMC*, was certified gold in the United States, the first rap album to gain this honour. A year later, they appeared in *Krush Groove*, the first ever rap movie. In 1986, they signed a six-figure sponsorship deal with **Adidas** after their hit single, **'My Adidas'**, alerted the sports company to the band's willingness to promote their footwear. Spool forward a year, and the rap crew's alliance with legendary rockers **Aerosmith** on the classic **'Walk This Way'** was also a first of its kind, while in 1991, they became the first rappers to release a greatest hits album (most rap acts aren't together long enough to warrant such a testament of durability). And with a new album imminent (their eighth), they ain't finished yet.

SADE

Back in the mid-80s, the sleek, soulful, seductively urbane Sade was the very personification of **sophistication**. If the music of Sade didn't seep from the speakers of your local restaurant or wine bar, it simply wasn't worth frequenting. It was 1984 when her debut album, *Diamond Life*, made her one of the most successful female artists of all time. Her music was soul and jazz, drenched in an eiderdown of **elegance** courtesy of a singer who could well have been mistaken for one of the world's most **beautiful** women. If back then she was ubiquitous, the following years saw the daughter of a Nigerian father and English mother retreat into hiding, moving first to Spain, then back to England. While further albums *Promise*, *Stronger Than Pride* and *Love Deluxe* all sold well, Sade became something of an enigma, who appeared to have little time for fame. The **majesty** and poise she exerts over all her records, however, has nevertheless influenced innumerable bands today, and she remains among the most **respected** artists of recent times.

Salt-n Pepa shake their thang

SALT-N-PEPA

Not only are Salt-n-Pepa rap's most successful and celebrated duo, they can also lay claim to the greatest album title the genre has yet seen in *A Salt With A Deadly Pepa*. Very funny, that. Back in the middle '80s, Ms Salt and her friend Ms Pepa, both from Brooklyn, New York, had set their sights on becoming nurses. (Incidentally, for the record, "Salt-n-Pepa" are not their real names: the former was actually christened **Cheryl James**, the latter **Sandra Denton**.) But, the riches of rap proved a little too attractive and before long Salt-n-Pepa had secured a deal and, with their resident DJ, **Spinderella**, in tow, scored a huge crossover hit in 1988 with the irrepressible **'Push It'**. They've remained on the scene with admirable consistency ever since, scoring a string of hit singles. Admirable, because rap is a world notorious for one-hit wonders, acts who barely even manage 15 minutes of fame before being usurped by **The Next Big Thing**. Salt-n-Pepa, on the other hand, are here for the duration.

THE SCORPIONS

The Scorpions formed in Hanover, West Germany, in 1975, and went on to become one of the world's biggest selling rock bands. Fittingly, they wore their hair long and bleached blonde. Throughout the '80s, the band were a constant at **Monsters Of Rock** festivals across Europe (audiences of 70,000 plus), and in America, after a profile-raising arena tour with **Bon Jovi** in 1984, they soon attained **platinum** status. In 1988 they were invited to perform ten concerts (15,000 people a night) in Leningrad, USSR, a reportedly life-changing event that led them to write what was to become one of their biggest hits, **'Wind Of Change'**.

The Scorpions in Moscow

SEAL

In many ways, the emergence of Seal as a major sex symbol of the 1990s was of immeasurable comfort to many teenagers unhappy with their complexion. At the age of 23, Seal contracted lupus (a particularly unpleasant skin disease that produces ulcers), which left him with distinctive facial scars, but this didn't stop him being voted The **World's Most Beautiful Man**. Quite right, too - there really are few people with the stature and handsome good looks of the man born with the improbable name of **Sealhenry Samuel**. And there are even fewer with a voice as rich as his (think melted chocolate, a lot of it). Seal first found exposure providing the vocals for **Adamski**'s huge international hit **'Killer'**, before embarking on a solo career that would lead to him becoming one of the most successful male singers of the decade. Two albums, both eponymously-titled so as to avoid confusion, took '90s soul to an all-new elegant plateau, before the use of his expert ballad, **'Kiss From A Rose'**, from the *Batman Forever* film, shot him into the stratosphere. The video rarely left MTV's screens, while over in America, it went on to become the most played single on national radio - ever.

MUSIC TELEVISION®

SHAGGY

Elastic of limb and rubbery of smile, Shaggy's entire image is much like the music he makes. Since 1993, the Jamaican-born, Brooklyn-raised ragga star has courted worldwide success. His No.1 single, **'Oh Carolina'**, was a re-working of the old **Prince Buster** classic, a song so irrepressibly cartoonish that it instantly endeared him to a nation of millions as a PG-rated alternative to the subversive and often homophobic reggae of **Shabba Ranks** and his ilk. Two years later, he scored even greater success with **'Boombastic'**, another caricature of ragga with its fat rhythms and growling, baritone vocals. Used in England as a Levi's TV advertising theme, and further boosted by a very entertaining claymation video (which hogged MTV for months), the song made him one of the most successful ragga artists ever. Predictably, the man has not stopped smiling since.

Mr Boombastic: Shaggy

SHAKESPEARS SISTER

Siobhan Fahey spent most of the '80s as one third of Bananarama, the most successful British female pop band until the Spice Girls. But Fahey was far from happy, being constantly at odds with the trio's hyper-efficient producers (**Stock Aitken & Waterman**). So she decided eventually to quit the band and join forces with Los Angeles singer-songwriter **Marcella Detroit**. And so, Shakespears Sister was born, so named after a song by Fahey's favourite band, **The Smiths** (its misspelling and lack of punctuation, incidentally, was a typographical error that somehow stuck). After a mild response to their 1989 debut album, *Sacred Heart*, the pair finally struck gold three years later with the million-selling single **'Stay'**, a beguiling ballad that offset Detroit's magnificent full-throttled voice against Fahey's more sardonic, almost disinterested drawl, and which came with a fabulously dramatic video (high camp meets high kitsch) to match. But again, Fahey was unhappy and the pair split, following careers which have yet to scale the heights they found together (although Fahey kept the name Shakespears Sister).

SIMPLE MINDS

As an image, it proves hard to forget. It is somewhere around the late 1980s and Simple Minds are playing stadia across Europe. The music is as chest-beatingly defiant as required, while up front, a man with long flowing hair, an enormous, over-sized white shirt, and what looks suspiciously like black Lycra leggings, is standing stage-front, one fist in the air, the other pressing the microphone tight to his lips, singing songs of PRIDE. **Jim Kerr** (for it is he) was pretty much the consummate '80s frontman. Simple Minds, who formed in Scotland back at the arse-end of the 1970s, dominated the '80s with only **U2** for company. Both were political, polemical and passionate, both wrote songs tailor-made for vast open spaces, and both went head-to-head for world domination. U2 later won convincingly by kicking themselves into the '90s, while Kerr and co continued to tread the same path over and over. Nevertheless, in 1986 there was no more rousing a record than their *Once Upon A Time* album, back when Kerr, replete in aforementioned "costume", looked like David taking on Goliath - and **winning**.

SIMPLY RED

As incongruous a vision as it may be, the ginger-haired **Mancunian** with the jewel-encrusted smile has one of the finest soul voices ever bestowed upon a white man. Yes, despite being born and bred in the north of England, **Mick Hucknall** sounds on record like he grew up in every soulboy's Utopia, **Motown**. Formed after Hucknall disbanded his punk band, **The Frantic Elevators**, Simply Red released their seminal debut album, *Picture Book*, in 1985. The languorous mood of the album, which featured the elegiac strains of *'Holding Back The Years'*, made it the year's No.1 seductive soundtrack. Quickly gaining an international reputation not only as a superlative singer but also something of a Lothario, Hucknall became perennial tabloid fodder, attending European premières and parties with a variety of attractive women on his arm (among them, tennis legend **Steffi Graf**). Hucknall later bought a place in his spiritual home, Italy, where he not only wrote songs but held innumerable dinner parties, which allowed him to show off his other major talent, cooking. The release of the *Stars* album, in 1991, kicked the band into the stratosphere with worldwide sales of eight million. Hucknall remains a very famous boy indeed.

Mick Hucknall of Simply Red and Manchester United

SISTERS OF MERCY

For many, much of the '80s were spent in the grip of goth, but if bands such as **The Cure** and **Siouxsie & The Banshees** were the genre's chart-friendly exponents, then Sisters Of Mercy represented what happened to goth after midnight. Essentially, it got very strange indeed - rather grave but with just a hint of an ironic twinkle in its solemn eyes, perhaps too wry to be goth at all. Formed in 1980 by the gaunt **Andrew Eldritch**, the Sisters created fearsome, compelling records such as 1985's *First And Last And Always* (finest cut: **'Amphetamine Logic'**) and 1987's *Floodland* (finest cut: **'This Corrosion'**, aided by the Wagnerian production talents of **Meat Loaf** collaborator **Jim Steinman**). It was magnificent, brooding music. By this time guitarist **Wayne Hussey** had left to form his own version of goth, **The Mission**. *Vision Thing* was released in 1990, by a line-up including ex-**Sigue Sigue Sputnik Tony James** on bass and **All About Eve** man Tim Bricheno, and the band have continued to tour occasionally, with various line-ups. Eldritch - ever the teasing enigma - lives behind mirrored shades in Germany, in isolation, leaving fans to wonder whether another album will ever appear.

SKUNK ANANSIE

A black bisexual with big boots, a bald head and a T-shirt advertising the sharp-toothed wonders of **"Clit Rock"**, this particular band's lead singer isn't about to go unnoticed by anyone. Fact is, there is little in the way of subtlety surrounding anything that Skunk Anansie do. And what exactly Skunk Anansie do "do" is rage. Skunk Anansie seethe with verbose malevolence. They articulate anger and frustration until they froth at the mouth and burst a blood vessel.

Skin of Skunk Anansie

Singer **Skin** has a voice that can switch from the melodic (**'Charity'**) to ear-splitting screeching (**'Selling Jesus'**), and that's some range. And when you hear tracks such as **'Intellectualise My Blackness'** and **'Little Baby Swastikkka'** (both from their debut album *Paranoid & Sunburnt*), you realize that Skin could take on all of **Rage Against The Machine** with one hand tied behind her back - and win. One of the more assertive British bands currently doing the rounds at the moment, Skunk Anansie, whose second album *Stoosh* lit up 1996 like a firecracker, are seven shades of wonderful at the very least.

SMASHING PUMPKINS

Smashing Pumpkins are a band who perennially teeter on the precipice.
In 1991, that precipice was worldwide recognition for their fantastic debut album, *Gish* (they were ultimately overlooked when **Nirvana**'s *Nevermind* introduced the world to grunge, and grunge to the world). In 1994, they tipped over the precipice into too much of, well, too much of everything: fame, success and overwhelming pressure. Come 1996, and they were staring self-destruction in the face as the group's sometime keyboard player, **Jonathan Melvoin**, died from a heroin overdose, which later resulted in the sacking of drummer **Jimmy Chamberlain**. But for these very reasons - this permanent sense of high drama - the Pumpkins have proved to be one of America's most exciting bands of the last decade. Their second and third albums, '93's *Siamese Dream*, '96's *Mellon Collie And The Infinite Sadness*, proved that rock histrionics were by no means a thing of the past, and both albums boasted a visceral power. Indeed, so intense was the latter record that singer **Billy Corgan** ceremoniously shaved his head for added effect, then spent some months perfecting his satanic stare. A bonafide classic rock act, Chicago's Smashing Pumpkins have earned their place in rock's rich pageant.

SNAP

Coming out of America, via Germany, at the turn of 1990, Snap exerted a brief but formidable hold over the mainstream dance scene courtesy of their almighty introductory single, **'The Power'**. A duo comprising the screeching vocals of **Jackie Harris**, and the big, bad, butch barking tones of one **Turbo B** (believed not to be his real name), **'The Power'** was as successful as it was controversial; accusations of plagiarism dogged it constantly (the chorus of **"I got the power"** was sampled from **Jocelyn Brown**'s **'Love Is Gonna Get You'**, the tune inspired by **Chili Rob G**'s **'Let The Words Out'**). Surviving the flak while continuing to court a different kind of controversy (by admitting to some particularly questionable ethics), they scored several other hits, including **'The Cult Of Snap'**.

SNOOP DOGGY DOG

Hard as it may be to believe, Snoop Doggy Dog began his singing career in church with the local Baptist choir. But instead of growing up to become **Whitney Houston**, Snoop turned instead to crime and within a month of leaving school, he was sentenced to one year in county jail for selling cocaine to an undercover agent. As soon as he was released, he promptly returned (for violating his parole). With a lot of spare time on his hands, he turned his attention to rapping. Once out, he hooked up with **Dr. Dre** on the latter's *The Chronic* album, but soon after was arrested yet again, this time accused of participating in a drive-by murder (for which he was eventually acquitted three years later). Such sour controversy didn't hinder his career. Later that same year (1993) his own debut album, *Doggystyle*, went straight to the top of the US chart, going on to sell four million copies. A languid West Coast-style rap mixed with classic '70s funk, the actual quality of his music was often overlooked in favour of the man's lewd lyrics and his obsession with fat-bottomed girls. In 1995, he was charged with possession of marijuana and drug paraphernalia, proving that he is nothing if not consistently **baaad!** His musical career continues with *Tha Doggfather*.

The gloriously noisy Sonic Youth

SONIC YOUTH

The position Sonic Youth hold in popular music is a peculiar, possibly unique, one. Formed in New York back in 1981 (when most of today's American guitar bands were still in diapers), they quickly became regarded as the perfect alternative US rock band. They went into the studio and emerged with a glorious noise. This glorious noise then became an album, and the album became roundly celebrated. Cult status immediately befell them, and every band that followed in their wake had at least one Sonic Youth T-shirt permanently about their person. By the time of grunge, they were promoted to godfather status, and without them **Nirvana** and just about everybody else wouldn't even have existed. *Goo* (1990) was a seminal album, as was 1994's *Experimental Jet Set, Trash & No Star*, if only for its magnificent title. By the mid-1990s, Sonic Youth had still failed to score a bonafide crossover hit single, and yet **Thurston Moore** and **Kim Gordon** were practically household names. At **David Bowie**'s recent 50th birthday celebrations at Madison Square Gardens, the Youth were hand-picked to appear. They remain the best kept secret around, a stubbornly underground proposition.

SOUL ASYLUM

Despite becoming very successful indeed at the tail end of the grunge era (1992), Soul Asylum's history actually dates back to 1981. Led by the very handsome **Dave Pirner**, who had previously been the singer in the delightfully named **The Shits**, they created a rather frantic mess of punk, rock, country and folk. Often, the response such a hybrid garnered was a massive question mark. Come the '90s, however, and Soul Asylum became soft rock personified, a little like **Bruce Springsteen** meets **The Lemonheads**. *Grave Dancers Union* came with a seamless production and several excellent hit singles in the shape of the all-American **'Black Gold'** and **'Runaway Train'**. Pirner then became famous outside of music for two main reasons. The first was that he claimed never to wash his hair (which explains why it looks like a particularly unkempt bird's nest), while the second was his very public relationship with Hollywood's latest golden girl, **Winona Ryder**.

**Dave Pirner
of Soul Asylum**

SOUL II SOUL

In the history of British dance music, Soul II Soul couldn't occupy a more integral role. The band grew out of a North London sound system in the early 1980s, and was led by the ultra-cool **Jazzie B**, **Philip 'Daddae' Harvey** and producer/arranger **Nellee Hooper** (who would go on to work with **Massive Attack**, **Björk** and **Madonna**, achieving iconic status along the way). They started out organizing warehouse raves before becoming a band in their own right. In 1989, with vocalist **Caron Wheeler** at the microphone, they released the classic **'Keep On Movin'** single, whose underlying drum beat would go on to launch countless dance records. **'Back To Life (However Do You Want Me)'**, became a UK No.1, while shortly afterward, their *Club Classics Volume One* album was hailed as one of the most important British album releases of the era, with Jazzie B not only a formidable frontman but also a budding entrepreneur (with a chain of shops, a record label, and even a proposed - though never fulfilled - hospital). The band's success dipped thereafter, going through a succession of featured vocalists, none of whom fitted as neatly as Wheeler (who was pursuing a solo career). Their imminent return, however, promises much.

SOUNDGARDEN

Soundgarden first came to global attention around the time of grunge. Unsurprising, really, because back in the genre's heyday (1991-92) anyone sporting long hair, a loud lumberjack shirt and an even louder guitar was promptly lapped up by an insatiable worldwide audience. But their history actually dates back to 1987, when they were one of the first Seattle bands to be signed to **Bruce Pavitt**'s then-fledgling Sub Pop label (the label that would later go on to define the Seattle sound of the early '90s). While, for convenience's sake, they were filed alongside the likes of **Nirvana** and **Pearl Jam**, their sound had more in common with the likes of **Black Sabbath**: their metal was heavy, their mettle unrepentant. They scored a huge mainstream hit with their 1992 album *Badmotorfinger*, which enjoyed excellent worldwide sales thanks not only to the record, but also due to the fact that singer **Chris Cornell** is rather beautiful, his sharp cheekbones and magnificent cascading locks attracting hordes of newly-converted female fans. Two years later, to coincide with the release of the *Superunknown* album, Cornell had chopped most of his hair off, tired of such unnerving attention. Soundgarden split in the first quarter of 1997, but he remains one of the more **attractive** Men In Rock nevertheless, a factor which probably dogs him on a daily basis.

SPICE GIRLS

To suggest that the Spice Girls are 1) the most revolutionary cultural force in POP music since **The Beatles**, 2) a zeitgeist-creating phenomenon of the late 1990s and 3) the best thing since sliced bread would, of course, be veering toward exaggeration. But they could be. For the emergence of **Mel C**, **Mel B**, **Victoria**, **Emma** and **Geri** proved the uncontested highlight of 1996. An all-singing, all-dancing sensation, they appeared out of nowhere, straight into the No.1 position the world over with **'Wannabe'**, a song with more natural effervescence than Perrier. While every nation's more scurrilous "news" papers immediately (and desperately) attempted to dig up a little dirt on the suddenly-famous quintet, everyone else had far more serious subjects to ponder. Specifically: which is your favourite Spice Girl? It was the question on everybody's lips and proved a greater subject of discussion than the single European currency. By Christmas, their debut album, *Spice*, had slain all in its wake, (in the States, too), while their third monster hit, **'2 Become 1'**, was a song so overtly romantic that the entire world fell suddenly in love with one another. Their significance, then, cannot be overstated: Spice Girls, in a very real sense, rule.

SPIN DOCTORS

The Spin Doctors are your classic misfits. Beauty sits not upon their features, nor in their immediate vicinity. Instead, they are somewhat geeky: sallow complexions, lank hair parted down the middle and elbow- and knee-joints that work like those of a flamingo. Speaking musically, they are **Grateful Dead** disciples. And they are rather successful. The Spin Doctors' 1992 debut album, *Pocket Full Of Kryptonite*, initially sold between 60 and 70,000 copies to the band's die-hard following of neo-hippies. But then MTV - followed by Britain and, indeed, the rest of the world - picked up on the band, particularly their two hits **'Two Princes'** and **'Little Miss Can't Be Wrong'** and suddenly New York's latter-day Grateful Dead started to take off. Off into the big time, a place where records sell in units totalling several million, and a place where fame, success and lots and lots of money suddenly become part of your everyday life. Since then, however, they've reverted back to their previous status, that of eternally popular cult band whose very lack of image remains the key to their appeal.

BRUCE SPRINGSTEEN

The music of Bruce Springsteen embodies America in its entirety. It unites liberals with rednecks, the East Coast with the West Coast and all points in between. This is a commonly-held belief by, seemingly, everyone except **The Boss** himself. When his most famous song, **'Born In The USA'**, was seen as a fist of defiance in the face of war (in this case, The Gulf Conflict), Springsteen went to great pains to explain that the song was actually vehemently anti-war. Similarly, when certain politicians decided to adopt the very same song as a political rally cry, Springsteen immediately threatened legal action. However, what all this proves is that his songs appeal to every blue-collar citizen in the land. Thirty years in music has made Springsteen a permanent resident in America's **Hall Of Greats**, in which time he's gone from Angry Young Man to Thoughtful Muse, from *Born To Run* (anger and revolt and the youthful pursuit of dreams) to *The Ghost Of Tom Joad* (middle-aged introspection and worldly contemplation). His soundtrack work on recent films (*Philadelphia*, *Dead Man Walking*) has been exemplary, suggesting that although he's slowed the pace, his music is as valid today as it ever was.

The Boss

MUSIC TELEVISION®

STAKKA BO

How does that saying go: If the mountain won't go to Mohammed then Mohammed must go to the mountain? Well, while over in the UK in the early 1990s the **Stereo MCs** were redefining hip hop as we know it, and cleaning up accordingly, sprightly Swede Stakka Bo launched his own Stereo MCs tribute act and became one of his country's most successful and, more importantly, least embarrassing musical exports (this was the time of **Dr. Alban**, remember). His superb debut single, **'Here We Go Again'**, was the greatest song **Rob Birch** and co had never written and suddenly everyone viewed Sweden as a very funky proposition indeed. With the release of his album, *Supermarket*, Bo proved himself as much more than a mere wannabe, revealing a bright sense of melody, verbal sophistication and of course a terrific sense of humour. A ubiquitous presence on the Swedish dance music scene, he returned in 1996 with *The Great Blondino* album, and teamed up with Titiyo early in 1997 for the single **'We Vie'**.

STEREO MCS

Stereo MCs are, without contention, the decade's most famously inactive band. Probably the most respected rap band to come out of Britain so far, their reputation was created on the promising *Supernatural* album (1990), but was truly cemented with the *Connected* set two years later, an album that won two **Brit Awards**, scored several hits (**'Ground Level'**, **'Step It Up'**), and spawned an entire nation of copyists. Led by the ferret-like Rob Birch, the Stereos personified laidback rap mixed with a pop nous that appealed equally to clubbers and armchair enthusiasts alike. Their popularity spread like wildfire, in both Europe and America, but instead of capitalizing on this, the band promptly did...nothing. After a series of incredible live dates in 1993, Stereo MCs disappeared into the studio, supposedly to work on a follow-up. The band's inactivity became almost legendary, not least because every scheduled release date passed without incident. The current rumour has it that there will be a new album out in Autumn '97, but fans are advised not to hold their breath.

Stereo MCs take time out from a busy recording schedule

STING

Some things about Sting. Sting is from Newcastle in the north east of England. He is a former teacher. He starred, in 1979, in the seminal film *Quadrophenia*. Between 1977 and 1985, he enjoyed 15 UK hits and five UK No.1s with **The Police**, during which time they attained legendary status. He continues to act in films, meanwhile, some very good, some not so good. Post Police, he carved out a solo career with typical efficiency, each album selling vast quantities, and before long he became one of the most recognizable pop stars on the planet. Rumour has it that not an hour goes by on South American radio without them playing at least one song by Sting. He spent much of 1986 touring with **Amnesty International** alongside **Peter Gabriel**, **Bob Dylan**, **Tom Petty** and **U2**. In 1989, led by his conscience, he went on a promotional tour to publicize the plight of the Kayapo Indians and to help save the Brazilian rainforests. In interviews, meanwhile, he began to talk of his love of yoga and how its discipline has enabled him to sustain sex for many hours. Naturally, he is admired by millions and envied by even more.

The Stone Roses at the Reading Festival, 1996

STONE ROSES

The first incarnation of Stone Roses emerged in **Manchester** way back in 1983. But, with the kind of studied nonchalance that would later typify their career, the band's eponymously-titled debut album didn't emerge until a whole six years later, in the spring of 1989. When it finally saw the light of day, however, it was instantly hailed as a classic. Along with fellow Mancunians **Happy Mondays**, the Roses spearheaded the triumphant '**Madchester**' scene (indie meets dance and takes some drugs) and its enduring influence continues to shape music to this day. By the time they headlined Spike Island, in Cheshire, England, before 30,000 fans, they had become one of the most celebrated bands in British history. Thereafter, however, things went somewhat awry. Two drawn-out court cases with former record labels followed, then, after the band signed to **Geffen Records** for a reputed $4 million, nothing further was heard from them for almost four years. By the time they finally re-emerged with the swaggering *Second Coming*, the strain was only too visible, with one member leaving, then another, and by the summer of 1996, the greatest band of their generation were history, leaving only a lingering legacy.

STONE TEMPLE PILOTS

After **Nirvana** and **Pearl Jam** opened the floodgates for a myriad of vaguely alternative American rock acts, it suddenly appeared as if every new US band had a grunge element to their sound. This naturally made the music press somewhat cynical in their view toward the genre, and one band in particular who suffered from this was San Diego's **Stone Temple Pilots**. Formed in 1991, they had a four-million selling debut album in *Core* within a year, their decidedly Pearl Jam-like music finding instant favour with fans who were merely hungry for more of the same, and who were not particularly aware of any bandwagon-jumping. A second album, *Purple*, followed shortly afterward and again afforded them many platinum discs. But, despite this, the band were constantly dismissed by critics who accused them of plagiarism. As the band's success grew, so too did singer **Scott Weiland**'s drug use. In and out of detox, he would also mysteriously "go missing", causing the band to pull out of commitments, thus suggesting that their future is anything but certain.

The Stone Temple Pilots in concert

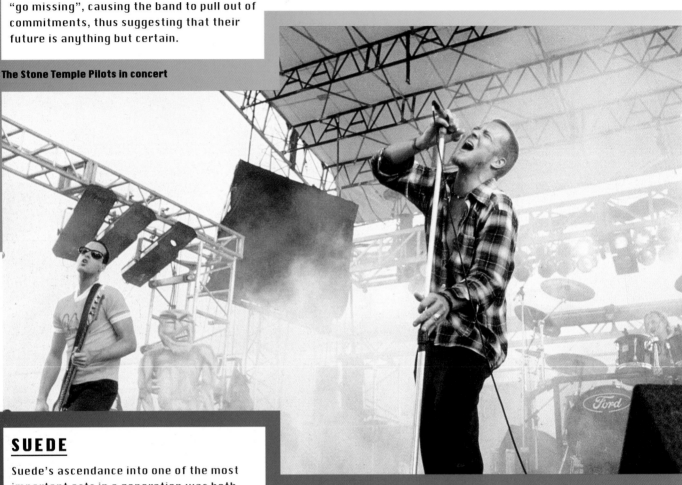

SUEDE

Suede's ascendance into one of the most important acts in a generation was both swift and, up until recently, unprecedented.
At the beginning of 1992, shortly after **Justine Frischman** left to form **Elastica**, Suede started getting the kind of attention they had craved. By year end, they were omnipresent, their name on the tip of every tongue that wagged. The following year, their eponymously-titled first album became the fastest-selling UK debut album since **Frankie Goes To Hollywood**'s *Welcome To The Pleasure Dome* nine years before. Incredibly precocious and acutely aware of their own worth, their 1994 album, *Dog Man Star*, was recorded with the specific intention of being hailed a classic the moment it hit the streets. It was. Then **Bernard Butler**, their genius guitarist, left the band, **Britpop** happened, and Suede were suddenly cast adrift, misunderstood and overlooked. Their foppish theatricality had suddenly become very old hat as **Oasis** brought no-nonsense rock to the fore. Down but not beaten, Butler's 17-year-old replacement, **Richard Oakes**, was later joined by keyboardist **Neil Codling**, and the band returned in 1996 with the excellent *Coming Up* album. While their success may not quite be on the stratospheric level they feel they deserve, Suede nevertheless remain one of the most respected British acts in a long, long time.

SWING OUT SISTER

In Swing Out Sister-land, the sun always shines. It is always late spring/early summer, everyone is always happy, and the urge to skip off into the park wearing very neat threads is inevitably far too irresistible to ignore. An over-simplification, of course, but upon hearing their eternally young breakthrough single, it is nearly impossible to come to any other conclusion. Swing Out Sister broke out with **'Breakout'** in 1986, a song that boasted more *joie de vivre* than any other song of its era bar, perhaps, **Katrina & The Waves'** 'Walking On Sunshine'. A duo comprising **Andy Connell** and **Corinne Drewery**, Swing Out Sister combined the influence of **Northern Soul** with cappuccino jazz and sublime pop inflections through four albums-worth of music that had much the same effect on the ears as a Jacuzzi does on an aching back. In a word (or, in fact, three): pure aural sophistication.

TAKE THAT

Take That revolutionized the way the world saw boy bands. And for this reason alone they shall command eternal respect. When the five young men - **Gary Barlow**, **Robbie Williams**, **Jason Orange**, **Howard Donald** and **Mark Owen** - first got together in 1991, it was under the strict supervision and tutelage of manager **Nigel Martin-Smith**, who wanted to create a British version of New Kids On The Block. Up until that point, boy bands had existed solely for impressionable young girls in the mad grip of puberty, who adored their perfect complexions and toothpaste-bright smiles. For everyone else, boy

bands were merely puppets worthy only of derision. But, slowly, Take That began to increase their appeal. Barlow, it soon became clear, was a budding **Elton John**, someone who could certainly write a well-crafted pop song, while Robbie Williams supplied the band with a cocksure, entertaining image that girls and boys of all ages could easily appreciate, even admire. By 1995, and the magnificent single **'Back For Good'**, Take That were a ubiquitous presence. For boys as famous and as young as they, it was incredible that they could still appear so carefree, with no visible stress, tension or friction. In July, however, the bubble suddenly burst. Williams, who had been hanging out with **Oasis**, either quit or was kicked out of the band (depending on which version you read), and immediately started cultivating a drug habit. (This would soon have him asking for Elton John's help and advice on how to clean up.) Meanwhile, the band attempted to carry on as before, but by February '96, they announced that they were to split while on top. They may reform some time in the future, they suggest, but for now they each wish to concentrate on solo careers. Thanks for the memories.

Take That: gone for good

TALK TALK

Talk Talk were a band who took the entire notion of production to a new level. They would take what they'd written into a hermetically-sealed studio and lay down layer after layer of sound as if it were paint on canvas. What they would emerge with sometime later was music thick with sound and style that overlooked nothing and was therefore filled with delectable intricacies and a multitude of instruments. The result was uniformly wondrous, if occasionally slightly overcooked. Their *It's My Life* (1984) album, which contained the singles **'Such A Shame'** and **'Dum Dum Girl'**, proved a huge success across Europe, while its follow-up four years later, *The Colour Of Spring*, which produced the landmark single **'Life's What You Make It'**, became something of a classic. Meanwhile, 1991's *Laughing Stock* proved somewhat interminable, and also proved to be their last album, as the band have remained virtually silent ever since.

TALKING HEADS

Before **R.E.M.** went *Green* and became the doyens of alternative American rock, that mantle rested squarely on the oversized shoulder pads of New York's Talking Heads. Formed in 1974, they quickly became noted as the finest of the so-called **CBGB**-era bands (which also included **Television**, **Patti Smith** and the **Ramones**), and a short half decade later, were among the most idolized "art rock" bands on the planet. A liquid gold rhythm section of drummer **Chris Frantz** and bassist **Tina Weymouth** played alongside keyboardist **Jerry Harrison** and frontman **David Byrne** (who cultivated a self-consciously nerdy presence and sublimely neurotic vocals). Talking Heads were a delectably stylized enigma and were universally admired.

David Byrne and Tina Weymouth of Talking He

Video was a favoured medium, and typically innovative promos accompanied two of their most magnificent songs, **'And She Was'** and **'Road To Nowhere'** (both 1985). By 1988, however, after fourteen fruitful years, singer David Byrne decided to take a little time out. He planned, in time-honoured fashion, to "do other things", maybe a little film work or the occasional solo album. Then, once refreshed and re-invigorated, he would return to the band. That, however, never happened, and in 1996, much to the singer's chagrin, the band continued without him under the moniker of **The Heads**.

TEARS FOR FEARS

It is 1983 and the two young men who make up Tears For Fears - **Curt Smith** and **Roland Orzabal** - have terrible haircuts. Not as bad as, say, fellow early-'80s act **Flock Of Seagulls**, but bad enough. Thankfully, this doesn't stop them having hits, and their debut album, *The Hurting*, is an unusually thoughtful record for ones as young as they (much of it is influenced by the writings of **Arthur Janov**). Two years later and the band release the *Songs From The Big Chair* album, which includes the massive hit **'Everybody Wants To Rule the World'**. Although the album goes on to sell over five million copies in America alone, the band's sole songwriter, Orzabal, still rarely manages a smile - he is notoriously serious. Their next album (*The Seeds Of Love*) is hugely expensive and overly ambitious, while in 1992, Smith exits the band. Orzabal continues alone, but further album releases, *Elemental* and the rather pompous *Raoul And The Kings Of Spain*, fail to match previous successes. Since their inception, however, both Smith and Orzabal have allowed stylists to work wonders to their hair, despite the ongoing threat of baldness.

TEXAS

Like many of their peers, Scotland's Texas were obsessed with the music of America, and set about approximating the style right down to every meticulous six-stringed twang. The band's breakthrough single, 1990's **'I Don't Want A Lover'**, was a slide guitar classic, every bit as cinematic as anything by **The Eagles** or **Ry Cooder**. The accompanying album, *Southside*, followed a similar path and the band quickly found their niche, albeit a secondhand one. Two further albums of sensible AOR followed, which succeeded in making them superstars in France, but not very credible anywhere else. Their latest album has changed all that, however. Having disappeared from view in 1994 for a major re-think, Texas returned this spring with their exceptional fourth album, *White On Blonde*, a modern-day soul record that boasted current influences (including trip hop) to quite spectacular effect. The result was a No.1 record, and the deification of singer **Sharleen Spiteri**, who has since become something of a diva. It remains one of the decade's more impressive turnarounds, from potential obscurity to sleek, soulful greatness - all thanks to one career-saving record.
Texas are currently busy becoming very famous indeed.

Sharleen Spiteri of Texas

THE THE

No matter how ironic or post-modern it was supposed to be, "The The" remains one of the worst band names in history. Fortuitously, though, the band themselves (essentially Londoner **Matt Johnson**) were to prove a far more thought-provoking proposition. Formed in 1979 as **Margaret Thatcher** took power in England, Johnson created some intriguing music, which combined spidery guitar work, a nascent sense of prowling ambience, skewed poetry and a neat pop sensibility. In other words, here was someone tailor-made for major cult worship. In 1986 he released the classic *Infected* album, which concerned itself with social decay, the power of America and an obsession with sex. In 1992 came *Dusk*, a musical film noir again infused with a creeping sense of paranoia and an almost unerring majesty, despite the often sour subjects dealt with in his songs. A decidedly singular artist, Johnson is also one of the more intriguing British singer-songwriters to have emerged in recent times, a man only blighted by his own murderously slow work-rate.

THERAPY?

There are ways and ways to run a band. **Stone Roses** take five and a half years to record an album. Therapy? take five and a half minutes. Now that's progress. Therapy?'s workrate has been little short of magnificent since they first formed in Belfast in 1987. They've gone from mini-albums on mini labels (*Baby Teeth* and *Pleasure Death*) to juicy big albums on big labels (*Nurse*, *Troublegum*, *Infernal Love*) with barely a pause. And each has brought them to a wider audience, first homegrown, then European (where collective sales top half a million), then over in America where the college charts have made them feel most at home. Their music is at once dark, brooding and ferociously loud, while peppered with a magnificent streak of juvenile humour. Fittingly, then, they quickly found acceptance across the board and were tagged as exponents of "postmodern metal", while frontman **Andy Cairns** experimented with hair dye, every variation on the goatee you could possibly imagine, and even went through a brief **Elvis**-meets-**Bono** period that suggested his chief goal with Therapy? was to have fun, and a lot of it.

Therapy? No, just a good tailor

TANITA TIKARAM

Possessor of the most phonetically-pleasing name since **Dave Dee, Dozy, Beaky, Mick & Tich**, Tanita Tikaram went straight from the school classroom to considerable international success, seemingly overnight. A highly individual artist, Tikaram looked like a very young, and very beautiful, **Elvis Presley** and sounded like no one else on earth. Her voice was a strange instrument, deep and husky, warm and quite enchanting. She sang literary, bookish songs with titles such as **'Twist In My Sobriety'**, that no one quite understood, but which everyone admired nevertheless. Between 1988 and 1995, she released five highly individual albums (her debut, *Ancient Heart*, was also her best), before deciding, at the grand old age of 26, to take time out of music, pursue other interests, and only return when she feels the time is right. She has plenty of time yet.

DIE TOTEN HOSEN

Should any German rockumentary maker ever feel the need to immortalize the lives and times of local heroes Die Toten Hosen on film, then it would probably prove more entertaining, more unreal, than **Spinal Tap**'s adventures in rock'n'roll. Die Toten Hosen are not like other bands. They are, simply, more...of everything. It seems that the band formed because **Andreas Frege** and **Andreas Meurer** were hungry late one night in 1982. They ordered a pizza, the delivery boy, **Michael Breitkopf**, arrived and boasted of a certain prowess on the guitar and, hey presto, the band was born (and the pizzas grew cold). A punk band who are wont to donate their entire concert proceeds to the **Dusseldorf Appeal Against Racism And Racial Prejudice**, Die Toten Hosen have, in between selling vast amounts of their albums *Damenwahl, Bis Zum Betteren Ende - Live* and *Reich & Sexy*, lived in squats, played mental hospitals, convents, prisons and old peoples' homes, toured with **Faith No More**, **U2** and **The Rolling Stones**, have bought two professional football players for **Fortuna Dusseldorf**, their favourite team (to no avail - the team were still relegated at the end of the season), have held a grudge ice hockey match against Russia's **Leningrad Cowboys** before 10,000 spectators, and have attained legendary status in their own country, as well as throughout much of the rest of Europe. Record sales now total over four million. They have a reputation that precedes them wherever they go. Surely it is only a matter of time before **Pizza Hut** adopt them as their latest mascots. It'd do wonders for the sales of margheritas.

Die Toten Hosen at the Phoenix Festival, 1995

TERENCE TRENT D'ARBY

Few artists possess such natural star quality as Terence Trent d'Arby. This former American soldier, stationed at **Elvis Presley**'s old army base in Frankfurt, West Germany, exploded on to the scene, circa 1987, like a **Second Coming**. A beautiful man with songs as lithe and muscular as his bare torso, his debut single (**'If You Let Me Stay'**) was as perfect as any debut single could ever be, and the accompanying album (*Introducing The Hardline According To...*) had STAR written all over it. Ever so slightly full of himself, a typical quote ran thus: "I think I'm a **genius**. Point fucking blank". Perhaps predictably, however, his ego ran amok and his second album, *Neither Fish Nor Flesh*, was widely proclaimed a disaster. Undaunted, he returned in '93 with the *Terence Trent d'Arby's Symphony Or Damn Exploring The Tension Inside The Sweetness* album. To promote it, he appeared naked, but for a delicately placed fig leaf, on the cover of *Q* magazine. Two sandwiches short of a picnic, say some; a maverick genius, say others. The downright sexy *Terence Trent d'Arby's Vibrator* album followed in '95, selling poorly but confirming once more that here is an artist whose talent is very nearly as sizeable as his ego.

Tricky: obviously feeling a little horny

TRICKY

Back in the not too distant past, Tricky was merely an acolyte of Bristol's premier trip-hop exponents, **Massive Attack**, who, when not lighting up and lying back, would collaborate with them on experimental jams that would sometimes end up on vinyl, sometimes not. But then he developed an itch, felt like he had to scratch it, went away, and did just that. The result was awesome. Very much so. His debut album, *Maxinquaye* (1995), was a disarmingly beautiful creation, the music languid and torch-lit, pensive and cool blue, exhaling smoke rings up into the darkness above. But, unlike its peers, this record adhered to even fewer musical conventions. Following its own map of consciousness, it wrong-footed anyone who even attempted to compartmentalize its weird, wonderful mixture of hip hop, trip hop, rap, soul and pop sensibilities. It deserved excessive hyperbole, which it duly received. Suddenly, Tricky and his co-singer/sometime girlfriend/mother of his child, **Martina**, had arrived. Over the space of two further albums, *Nearly God* and *Pre-Millennial Tension*, Tricky rightly became recognized as the decade's most idiosyncratic act, a creative force with the power to bewitch, confuse and always dazzle.

TUPAC SHAKUR

When Tupac Shakur was gunned down on September 7, 1996, in Las Vegas, reaction and opinion was predictably divided across America. On the one hand, Shakur was the quintessential gangsta rapper who died as a direct result of gangsta life. He was a caricature of evil, and a convicted sex offender. He had **"Thug Life"** tattooed on his stomach and courted violence on a seemingly daily basis - he had previously been shot (five times) at a studio in Manhattan two years earlier and had several enemies in and out of the music business. To his fans, however, his death robbed the genre of its greatest blossoming star, a larger-than-life anti-hero, whose potential was only just beginning to reveal itself. A multi-platinum recording artist, whose *Me Against The World* album (1995) debuted at No.1 in America, Shakur, was also pursuing a career in cinema, having appeared in *Poetic Justice* with **Janet Jackson**, and *Gridlock'd*, alongside **Tim Roth**. His death, from a drive-by shooting, remains shrouded in mystery: there were no apparent witnesses, except for Shakur's cousin, **Yafeu Fula**, who was shot dead a few weeks later. No arrests have been made, and the investigation inevitably continues, as does the intriguing rumour that the rapper is still alive, having faked his own death.

TINA TURNER

There should be very little doubt in anyone's mind that Tina Turner is the nicest woman in the business. That she still appears so good natured after everything she has gone through - and she has gone through more than most - is little short of miraculous. Born **Annie Mae Bullock** in 1938, the young Tina Turner enjoyed considerable success in the 1960s with mentor-turned-husband Ike, having hits such as **'River Deep Mountain High'** and, later, **'Nutbush City Limits'**. But by the mid-70s her marriage had fallen apart. (Tina revealed that her drug-addicted husband regularly beat her.) She left home with only 36 cents to her name, and spent the next five years playing the chicken-in-a-basket circuit, amassing debts of over $500,000.

1983, however, saw a change in fortunes as her cover of **Al Green**'s **'Let's Stay Together'** became a huge hit and *Private Dancer*, her comeback album, went on to sell 15 million copies. She became one of the planet's biggest live draws (playing before 182,000 in South America in 1988, a world record), acted alongside **Mel Gibson** in *Mad Max: Beyond Thunderdome*, and despite the inevitable passing of years, retained her looks in a fashion that has since become the envy of women everywhere.

Tina Turner in concert in Sydney, Australia

UB40

Named after the identification code of the UK unemployment benefit form, UB40 went, with impressive ease, from life on the dole to a life of fine wines and Jamaican beach holidays. The eight-man line-up formed in Birmingham in 1979, releasing a series of politically-infused, reggae-influenced songs that took them to the top of the charts on both sides of the Atlantic - a rare feat indeed, because unless your name was **Bob Marley**, then reggae rarely saw the inside of the Top 10. Much like **The Fugees** today, UB40 excelled in taking classic songs (in this case, **Neil Diamond**'s **'Red Red Wine'** and **Jimmy Cliff**'s **'Many Rivers To Cross'**) and updating them in a chart-friendly fashion, an approach that saw them still enjoying US and UK No.1 success as late as 1993, with their version of **Elvis**'s **'Can't Help Falling In Love'**.

Underworld go in
search of three lagers

UNDERWORLD

It comes right at the very end of *Trainspotting*, and it is the most memorable scene. It appears on the film's magnificent soundtrack, and although standing alongside such classics as **Iggy Pop**'s **'Lust For Life'**, **New Order**'s **'Temptation'** and **Lou Reed**'s **'Perfect Day'**, it is the album's finest cut. It is also the greatest nine-minute paean to drinking ever recorded. By now, of course, **'Born Slippy'** is a weight around Underworld's neck. They only chanted **"lager, lager, lager"** in the chorus (such as it is) for something to chant, but it has since become the beer boys' No.1 anthem, accompanying many a long night's drinking into the morning after and beyond. Part of the *Tomato* design collective, Underworld have a neat sideline in state-of-the-art "dance" music. They are techno, they are acid house, and ambient, and pop, and even occasionally 18-30 (see above), and are currently the coolest name to drop right now in any circle you happen to inhabit. *Second Toughest In The Infants*, their classic 1996 album, is to the dance genre what modern art is to the classics: one step beyond. Were you so inclined, you'd suggest that respect is altogether due.

VAN HALEN

Imagine, if you will, the rock'n'roll tale of Van Halen told in a feature-length movie. Directed with wanton madness by **Oliver Stone**, it would star **Jim Carrey** in a scene-stealing performance as **David Lee Roth**, the remainder of the band filled by three long-haired method types. Highlights would include the band in full rock opera/pantomime mode, as they travel the world on one of their many monstrous world tours. On stage would be Carrey/Roth acting the carefree, heavily made-up loon before his adoring crowd, dressed in nothing but a pair of very brief briefs, while backstage the band's entourage make sure that the gigantic bowl of **M&Ms** is as specifically colour-coded as requested. The movie would dwell lovingly on the hysterically expensive video shoots for such legendary hits as **'Jump'** and **'Hot For Teacher'** - the screen so stuffed with scantily clad girls that it resembles a glimpse of *Baywatch* heaven. It would follow Carrey/Roth's later solo career through songs such as **'California Girls'** and **'Just A Gigolo'**, revealing the singer to be, if anything, the perennial clown, and would provide the viewer with ample examples of just why Van Halen should be regarded as one of America's great rock acts. It would also come, quite naturally, with an 18 certificate.

LUTHER VANDROSS

Okay, picture the scene: it's the weekend, a Saturday night, the arrival of your date is imminent. The lights are low, the candles bright and Luther's voice - who else? - is slowly unfurling from the hi-fi's speakers, lending this scenario the perfect musical atmosphere. When Luther Vandross sings of love, he pronounces it **"lurve"**. To listen to Luther and not feel romantic is, frankly, to be dead from the eyebrows down. He's being making classic bedroom soundtracks for over 20 years now, has scored innumerable hits, has picked up even more awards and has sung with, and produced, such legends as **Dionne Warwick**, **Anita Baker**, **Whitney Houston** and **Mariah Carey**. One of the most consistent soul legends ever (he has had hits in the '70s, '80s and '90s), he is clearly a believer in the notion that love makes the world go round, for it is the subject of practically all of his songs. Now, let's get back to the aforementioned scene: dinner is dispatched and you've both moved into the lounge in front of an open-log fire. The song is the Vandross classic, **'So Amazing'**, and gradually nature takes over. In nine months time, you'll have at least two lasting reminders of this evening, one of which will be Luther's *Greatest Hits 1981-1995*.

Luther Vandross: he's a "lurver" not a fighter

VANILLA ICE

Unsurprisingly, Vanilla Ice was never very popular with rap's aristocracy, and he never quite managed to get the respect from the likes of **Ices T** and **Cube** that he felt he deserved. That said, however, he was briefly (very briefly) the biggest rap star on the planet. His 1990 debut single, **'Ice Ice Baby'**, which sampled **Queen**'s **'Under Pressure'**, appeared as if from nowhere and dominated the charts worldwide for an interminable amount of time. Hot on the heels of that other pop-rap king, **MC Hammer**, Ice was, he said, a street hoodlum turned good, and despite possessing possibly the worst hair "style" in recent years, wished to be a positive influence on the globe's youth through his good "vibes" and lyrical positivity. If nothing else, his ambitions were admirable, but they were never quite realized, as, with almost shocking alacrity, Vanilla Ice - the first rapper ever to have a *Billboard* US No.1 single, remember - disappeared from view as quickly as he had emerged. His whereabouts today are anyone's guess.

U2

See Legends of MTV pp. 28-29

WARREN G

Part of the Long Beach rap dynasty that emerged at the turn of the 1990s, Warren G followed quickly in the footsteps of his brother, **Dr. Dre**, and went into the world of hip hop. G first came to prominence as a DJ for local outfit **213**, which consisted of his best friend, **Snoop Doggy Dog**, and R&B king, **Nate Dogg** - both of whom went on to considerable solo success. In 1994, he released his own debut album, *Regulate...G-Funk Era*, which earned **Grammy** and *Soul Train* nominations in the US, and sold upward of a million copies at home alone. Like his peers, however, G wasn't satisfied merely with dominating the music scene, and has since pursued an acting career, appearing in several TV shows, including the sitcom *Clueless*, and also has a movie script in the works. His ethos is "continually pushing my limits", and, fittingly, he has spent much of 1997 increasing his musical clout with the mega-selling *Take A Look Over Your Shoulder (Reality)* album.

WEEZER

Weezer, the US "nerd" group that it was cool to dig, and who sang about pullovers and **Buddy Holly** and **Mary Tyler Moore** in cute four-part harmony, inadvertently struck gold and became very big indeed. Powered by an excellent video that was set within the classic US TV sitcom, *Happy Days*, the **'Buddy Holly'** single proved irresistible in 1995 and they got successful here, there, and all points north, south, east and west on the atlas. Suffering groupies, over-zealous fans and too much attention for too much of the time, they "kinda" flipped out. Quieter side-projects ensued and singer **Rivers Cuomo** went back to college. They chilled and tried to get their heads together, only they didn't altogether succeed. The second Weezer album, *Pinkerton* (1996), was the sound of sonic distortion and chronic disillusion, with melodies that sounded like schizophrenia feels. Songs about sex, the Japanese and loving lesbians (true!) confirmed that even if peace of mind wasn't achieved, inspiration was. Bitter, gritty, grating and bemusing, *Pinkerton* was the sound of warped entertainment, the sound of a band very unhappy about the prominent position they suddenly found themselves in. They are currently seeking an acceptable equilibrium.

Paul Weller: back from the brink

PAUL WELLER

It was the end of the '80s and it looked very much like the last nails had been hammered in the coffin of Paul Weller's career. His record label rejected the **Style Council**'s fifth album, the band were dropped and split up. All but confirmed, then: Paul Weller was washed up. At least he had the memories: with **The Jam**, Weller had fronted one of the most explosive groups in a generation. But, as it turned out, retirement wasn't on the cards. Two years later, Weller set up his own label and started to record. People were encouragingly responsive: he signed to **Go! Discs** (once home to **Portishead** and **Beautiful South**), and released *Wildwood*, an album of no little musical maturity. Cries of **"renaissance!"** could be heard from all quarters. And by the time he put out *Stanley Road* (1995), which debuted at No. 1 in the UK charts and went on to multi-platinum status, he became recognized as a genuine icon, revered as Britain's own **Neil Young** (only less grizzled). Revisiting the assured R&B of 1970s band **Traffic** (with, coincidentally or not, **Steve Winwood** on backing vocals), *Stanley Road* bore all the hallmarks of great songwriting, of someone who realized that the balance between perspiring rock and understated subtlety is everything. He then helped **Ocean Colour Scene** from obscurity into major stardom and has been known to share a microphone on stage with one **Noel Gallagher**.

WET WET WET

Wet Wet Wet's career has been hampered, in no small way, by singer **Marti Pellow**'s smile. It has dogged their entire career. A rather handsome young man, Pellow quickly got accustomed to grinning in front of the camera, and this grin was so sweet that it simultaneously landed him thousands of female fans and a similar number of people who wanted to promptly wipe it from his face. Smug, they called it. Nevertheless, Wet Wet Wet are actually one of the more credible bands who just happen to have a large teenage following. Their music is influenced directly by American soul, and their first session upon signing to their record label was recorded in Memphis with Al Green's master producer, **Willie Mitchell**. By 1993, they were one of Britain's most popular bands, and their greatest hits tour played to sell-out crowds everywhere. But, improbable as it may sound, a year later they became even bigger when their treatment of the **Troggs**' 1967 classic **'Love Is All Around'** (from the **Hugh Grant** film *Four Weddings And A Funeral*) hit the UK No.1 spot and stayed there forever - actually, it was "only" 15 weeks, but felt noticeably longer. These days, Pellow attempts to smile less, while his band have become something of a national institution.

WHALE

It was the classic debut single to end all classic debut singles. Sweden's Whale emerged somewhere around the middle of 1995 with a single graced with the unforgettable title **'Hobo Humpin' Slobo Babe'**. It was a monster track built on a big fat bass line, raging hormones and a predilection for all things **Beastie Boys** and **Björk**, and for reasons unknown, the song was about a posh girl indulging in matters of a strictly carnal nature with a tramp she plucked from the streets. The accompanying video was brilliant - all style, day-glo weirdness and a cute girl singer with braces on her teeth - and MTV stuck it on heavy rotation. With such sudden success, the band were quickly forced to give up their day jobs (**Henrik Schyffert** was a radio and TV producer, **Gordon Cyrus** a hip hop producer and singer **Cia Berg** was an actress and TV presenter) to concentrate on their debut album. *We Care*, like the single, was a ridiculously riotous, wild and wacky delve into three very peculiar imaginations. It also possessed a musical style made up of profound idiosyncrasies, calling to mind everyone from **Prince** to **Deee-Lite**. This was music to get drunk to.

WHITE TOWN

It is perhaps the greatest underdog success story of the decade. **Jyoti Mishra**, the 30-year-old Indian man whose shadowy presence constitutes White Town, created **'Your Woman'** in his lo-fi bedroom studio and sent out five copies to Radio One, hoping for perhaps a couple of plays on specialist shows. DJ **Mark Radcliffe** picked up on it, however, played it to death on *The Breakfast Show*, and a sensation was born. Mishra promptly signed to a record company, refused interviews and photographs, and at the beginning of January, watched his single debut top the UK charts, selling over 100,000 copies in its first week. Turning the very concept of a new act's long trawl toward the limelight on its head, he was rightfully hailed as a DIY hero. His success, though, has also brought out the cynics, who believe him to be a one-hit wonder; this year's **Babylon Zoo**. But the confidence and playability of his debut album, *Women In Technology*, suggests that this shy, Derby-based pop sensation will have the last laugh, enjoying success very strictly on his own terms. Hats off.

THE WONDER STUFF

A very probable scenario: a teenage **Miles Hunt**, one day to become lead singer of The Wonder Stuff, sitting in his front room, watching television. Upon it he sees the **Sex Pistols**' singer **Johnny Rotten** sneering in quite magnificent fashion. The young Miles Hunt rushes to the mirror to attempt to match the scowl. He is immediately successful and, some years later, becomes quite famous for it. From 1986 until 1994 The Wonder Stuff wrote about many an English malaise (cynicism, greed, the weather) and set it to music delivered with drunken, vociferous passion. Soon enough, they became huge. *Never Loved Elvis*, their third album, saw them dominant throughout 1991 with hits such as **'Size Of A Cow'** and, later, a duet with Britain's finest comedy duo, **Vic Reeves & Bob Mortimer**, on the No.1 single, **'Dizzy'**. By this stage, the band appeared desperate to crack America, but they never quite managed it, a failure that inspired the barbed *Construction For The Modern Idiot* album in 1993. A year later they decided to go out on top and so, after headlining the inaugural **Phoenix Festival**, they split up, Hunt going on to a brief stint as an **MTV DJ**, the remaining members dipping into obscurity.

Mile Hunt shares a joke with the rest of The Wonder Stuff

YELLO

Yello, a deliciously odd Swiss duo comprising **Dieter Meier** and **Boris Blank**, are one of the most influential acts ever to come out of Switzerland. Indeed, outside of cheese, they are among Switzerland's most celebrated exports. Forming in 1979, their music took off where **Kraftwerk**'s left off, a form of computer-generated techno and house that went on to provide the backbone of 1990s dance. Despite considerable success, they remained elusive and profoundly enigmatic. While Blank made music his life's work, Meier, a millionaire, was alleged to be rather fond of gambling, not least because he possessed something of an interminable winning streak. Their greatest hit, easily, was the frenetic, beat-driven **'Oh Yeah'**, a song so bizarrely cool and coolly bizarre that it subsequently featured in several Hollywood films, including *Ferris Bueller's Day Off* and *The Secret Of My Success*. Film score work then consumed much of their time, but the mysterious duo still make the time to put out their idiosyncratic material, very much under their own terms.

NEIL YOUNG

It seemingly matters not to his vast legion of fans that 52-year-old Neil Young is something of an old man, for he remains an icon of the **X Generation**. Feeding the electric guitar with the kind of stunning power that **Jimi Hendrix** was once famed for, Young is the forefather of grunge and an inspiration to probably every lead guitarist on the planet. His career spans a 30-year period, during which he was part of the venerable **Crosby, Stills, Nash & Young**, before becoming something of a solo troubadour. While his reputation remained as concrete as ever throughout the '80s, it was with the advent of the aforementioned grunge movement that he became truly relevant once more. **Pearl Jam** never missed a single opportunity to talk of his inspiration, and went on to provide backing-band services for their hero as well as collaborating on his *Mirror Ball* album. In 1994, when **Nirvana** frontman **Kurt Cobain** quoted a line from one of Young's songs ("It's better to burn out than fade away") in his suicide note, rock's elder statesman was visibly shocked and returned with the maudlin *Sleeps With Angels* album, revealing a far more reflective, sombre side - just in case anyone took his words too literally again.

ZZ TOP

ZZ Top are cleverly named. Where in any musical encyclopedia some bands are omitted purely by accident (proving that the compilers are only human), ZZ Top are impossible to forget by virtue of the fact that they represent **The End**, the very last inclusion of any A-Z. Fortunately, however, this isn't their only point of interest. A trio who formed in Texas back in 1970, they became famous chiefly because two of them had these ridiculously long beards. The one without, incidentally, is called **Frank Beard** (ho, ho). With low-slung loud guitars, ZZ Top are capable of making rumbling rhythm and blues, but mostly send up the heavy rock genre in glorious fashion.

Their peak era was back in 1983, with their **multi-platinum** album *Eliminator*. Its fantastic tunes soon became ubiquitous, thanks largely to the singles **'Gimmie All Your Lovin'**, **'Sharp Dressed Man'** and **'Legs'**, and their accompanying videos. These splendid items, which may have been ironic, but then again may have not, featured the hoary old rockers surrounded by a plethora of beautiful, scantily-clad women who flashed their flesh with all the carefree abandon of a *Baywatch* lifeguard. Needless to say, these videos found much popularity among a large chunk of the world's male population and, accordingly, they've dominated MTV's request slots ever since.

ZZ Top: sharp-dressed men

If a year is a long time in politics, a decade is a lifetime in pop music. The rock world has changed so much since **Elton John** switched on MTV Europe on August 1, 1987, that the landscape is virtually unrecognizable. Back in 1987, the superstar triumvirate of Madonna, Prince and Michael Jackson bestrode the music world like colossi. Few would have predicted the turbulent decade that awaited all three. All survive now, at or near the apex of pop, but only after a slew of bizarre events including books of full-frontal photographs, surreal name changes, and unproven allegations of child abuse against the **King Of Pop** himself.

Yes, the music world that welcomed the inception of MTV Europe back in '87 was a very different one. A mere two years after Live Aid, charity gigs were in vogue, and huge shows in support of AIDS Awareness, Amnesty or freeing Nelson Mandela were a regular event.

ROCKS OFF

The rock hierarchy seemed set in stone in those days - David Bowie, Phil Collins, Annie Lennox, Bruce Springsteen, Elton John, and bad boys like Billy Idol and Guns N'Roses. Yet the pop world is never static, and only the fittest of the old guard were to survive the forces of change at work over the next decade.

It was early in 1988 that it became clear that a whole new movement was gripping the European music scene. The **Ecstasy-fuelled** house music explosion, which originated in the summer clubs of Spain and Italy, moved from the underground to the mainstream and created a new generation of music fans who were more interested in dancing and DJs than traditional rock stars.

New trends also emerged from the States. On a rock tip, the raging powerchords and troubled words of Nirvana shaped and influenced a generation of fans,

although the band's lynchpin Kurt Cobain had no desire for messianic status. When he blew his face off in Seattle in 1994, the shock waves echoed round the globe as they had at the death of John Lennon over a decade earlier.

The **seismic changes** in the world of rock were mirrored in rap music. MTV Europe's first decade began with Public Enemy as the undisputed talismen of the hip-

police charge. Snoop Doggy Dogg was acquitted of murder, yet stars like Tupac Shakur and Notorious B.I.G. were shot dead. It's a long way from '80s pop charity shows.

NEW 2

Not every member of the class of '87 ceded their place to the new breed. U2 underwent a staggering self-reinvention and produced the most exciting tours of the decade with the Zoo TV and Pop Mart **extravaganzas**. R.E.M. also built on their status as the biggest cult band in the world, and Simply Red and Wet Wet Wet spent ten years on top.

The '90s also witnessed a slew of brand new stars in the rock galaxy. Take That became the biggest boy band in the world, then broke hearts all around the globe in early 1995 when they called it a day. Boyzone looked set to inherit their crown, but were forced to give way as the **turbo-powered** Spice Girls burst through, with the three cutest kids in the States (Hanson, of course) close on their heels to Number 1-ship.

NEW KIDS

Alanis Morissette came to prominence with the startling success of her *Bitter Little Pill* album, and the dance scene spawned new talent such as The Shamen, Underworld and The Prodigy. And from Manchester came Oasis, setting new records for album sales and leaving tales of punch-ups, cancelled tours, drug abuse and scandal in their wake.

hop community, preaching righteous but controlled rage. Then, from the ghettos of South Central L.A., emerged Niggers With Attitude, with their street, outrageous and frequently misogynistic take on life.

NWA walked it like they talked it, and so did the so-called gangsta rappers who followed them. In the early '90s, virtually every hip-hop star faced some kind of

The late '80s had a band just the same: Guns N'Roses...

It's been a long, strange trip indeed...and it's only just begun. When MTV Europe celebrates its twentieth anniversary in 2007, will Oasis, Boyzone, Alanis Morissette and the Spice Girls have gone the way of Simple Minds, Bros, Yazz and Bananarama? There's only one way to find out - and that's to **stay tuned...**

George and Andrew, back again for a reunion at Wembley

Album of the Year

SIGN O' THE TIMES - PRINCE

Prince [see MTV Legends pp. 12-13] has undoubtedly
been the most prolific superstar of the '80s and early
'90s, invariably producing at least one album every year,
and many fans feel that this sprawling, sumptuous
double album was his creative apex to date. *Sign O' The
Times* was a mesmerizing, hypnotic riot of possibilities,
an almost unnaturally fertile and inventive smorgasbord
of just about every musical genre in existence - and a
few more besides. Prince spiralled and slalomed
between jazz-funk, rap, acid, blues and rock, and
sounded possessed and transfigured by glee. The album
spawned a slew of hit singles, from the hard-eyed social
comment of the title track to the delicious, delirious yelp
of 'If I Was Your Girlfriend' and the luscious 'I Could
Never Take The Place Of Your Man', and every track
resonated with the self-confidence of an artist working
at the peak of his mighty powers. The whole was a
fantastic, infectious ride into the stratosphere as Prince
played with a sense of fun and mischief, allied with a
genuine and profound love of music...and life. It also
goes without saying that *Sign O' The Times* was the
sexiest record of the year. Nobody tried to copy Prince
because nobody else could do this stuff. *Sign O' The Times*
was 1987's sublime musical high point and proved
beyond doubt that, in **Prince Nelson Rogers**, the music
world has a very special and really rather unique genius.

Elton turns on MTV Europe

When Elton John first switched on MTV Europe on August
1, 1987, the rock world was looking distinctly charitable.

Working for charity

MTV Europe's launch came just two years after the
famous **Live Aid** extravaganza, and huge charity
shows featuring rock's biggest names were still a
fixture of the music calendar. In particular, 1987
featured a series of high-profile gigs to raise public
awareness of AIDS and generate funds for research
into the life-threatening disease.

The biggest of 1987's shows was at Wembley Stadium,
London, and featured George Michael [see MTV Legends
pp. 22-23], Boy George, Elton John, Aswad, Meat

Loaf, Bob Geldof, The Communards, U2 [see MTV Legends pp. 28-29], Womack & Womack and Bananarama. The highlight of the show for many was a one-off reunion of Wham! featuring Michael and former cohort Andrew Ridgley.

Ferry Aid

Boy George and Bananarama also featured on 'Ferry Aid', a version of The Beatles' 'Let It Be' recorded by stars from the rock world, including Kate Bush, Mark Knopfler, Mark King and Pepsi & Shirlie. The single raised money for the families of victims of the **Zeebrugge** disaster, who were killed when a ferry sailing from the Belgian port to the UK tragically sank.

One further public-spirited project from the aristocracy of the pop world was an album called *Spirit Of Peace*, which set out to raise money for Amnesty International. Dire Straits and Peter Gabriel contributed tracks to this worthy cause, as did Simple Minds, Sir Paul McCartney and Tears For Fears.

Beastly Beasties?

It would be completely misleading, however, to imagine for one minute that every rock star in 1987 was dedicated solely to charity work and good causes. There were also plenty of artists still pursuing those sacred **shibboleths** of sex, drugs and rock'n'roll, and

filling various tabloid newspapers with their lurid exploits as they went.

The media's chief whipping boys for '87 were American rap band **The Beastie Boys**. The controversial trio enjoyed enormous success in both America and Europe with their debut album *Licensed To Ill* and singles such as '(You Gotta) Fight For Your Right (To Party)' but their subsequent tour of **Europe** with Run DMC was ridden with bad publicity and self-righteous tabloid accusations of boorish behaviour by the band.

Ad-rock arrested

The Beasties' problems began at the Montreux Rock Festival in May, when they were accused of insulting fans at a show that also featured Whitney Houston, Simply Red and Level 42. Later that same month the band hit Britain, and Ad-Rock was arrested in Liverpool and accused of hitting a girl in the face with a can of beer. One British newspaper also accused the trio of mocking and insulting disabled fans at one of their gigs, a charge which the band vigorously denied.

On a lighter note, **VW** car-owners came to loathe the Beasties, as their habit of wearing the metal VW badges from the bonnets of Volkswagon cars as jewellery led to many cars being relieved of their insignia by fans! Yet, overall, The Beastie Boys were guilty of no more than high spirits, and the media hype did their notoriety - and ticket sales - no harm at all.

The Beastie Boys: spreading fear among VW owners

Roses riot on

And the Beasties didn't have a monopoly on rock'n'roll bad behaviour: 1987 also witnessed the arrival of Guns N'Roses, who released their debut album *Appetite For Destruction* and left a trail of drink, drug and violence-related mayhem in their wake as they toured the globe to promote it. **The Daily Star**, a downmarket UK tabloid, coined a portentous phrase to condemn them: "They're even nastier than the Beastie Boys."

Stars at play

1987 was a major year for big-name world tours. **David Bowie** took his critically-savaged but commercially-successful Glass Spider show around Europe and the States, and U2 [see MTV Legends pp. 28-29], Tina Turner, Genesis, Madonna [see MTV Legends pp. 20-21], Bob Dylan, the Beach Boys, Tom Petty, Alison Moyet and The Cure could also be found out on the road. Madonna unveiled her latest feature film, *Who's That Girl*. U2 released *The Joshua Tree* and became one of the biggest acts in the world, and Michael Jackson [see MTV Legends pp. 18-19] followed up the colossal *Thriller* with the generally well-received *Bad*. **The Cure** gave the world the *Kiss Me, Kiss Me, Kiss Me* double album, Whitney Houston released *Whitney* and The Cult went *Electric*.

Axl Rose: Still got an *Appetite For Destruction*

New beginnings

However, 1987 was particularly notable for a succession of remarkable debut albums from artists who were to go on to become world superstars. George Michael celebrated the demise of Wham! by releasing the soulful *Faith* collection. US rap militants **Public Enemy** also emerged with the agitated and brilliant *Yo! Bum Rush The Show*.

Two major pop-soul acts to break through in 1987 were **Simply Red** with the album *Men & Women* and Scottish blue-eyed soul specialists **Wet Wet Wet** with *Popped In, Souled Out*. Great things were also predicted for **The Christians** (*The Christians*) and US singer-songwriter **Terence Trent D'Arby** (*Introducing The Hardline According To Terence Trent D'Arby*) but neither act managed to follow up the commercial success of their debut offerings.

Paula gets nasty

Paula Abdul was yet to rise to fame in '87 and was still working behind the scenes rather than making music herself. However, she did pick up a prestigious MTV award for arranging the choreography on the video for Janet Jackson's [see MTV Legends pp. 16–17] hit 'Nasty'. Def Leppard's *Hysteria* was huge Stateside.

Salt'N'Pepa released their debut album *Hot, Cool & Vicious* in '87, and the London-based bubblegum pop hit factory of producers Stock, Aitken & Waterman was also coming to prominence. SAW enjoyed hits with Rick Astley, Sinitta and Mel and Kim as well as a debut single - a cover of the '60's hit 'The Locomotion' - by Australian soap starlet Kylie Minogue.

Beatles are back!

One of the best-selling records of 1987, however, was 20 years old. EMI released The Beatles' *Sgt. Pepper's Lonely Hearts Club Band* on compact disc and saw it once again top album charts across Europe. Another oldie "enjoyed" a hit in somewhat surreal circumstances - Nina Simone's 30-year-old 'My Baby

MTV IN 1987

MTV Europe launched at 12.01am on August 1st, from the **Roxy Club** in Amsterdam. Elton John flicked the switch, to 1.6 million households. The first video shown was 'Money for Nothing' by Dire Straits. In September, MTV was granted a one-week cable and satellite exclusive on 'Bad', Michael Jackson's 16-minute video/film and in October, *Yo! MTV Raps*, Europe's first rap show, was launched.

Just Cares For Me' did well in Europe, where it was used in a TV advert, but the notoriously maverick Nina gave a series of press interviews in which she urged her fans not to buy the single because she wasn't making enough money from it!

The Smiths are dead

Serious and introverted young men and women across Europe went even deeper into mourning in '87 as cult UK band **The Smiths** split. Singer Morrissey began a solo career and guitarist Johnny Marr went to work with The Pretenders. Frankie Goes To Hollywood also split. Another tragedy - for different reasons entirely - was the worldwide success of *The Return Of Bruno*, a blues album by actor Bruce Willis, "moonlighting" with a second career.

Dave weds Siobhan

Rap star Scott La Rock was shot dead in '87, as was reggae legend Peter Tosh. Iconic pop artist **Andy Warhol** (who had just directed a video for British stars Curiosity Killed The Cat) also died, as did soul singer Fat Larry. On a happier note, Eurythmics star Dave Stewart got married - to Bananarama singer Siobhan Fahey.

Siobhan Fahey and happy Dave Stewart: Hitched in '87

88

Album of the Year
SURFER ROSA - THE PIXIES

The Pixies were a **turbulent** guitar-rock quartet from Boston, New England, and *Surfer Rosa* was enormous. The band had debuted the previous year with a scathing mini-album called *Come On Pilgrim*, but nothing could have prepared the casual listener for the primal power and urgency of their second record. The Pixies' sound was based on an **Iggy Pop**-style visceral, animal rock'n'roll, to which they added a dark, voluptuous and alien quality that was quite staggering. Singer Black Francis possessed a raw, crazed howl that tore open the very fabric of the songs, and bassist Kim Deal (later to become the mainstay of The Breeders) wrote and sang on the bittersweet lullaby *Gigantic*. The Pixies gibbered, ranted in tongues, beat up rock'n'roll real good and proved to be one of the most undercelebrated yet important underground bands of the decade. **Kurt Cobain** was to claim years later that The Pixies were one of the biggest influences on the music of Nirvana, and listening to *Surfer Rosa* now you can easily see why. This was the dark stuff, and no mistake.

The Pixies: Would influence a generation with *Surfer Rosa*

They call it aciid!

In many ways, 1988 was a year of great **change** for Europe's music scene. The old guard of stars, whose positions in the pop hierarchy had been consolidated by Live Aid, still held sway but a fresh new musical movement was coming up fast - the dance explosion was to dominate much of the next decade.

The **Acid House** movement, as it came to be known, originated in Chicago and Detroit but had its European roots in the clubs of Spain and Ibiza, where a host of DJs span **euphoric**, anthemic house music (known as Balearic Beat) to delighted party-loving young holidaymakers. These sunny months of '88 became known as the Summer Of Love, and over the following few months the tunes and ethos of Acid House penetrated Germany, the UK and the rest of Europe. Belgium had its own early, quasi-erotic variant known as **New Beat**.

A new order?

Acid House's "stars" were mainly faceless producers and studio technicians. At throbbing all-night raves, yellow **"Smiley"** badges and cries of "Aciied!" were ubiquitous. Inevitably, though, recognizable personalities and new stars emerged as the music began to penetrate the mainstream.

Inner City, D Mob, Bomb The Bass and S'Express all enjoyed Europe-wide hits during the year, and New Order's mid-80s classic 'Blue Monday' was reinvented as an Ibizan rave tune. New dance-influenced bands also became household names, notably Stone Roses and **Happy Mondays**. As 1988 ended it was clear that the new dance explosion had arrived, and it was to utterly transform the face of music.

Mandela day – a new star

Yet despite these turbulent changes at an underground level, on the surface the music world remained very much as before. Charity and "conscience" concerts continued to proliferate, and the major consciousness-raising event of '88 was the 70th birthday tribute to jailed African National Congress leader **Nelson Mandela**, which was held at Wembley Stadium, London, on June 11.

The bill for the Mandela show read like a rollcall of virtually every major name in the world of pop. Simple Minds and Peter Gabriel duetted on Gabriel's anti-apartheid epic **'Biko'** and also on the starladen bill were Meat Loaf, Chrissie Hynde, Eurythmics, Stevie Wonder, Bryan Adams, UB40, George Michael [see MTV Legends pp. 22-23], Whitney Houston and Sting. Fans of virtuoso guitar technique also enjoyed Eric Clapton making a guest appearance with Dire Straits.

Fast star

A new star was born at the Mandela tribute show. Black US singer-songwriter **Tracy Chapman** performed early in the day, but was later summoned back to the stage as an emergency stopgap when Stevie Wonder suffered equipment trouble. Chapman did a short acoustic set, performing songs such as 'Fast Car' from her eponymous personal/political debut album, which she had released earlier in the year to, at the time, little acclaim.

Chapman's unexpected Wembley performance was lauded by fans and critics alike and her album shot quickly to No.1, both in the States and throughout Europe. The 24-year-old singer's brilliant year was rounded off in September when she appeared on the six-week **Amnesty International** tour of the world's stadia, together with Bruce Springsteen, Peter Gabriel and Sting.

Tracy Chapman: Played for Mandela at the tribute show

Black goes back

1988 saw a slew of landmark album releases from major stars. The enigmatic Prince [see Legends pp. 12-13] had a strange year. He recorded *The Black Album* but then decided not to release it. Instead, he put out **Lovesexy**, which featured a picture of himself naked on the cover, then looked on helplessly as bootleggers who had managed to obtain illegal pressings of *The Black Album* put them on sale and made a killing worldwide!

Paula Abdul's *Forever Your Girl* vied for chart-topping status in the States with Bobby Brown, New Kids On The Block and Bon Jovi's *New Jersey* [see MTV Legends pp.14-15], and all became fixtures on MTV Europe.

The Sugarcubes: Björk's first taste of pop success

U2 rattle, then say "hmmmm..."

U2 [see MTV Legends pp. 28-29] enjoyed mega-success in '88. The band released a feature film, *Rattle & Hum*, together with a live double-album soundtrack, which featured guest appearances by legendary bluesmen such as **B.B. King**. The record, which paid homage to the roots of rock'n'roll, topped charts all over the world but was ridiculed by critics as bombastic, pompous and ludicrously overly-earnest. U2 retired to Dublin to count their money, lick their wounds and undertake the complete aesthetic reinvention that was to peak with the release of *Achtung Baby* three years later.

Hip-hop don't stop

Rap enjoyed a brilliant year. The talismanic **Public Enemy** released their second album, *It Takes A Nation Of Millions To Hold Us Back*, and promptly went platinum. Yet even Chuck D's outspoken and frequently controversial crew, who were fast becoming radical, quasi-official spokesmen for the young black community, seemed like elder statesman of hip-hop when compared to newcomers **Niggers With Attitude**.

NWA emerged from the ghettos of Los Angeles with the harsh, frequently vicious, *Straight Outta Compton*, which painted unflinching word pictures of life on the mean streets. They also virtually single-handedly invented the genre known as **gangsta rap**, which was praised for its brutalist, uncompromising honesty but condemned for its profanity and misogyny. NWA stirred up a hornets' nest of publicity Stateside, and quickly followed Public Enemy to platinum-selling status.

Roses' tragedy

Controversy also continued to dog Guns N'Roses - even when the rockers were not to blame. The band supported **Aerosmith** on their *Permanent Vacation* tour, yet were reluctant to submit to the headliners' "No backstage drink or drugs" policy. However, the low point of the Roses' year, which saw their debut album *Appetite For Destruction* pass five million sales worldwide, came in August when they played the **Castle Donington** heavy metal festival in England. Over 100,000 people crowded the festival site, and during the Roses' set two fans were tragically crushed to death.

Björk this way

On a happier note, R.E.M. [see MTV Legends pp. 26-27] released the critically-lauded *Green*, Whitney Houston cleaned up worldwide with her Olympics theme single 'One Moment In Time' and from Iceland came an extraordinary art-collective pop group called The Sugarcubes. Their debut album, *Life's Too Good*, was a rambling, **eccentric** yet

beguiling affair, but most reviews of the record emphasized the extraordinary alien vocal qualities of their striking singer, Björk.

Kylie unlikely?

The London production team of **Stock, Aitkin & Waterman** cemented their hit-factory status by completing the process of making a megastar of soap star Kylie Minogue, who released her debut album, *Kylie*. They also began work with her *Neighbours* co-star Jason Donovan. Bros enjoyed a string of hits with songs such as 'When Will I Be Famous?' and 'Drop The Boy', and released the album *Push*, and there were also Eurohits for **Vanessa Paradis**, T'Pau, Yazz, Tiffany, Pet Shop Boys and Glenn Medeiros.

Who are the Wilburys?

In addition, 1988 saw the formation of a new **supergroup**. Bob Dylan, George Harrison, Tom Petty, Roy Orbison and former Electric Light Orchestra-mainstay Jeff Lynne got together to form The Traveling Wilburys. They released a debut album, *Volume One*. Sadly, Orbison, one of the truly classic voices of rock, died of a heart attack that December.

MTV IN 1988

February saw MTV Europe open new studios at **Camden Town**, London, with a celebrity-packed party. In April a major campaign, Rock Against Drugs, was launched, featuring major artists talking honestly about their experiences with drugs. MTV went on the road for the first time as the "support act" on Sting's European tour in August and in the same month celebrated the channel's first birthday, with 3.5 million subscribers.

In October, Bon Jovi switched on MTV in Norway and in the same month a German viewer won a **competition** to fly to New York to watch Wet Wet Wet play Madison Square Garden and hang out with the band.

Kylie Minogue: Nick who? Duets with goth-kings evidently a *long* way off

89

Album of the Year

RAW LIKE SUSHI - NENEH CHERRY

Neneh Cherry was a breath of fresh air for the music scene of 1989. Neneh, the daughter of **jazz** trumpeter Don Cherry, had been knocking around the music industry for a few years, singing with experimental underground bands such as Rip, Rig & Panic and Float Up CP, but this was the first time she'd made commercial pop - and what a debut it was! *Raw Like Sushi* caught the zeitgeist perfectly, marrying hip-hop scratching, club dance beats and brilliant, infectious pop songs to Neneh's sassy, streetwise B-Girl persona. The single 'Buffalo Stance' was a joyful hymn to fun-loving, sussed teenage girls and hit big everywhere. The follow-up, 'Manchild', was a sympathetic wake-up call to stubborn males. Neneh Cherry and her posse were shrewd and smart enough to take the best elements from all areas of music and shape them into a potent and knowing pop that was very much their own - and Neneh's **chutzpah** and cocky rapping were a delight. *Sushi* was the taste of 1989.

Green the world

Interest in environmental concerns was decidedly *de rigeur* for all pop megastars in 1989. March saw the release of the *Greenpeace Rainbow Warriors* album, featuring tracks by artists such as U2 [see MTV Legends pp. 28-29], The Pretenders and the ubiquitous Sting. Sting also boldly set out to protect the Kayapo Indian tribe and save the Amazon rainforest, and Sir Paul McCartney joined in by donating $100,000 to the Friends Of The Earth organization.

Other rock-related good works in '89 included various AIDS awareness shows in the States, with a major concert in San Francisco starring the Grateful Dead and Tracy Chapman. However, the ever-troubled **Guns N'Roses** were removed from the bill of a similar show in New York after protests by gay-rights pressure groups about a line in the Roses' song 'One In A Million', which ran, "Immigrants and faggots, they make no sense to me"!

Nenah Cherry: Raw but not fishy

Another dud year for the Roses?

Indeed, 1989 was a vintage year for Axl Rose's rock'n'roll heroes/villains. Guitarist Izzy Stradlin had a bust-up with Mötley Crüe singer Vince Neil backstage at the **MTV USA Awards**, although nobody seemed quite sure why. Then in October the Roses supported The Rolling Stones in Los Angeles and Axl announced from the stage that certain members of the band were about to be fired for "dancing with Mr Brownstone" - a not-particularly-veiled reference to heroin abuse.

The other Roses

Stone Roses, an independent band from **Manchester**, England, released their eponymous debut album and it was soon recognized as a musical landmark. The Roses combined the funky, clubby rhythms that character-ized the underground dance music explosion of the late -'80s with classic, shimmering harmonies and melodies that appealed to old-school guitar rock fans of bands such as **The Byrds** and Love. Topped by the sneering, tuneless-yet-endearing vocal of singer Ian Brown, the Roses quickly became a phenomenon, capturing the moment and shaping the zeitgeist.

Madonna Vs the Pope!

Madonna [see MTV Legends pp. 20–21] dominated the pop world in 1989, which naturally meant that she - like Guns N'Roses - was also at the centre of even more controversy than ever! In March the singer released her album *Like A Prayer,* and also a single of the same name, which featured a **gospel** choir. However, the Vatican strongly condemned the video for the single, which featured semi-erotic scenes between Madonna and a black Jesus, and there was the bizarre spectacle of the singer, whose image had always played heavily on her Catholicism, being threatened with the prospect of **excommunication**!

Madonna survived that danger, but did lose her $5,000,000 sponsorship deal with Pepsi as a result of the outcry. And this wasn't the only setback for the star: she also filed for **divorce** from her husband, actor Sean Penn, after dropping charges of assault and battery against him.

Rap's new tune

With many pop fans tiring of the rapaciousness and brutalism of gangsta rap, critics welcomed the emergence of a gentler, more mellow school of hip-

Sting: Supporting the rainforests with Raoni

hop. De La Soul's *3 Feet High And Rising* was a daffy, quirky mix of obscure samples, **new age** positivism and spirituality and meandering free-association stream-of-consciousness rapping. This new strain of rap quickly became known as Daisy Age, and later proponents of the style included PM Dawn and Canada's Dream Warriors.

Naturally, however, the hip-hop world wasn't without its controversies, and June saw Public Enemy leader Chuck D announce that the group's "Minister Of Information", Professor Griff, had been kicked out of the band after allegedly making "anti-Semitic" comments in an interview with the New York arts newspaper *The Village Voice*.

Major releases

Janet Jackson [see MTV Legends pp. 16–17] continued to mirror her brother Michael's progress to the apex of the pop world with the release of the funky, hard-edged album *Rhythm Nation 1814* (R and N being the 18th and 14th letters of the alphabet respectively). Simple Minds returned with the epic, sprawling *Street Fighting Years* and **Simply Red**'s third album, *A New Flame*, confirmed the red-haired soul merchant's position in the top division of music's superstars.

Veteran UK act The Cure released the intensely introspective *Disintegration*, their darkest, most desolate album for years, and then set off on a round of interviews in which they denied the album was at all depressing! The band were all shaken by inner turbulence - singer Robert Smith sacked founder member and keyboardist Lol Tolhurst in a move that triggered legal action, which was to drag on for years. The band also set out on tour to promote *Disintegration*, travelling to America on the cruise ship the QE2 in order to circumnavigate Smith's legendary and unshakeable fear of flying!

Prince goes bats

Prince [see MTV Legends pp. 12–13] released the ambivalently-received but commercially successful soundtrack album to *Batman*, which starred Michael Keaton and **Jack Nicholson**, and ethereal British songstress Kate Bush delighted many fans by breaking a long silence and releasing a new album, *The Sensual World*. However, **David Bowie**'s new band and album, both called *Tin Machine*, received one of the most disappointed and derisory responses afforded to a major star by critics for many years.

Soul II Soul: They were the
club classics in 1989

Let Lenny rule

Dreadlocked and **paisley-draped** cosmic
US rocker Lenny Kravitz made his debut
in '89 with an album called *Let Love Rule*,
which combined funk and soul with
heavy-duty blues riffing and had some
commentators reminiscing fondly about
the halcyon days of Jimi Hendrix.
Soul/swingbeat star Bobby Brown's
second album, *Don't Be Cruel*, had topped
the US charts in '88, and this year it
mirrored that triumph in Europe.

From London came the fascinating,
positivist rapper Jazzie B and his Soul II
Soul musical collective. Their debut
album *Club Classics Vol 1* combined
classic soul structures with the pulse and
spirit of the emerging house scene, and
for a few months the "funky drummer"
rhythms spawned and popularized by the
band became utterly ubiquitous. **Fine
Young Cannibals**, featuring heartthrob
singer Roland Gift, also enjoyed huge
worldwide success with their second
album, *The Raw And The Cooked*.

 ## IN 1989

On March 1, MTV launched in
Hungary, and June included
Environment Week, "green"
programming to coincide with
World Environment Day.
Second-birthday celebrations
in August were seen by MTV's
ever-increasing audience - the
figure had now risen to 10
million subscribers! Later that
month MTV hosted the **Moscow
Music Peace Festival** and went
on the road with Simple Minds.
In October, Lenny Kravitz
performed an acoustic set in
MTV's London studios. In
November MTV Europe
broadcast its first live feed to
East Berlin – and the Berlin Wall
came down the very next day!

Tasteless Vanilli

Early in 1989, **Milli Vanilli** (aka Rob Pilatus and Fabrice Morvan)
released an album that was called *All Or Nothing* in Europe and
Girl You Know It's True in America. The band were a huge hit,
chalking up six million album sales in the States and scoring three
No.1 singles with 'Baby Don't Forget My Number', 'Girl I'm Gonna
Miss You' and 'Blame It On The Rain'.

Milli Vanilli were even awarded a Grammy for Best New Artist -
which was when their whole world fell apart. The band's manager
Frank Farian, who had previously discovered and managed '70s
bubblegum superstars Boney M, revealed that Pilatus and Morvan
didn't play a note or even sing on the album. They had been hired for
their looks alone, and all of their music had been recorded by
anonymous German session musicians!

Milli Vanilli were **disgraced**, handed back their Grammy, and were never
heard from again. Even in a pop world that naturally thrives on hype and
inventive scams, theirs proved a surreal and highly salutary tale.

Deee-Lite: The lightest, sweetest flavour of 1990

Album of the Year

WORLD CLIQUE - DEEE-LITE

"From the global village, in the age of communication!" chirped a tongue-in-cheek Lady Miss Kier, and so began the most infectious, irresistible album of 1990. The gloriously **camp** and funksome Deee-Lite were a funloving threesome from New York City, who set out to rehabilitate the dread word "disco" (which had for so long been used as an insult by the intelligentsia of the music world) and succeeded effortlessly. *World Clique* sounded like a great, joyous night out with your own best friends anywhere at all on the globe. 'Groove Is In The Heart' was the big hit single, a sexy and knowing dance delight with a hook to die for, but the whole album was rammed with ace **club** rhythms, neat parodic sloganeering and mock-religious paeans to the power of the beat. It all sounded sharp, sublime and fluffily inspiring, and in 1990 the whole world fell in love with Deee-Lite.

Wall comes tumbling down

The '90s began with dance music culture inexorably on the rise and sampling and remixing ever more prevalent. Many people felt that the musical decade would be the most exciting and radical since the '60s. However, one of the most spectacular early events of the '90s looked not forward, but back. To celebrate the demolition of the Berlin Wall in November 1989, Roger Waters staged a version of his former group Pink Floyd's epic work *The Wall* at the wall's former site on July 21, 1990. Naturally, this necessitated building another wall, this time out of styrofoam, which was then knocked down at the show's supposedly spectacular climax.

John Lennon tribute: We all shine on

Around **200,000 people** turned out for the extravaganza, which starred Bryan Adams, Van Morrison and Sinead O'Connor alongside Waters, and featured a host of flamboyant special effects. However, the event was not an unqualified success. There was a series of power failures, the final demolition of the wall was peculiarly messy and many critics felt the reconstruction of this dread symbol of **oppression** and fear for the purposes of a mere rock show was in distinctly questionable taste. Waters' "Wall" was possibly a brick too far.

Mandela rocks out

A happier event occurred at Wembley Stadium, when two years after the Nelson Mandela 70th birthday concert, Mandela himself attended a second event to celebrate his release after **27 years** in prison. The day was a moving and emotional one as the elderly statesman - who was soon to become South African president - enjoyed the applause of the crowd and watched sets by artists including Simple Minds, Tracy Chapman, Peter Gabriel, Neil Young and Lou Reed.

Lou Reed also travelled to Liverpool, the birthplace of The Beatles, during the early part of the year, and joined **Yoko Ono**, Wet Wet Wet, Terence Trent D'Arby, Kylie Minogue, Lenny Kravitz and Joe Cocker to play a tribute concert to John Lennon, who had been murdered ten years earlier.

Blonde faith

Madonna [see MTV Legends pp. 20-21] cemented her status as arguably the world's most famous woman by taking her **Blonde Ambition** tour around Europe and the rest of the globe. The show was a joy, packed with wit, invention and humour, yet generated the predictable outcry from the Catholic Church and other self-appointed guardians of public morals, who objected to some scenes of sado-masochism, simulated masturbation and alleged **blasphemous** imagery. Yet the tour was big, big fun and made it abundantly clear that Madonna was laughing both at her prudish critics and at herself. She also linked with MTV, allowing us to give away her Jean Paul Gaultier-designed stage costume to a lucky competition winner from England.

Prince takes it to the bridge

Madonna's rival Prince [see MTV Legends pp. 12-13] was also busy, staging his **Nude** tour in the early part of the year, then producing the *Graffiti Bridge* film and releasing the movie's soundtrack as an album. However, these projects were received with, at best, lukewarm enthusiasm by the critics who normally drooled over his every utterance, and the pop world began to receive the first signals that all was not well inside **Paisley Park**. Prince did, however, pen a glorious single called 'Nothing Compares 2U' for a certain shaven-headed young Irish star named Sinead O'Connor.

Conservative pressure groups in America frequently attacked what they regarded as obscene content in rap songs, and near-the-knuckle group 2 Live Crew had a torrid 1990. Some retailers were prosecuted simply for selling their album, *As Nasty As They Wanna Be*, and matters came to a head when they were arrested after a show in Florida and prosecuted for obscenity. The band were later acquitted of all charges, helped in part by Bruce Springsteen speaking out on their behalf and letting them sample 'Born In The USA' for their single 'Banned In The USA'.

Another band in legal trouble were England's Stone Roses, who were fined for breaking into their former record company HQ and throwing paint around the building. The effort must have exhausted the band: they retired to a studio in Wales to record the follow-up to their much-lauded groundbreaking debut album and didn't come out until 1994!

White Mariah

When a little-known singer named **Mariah Carey** released a debut single called 'Visions Of Love' a few critics surmised that she could become a white Whitney Houston - but few people genuinely took much notice. However, by the end of the year her self-titled debut album of soul ballads and power-pop had gone platinum and it was very clear that a major new star was born.

And 1990 also saw the emergence of a turbulent, aflame and engagingly **baroque** rock band from Los Angeles called Jane's Addiction. Their album, *Ritual De Lo Habitual*, was a surreal, breathtaking slalom through rock history and convention, and poetic singer Perry Farrell seemed to want to hold the whole world in his hands. Few would have bet against him.

Depeche in mode

Depeche Mode had enjoyed Europe-wide **cult** status since their early days as an experimental electro band in England, but this year's release of their rapacious *Violator* album, plus strong support from MTV, confirmed their position in rock's big league. However, a lesser response was afforded Soul II Soul: their album *1990: A New Decade* was regarded as a large disappointment after the rave reviews for their debut.

Trance dance

Dance and club music continued to exert a strong influence over Europe's charts, with ambient bands such as **The Orb**, The Grid and KLF coming to the fore.

Unprejudiced George

George Michael [see MTV Legends pp. 22-23] had a superlative-laden 1990, following up the success of *Faith* by releasing **Listen Without Prejudice: Vol 1**. The title, he explained, was aimed at bigots and knockers who sneered at him because of his past in boy-band Wham!

Rap under the hammer

One of the most surprising successes was that of baggy-trousered rapper MC Hammer, who arrived with the smash single 'You Can't Touch This' and the album *Please Hammer Don't Hurt 'Em*, and staged an elaborate live show that often seemed more like a pantomime than a concert. Purist rap fans **shuddered** at Hammer's commercial dilution of the hip-hop ethos but young pop fans adored him.

The Orb: Pink, fluffy and part of the new wave of electronic music

Adamski's 'Killer' hit big all over Europe and introduced the vocal talents of **Seal** to the world, while Snap!'s 'The Power' was virtually inescapable.

(Broken) bone Idol

Rock stars in the wars included **Billy Idol**, who damaged his leg so badly in a crash on his Harley Davidson in Hollywood that for a while surgeons thought his leg would have to be amputated. The crash meant that he had to decline a part as Jim Morrison's best friend in **Oliver Stone**'s film *The Doors* (although he did make an appearance in a smaller part), but Billy was soon up and touring to promote an album called, fittingly, *Charmed Life*.

Gloria Estefan was also in the wars, breaking her back when her tour bus crashed in Pennsylvania. Gloria was hospitalized for a long spell, but luckily made a full recovery.

Less fortunate was soul giant **Curtis Mayfield**, who was paralysed from the neck down after a lighting rig collapsed on him during bad weather at a Martin Luther King memorial concert in New York. And singer Mel Appleby, one half of the Mel & Kim singing duo, died of pneumonia after a long battle against cancer.

Zappa Czechs out

Finally, one of the strangest rock tales of 1990 found Frank Zappa appointed the new **Cultural Liaison Officer** for the nation of Czech Republic! Zappa was awarded the post by Czech president Vaclav Havel, a long-time fan, when the singer visited Prague. Sadly, Havel reversed the appointment shortly afterward - and never told anybody why.

 IN 1990

MTV launched in Poland and Czechoslovakia in February, the same month as a Belgian viewer won MTV's *Ghostbusters II* competition and was presented with the Ectomobile (the vehicle used by the Ghostbusters when they went out to "kick some slime"). Israel became part of the MTV family in March, and in the summer Italian pop star Jovanotti joined as a part-time VJ.

October turned out to be a particularly busy month. MTV arrived in Iceland, and then in the same month made its debut in the Soviet Union. MTV also presented Billy Idol's European tour and staged a competition to give away a Harley Davidson motorbike. The winner was a 50-year-old Yugoslavian whose son entered the competition on his behalf! Billy presented the ageing biker with his prize in London. December saw MTV exceed the **20 million** household mark and reach over 50 million viewers.

91

Album of the Year

ACHTUNG BABY - U2

In 1991, U2's **Achtung Baby** [see MTV Legends pp. 28-29] both delighted and amazed the music world. The Irish band had long been rock heavyweights, one of the biggest bands in the world, as sales of their previous albums *The Joshua Tree* and *Rattle & Hum* had proved. However, they'd become associated with a pomposity, an over-earnestness, which some critics found off-putting. *Achtung Baby* represented no less than a total aesthetic re-evaluation and refocusing for U2 - in short, a creative leap. Producer Brian Eno lent a hand by transforming U2's traditional sound from powerchord rock into a more subtle, blanched soundscape, but it was the band themselves who were superbly on form. Bono, in particular, was worthy of note for his oblique, witty and lyrical lines, which evoked and cast spells. The most outstanding track was **'One'**, the best love song U2 had ever written. The fascinating, mesmeric post-modern melange that is *Achtung Baby* was later to spawn the amazing Zoo TV tour and *Zooropa* follow-up, and confirmed to all doubters that U2 were still a relevant, striving and deeply important band.

Dig the new breed

The map of contemporary rock was redrawn in 1991, as most of the acts who had ruled music throughout the '80s - Dire Straits, Genesis, Eric Clapton, Simple Minds - released largely **disappointing** albums, which performed well below expectations. A new wave of bands emerged to sweep them aside, and at their head was Nirvana [see MTV Legends pp. 24-25].

Kurt Cobain's Seattle-based trio had built up a hardcore alternative following through constant gigging and a stream of singles on US independent label **Sub Pop**, but the success of their second album, *Nevermind*, took everybody by surprise. Finding its roots in the alienation

and the nebulous, aching dissatisfaction that gripped America's **"slacker"** generation, and clearly much influenced by punk, *Nevermind* was a brooding, visceral and affectingly honest record. Normally sceptical critics loved its tone of angstful yearning and queued to laud it as a masterpiece.

Nevermind spawned the monster single 'Smells Like Teen Spirit', which soon acquired the (very much unwanted) status of a 'Stairway To Heaven' for the '90s. It launched Nirvana and the sensitive and troubled Kurt Cobain on the path to worldwide fame, and also smoothed the way for similar **"grunge"** bands such as Pearl Jam, Soundgarden and Alice In Chains to penetrate the mainstream.

Nirvana were reluctant pop stars, but it seemed they had little choice in the matter. A major new movement had begun, and they had been unanimously voted in as its leaders.

Jane's Addiction: A new slant on the rock ritual

Trent Reznor: Attacking pop with nine inch nails.

Taking the rap

In 1991, outspoken rap music and the delicate sensibilities of **Middle America** clashed head on. The US record industry, after pressure from right-wing politicians and religious groups, meekly agreed to sticker certain records with warnings of their obscene lyrical content. The decision was taken largely in response to the furore over the lyrical sex and violence on NWA's second album *Efil4Zaggin*, which contained tracks such as 'To Kill A Hooker' and 'Findum Fuckum And Flee'.

Former NWA man Ice Cube starred in a Hollywood movie, *Boyz N The Hood*, then released a **vicious**, aggressive yet fascinating album called *Death Certificate*. Some tracks verged on the anti-Semitic, one song suggested that the remaining members of NWA should murder their Jewish manager. The record caused yet more outrage, reopened the censorship debate and entered the American charts at No.2.

Hip-hop godfathers **Public Enemy**, meanwhile, recorded a single called 'Bring The Noise' with thrash metal band Anthrax and set out on a US and European tour in an attempt to knock down barriers and bring fans of the two different musics together.

Rock on the road

Jane's Addiction's visionary singer Perry Farrell had long wanted to translate the spirit of European rock festivals such as Reading or Roskilde to America. This year he did it - and then he took it out on the road. The **Lollapalooza** tour (the name means a bizarre event) transported Nine Inch Nails, Ice T, Henry Rollins, Living Colour, Butthole Surfers, Siouxsie And The Banshees and Jane's Addiction across 26 dates in 21 cities - all of which sold out. Farrell's brainchild was a triumph, a beacon for the slacker generation, and was to become a major **annual** event in the US alternative rock calendar.

The beat goes on

While America was embracing grunge, Europe was still turning to **techno**, club music and the aftermath of the dance explosion. Bands such as Prodigy, Altern-8, SL2, KLF, 808 State, Primal Scream and The Shamen rode high in the charts, although The Shamen were tragically depleted when Will Sin, the Scottish band's programmer and ideas man, was drowned off the coast of Spain during a video shoot just as the band stood poised for superstardom.

The eponymous debut album from **Seal** was also heavily dance-tinged, reflecting the singer's earlier work with UK DJ and club guru Adamski.

Old guard fight back

Various mainstays of the pop world naturally refused to bow down before the shock of the new. **Prince** [see MTV Legends pp. 12-13] maintained his high levels of productivity with *Diamonds And Pearls* and Metallica's self-named album was arguably metal's high point of the year. R.E.M. [see MTV Legends pp. 26-27] pleased just about everybody with the *Out Of Time* album, but didn't want to tour and so played only two shows - at The Borderline (a tiny London club) under the pseudonym Bingo Hand Job!

Simply Red released *Stars*, a colossal blue-eyed-soul album, which was to go on to become one of the biggest-selling records of all time. **The Pet Shop Boys** toured Europe and wowed fans with their deadpan yet luscious music and their extravagant show. Sting was also busy, putting out a new, jazz-tinged and introspective album called *The Soul Cages*, and Eurythmics' *Greatest Hits* collection was a mammoth smash.

Jacko – black or white?

Michael Jackson [see MTV Legends pp. 18-19] had a strange and pressurized '91. Feeling his status as "King Of Pop" threatened by brash newcomers such as **MC Hammer** (who challenged him to an onstage dance-out to see who was the best mover!), and having been upset by his brother Jermaine's betrayal (whose single 'Word To The Badd' criticized Michael's skin grafts and plastic surgery), Jacko took stock and tried to come out fighting. His album *Dangerous* strove hard to justify its title, while the single 'Black Or White', featuring **Slash** from Guns N'Roses, was a funky but lightweight affair. The real triumph was the video, an extraordinary multimillion dollar production featuring Macauley Caulkin, Bart and Homer Simpson, Norm from *Cheers*, Red Indian tribes and a model of the Statue Of Liberty. Why? Nobody really knew.

Seal: Building on the dance explosion

Snapped Axl

Guns N'Roses returned to the **fray** with the long-awaited follow-up to *Appetite For Destruction*, and unveiled not one but TWO double albums, going under the names of *Use Your Illusion I & II*. The consensus was that they were patchy, somewhat disappointing releases. However, Axl Rose ensured that the band maintained their controversy quotient by leaping from the stage in St Louis to attack a fan who took a photograph of him! In the resulting uproar a **riot** broke out, the show was abandoned and Axl was charged with assault.

Madonna goes to bed

Madonna [see MTV Legends pp. 20-21] had a quiet 1991, releasing only two singles in Europe ('Justify My Love' and 'Rescue Me'), but kept a high profile by putting out her tour video, **In Bed With Madonna**, in which she talked dirty, dirtier and dirtiest, described her erotic fantasies in minute detail and memorably humiliated the actor Kevin Costner. What on Earth could she ever do to top that? Well, 1992 was to hold the answer.

Everything I do...
and do...and do...and do...

The tune of 1991, by a long, long way, was '(Everything I Do) I Do It For You', the **lugubrious** ballad by Canadian rocker Bryan Adams. Originally featured in the film *Robin Hood: Prince Of Thieves*, the single topped the chart in the UK for a record 16 weeks, performed similarly well all over Europe, and went on to sell a massive 10 million copies worldwide. By the end of the summer, every milkman in the western hemisphere was whistling the song, and even Adams thoroughly hated it!

Mercury falling

November 24, 1991, marked the music world's first high-profile death from AIDS, when Queen-singer **Freddie Mercury** passed away from the killer disease. Mercury had been fighting the illness for many months, but refused to make public the nature of his sickness until the last few days of his life.

To mark the sad event, Queen's greatest hit, the '70s bombastic epic 'Bohemian Rhapsody', was re-released and went straight to No.1 in many countries, and the music industry set to work to plan a huge 1992 tribute concert for Freddie. The remaining members of Queen issued a **statement**: "We have lost the greatest and most beloved member of our family".

IN 1991

January saw the launch of MTV's highly acclaimed **Unplugged** series in Europe, with performances from The Cure and Sir Paul McCartney. The same month saw the debut of *Dial MTV*, the interactive viewers'-choice chart.

In March MTV became the first non-Soviet channel to be broadcast around the clock on the Leningrad (now St Petersburg) cable TV network. In May, Monaco became the 27th country in the world to receive MTV. Over 25 million homes witnessed the fourth-birthday celebrations and MTV launched in Italy.

And, finally, Bryan Adams very kindly added an extra date to his **European** tour when he played in a small village near Hamburg, exclusively for the winners of MTV's *Waking Up the Neighbours* competition.

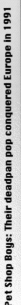

Pet Shop Boys: Their deadpan pop conquered Europe in 1991

Album of the Year

AUTOMATIC FOR THE PEOPLE - R.E.M.

The **enigmatic**, gently sensitive R.E.M. [see MTV Legends pp. 26-27] have long been the rock band loved by people who don't normally like rock bands. *Automatic For The People* was decidedly their creative high water mark to date, a wilful and beautiful masterpiece. Peter Buck's spectral, plangent guitar lines shaped a gorgeous wide canvas for Michael Stipe to craft and spell his nuance-heavy, angled words of dreams and loss, and the album resonated with power and passion. 'Everybody Hurts' soon became the lovelorn hymn for melancholics everywhere, 'Nightswimming' was almost unbearably lovely, and the poet Stipe lifted R.E.M. way, way above just about everybody else. In suitably contrary fashion, R.E.M. declined to tour their most **successful** album to date. This, it seemed, was a band who would do anything except for the expected.

Hip men wear plaid

This was the year that the **nihilistic**, troubled school of guitar rock that became immortalized as "grunge" truly came to prominence and dominated popular culture on both sides of the Atlantic. The words to drop were "slacker" and "Generation X", and even fashion gurus were designing "grunge" ranges of plaid shirts, ripped jeans and sneakers.

Pearl Jam were the first band to follow Nirvana [see MTV Legends pp. 24-25] successfully away from the alternative fringes and into the limelight. Eddie Vedder's band were more quasi-metal and prog-rock than Nirvana, but their debut album, *Ten*, equalled the phenomenal success of *Nevermind*. Soundgarden and **Smashing Pumpkins** enjoyed good years and Stone Temple Pilots released their debut, *Core*, in November.

Nirvana released only a handful of singles during the year but still remained at the centre of the media agenda, partly because of public fascination with Kurt Cobain's relationship with his wife, Hole-singer Courtney Love. The couple had a baby, Frances Bean, but an article in US magazine ***Vanity Fair*** claimed that Love had taken heroin while pregnant, at the risk of damaging her child. Cobain was rushed to hospital in Belfast with "stomach pains" after a Nirvana show in June, then later in the year told the *Los Angeles Times* that while he had used heroin, he intended to quit now that he was a father.

Ice dream

The rap-vs-censorship debate skewed off in a whole new direction this year when rapper Ice T and his offshoot thrash metal band, Body Count, recorded a track called 'Cop Killer'.

Ice T claimed the song was merely a condemnation of **racism** and police brutality but encountered a tidal wave of opposition and moral wrath from the authorities, especially when the Los Angeles riot erupted in April after the police officers who had been captured on camera brutally beating a black man, Rodney King, were cleared of all charges.

Pressure grew on Ice T's label, Time-Warner, to withdraw the track, with electioneering president **George Bush** describing 'Cop Killer' as "sick" and veteran actor Charlton Heston, a Warner shareholder, disrupting a company general meeting by reading out the lyrics to another Body Count song, 'KKK Bitch'. Another actor, Mickey Rourke, blamed Ice for the LA riots!

Time-Warner at first supported Ice, but were finally forced to bow to pressure and withdraw the track. Ice T was **unrepentant**, though, continuing to play the song at live shows despite police warnings and saying, memorably, "I could run for President. I got the whole country split right down the middle, and who's to say I don't have the majority?"

No more charity?

The '90s music world of nihilistic grunge rockers and **outrageous** gangsta rappers was far less disposed to pious shows of concern than its '80s predecessor, and 1992 witnessed only one major charity event: the Freddie Mercury Tribute for AIDS Awareness in London, in April.

The hierarchy of '80s pop showed up to pay tribute to

David Bowie: Remembering Freddie Mercury

Unhappy days

Happy Mondays, who had risen in the wake of the dance and club revival to be one of the biggest pop bands around, flew to **Barbados** in April to record their third album with ex-Talking Heads Chris Frantz and Tina Weymouth producing. The trip was a disaster. Percussionist and dancer Bez broke his arm twice in a series of car crashes on the island and singer Shaun Ryder developed a crack habit. The band returned to London with only one track completed and Ryder went straight to detox. The album, ...*Yes Please!*, was dreadful and the band split early in 1993.

Morrissey, the singer with cult '80s band The Smiths, was also in the wars: supporting Madness at one of their reunion concerts in London, he appeared on stage wrapped in a British flag and was promptly bottled off by a deeply unimpressed section of the crowd. Morrissey was due to play again the next day, but cancelled.

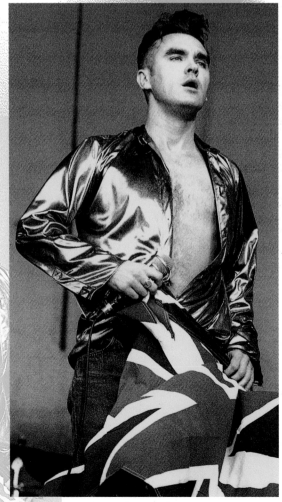

Morrissey: Union Jack couture was not in favour.

Freddie. Annie Lennox, Elton John, Bob Geldof and Lisa Stansfield turned up, and David Bowie sank to one knee to recite **The Lord's Prayer** in a gesture that was interpreted as either moving or absurdly mawkish. Metallica played, but seemed oddly out of place, and Axl Rose appeared despite having been turfed off the bill of an AIDS awareness show in New York because of Guns N'Roses' "homophobic" lyrics.

Madonna bares her...soul?

Indeed, '80s pop icons seemed to be going to ever more desperate lengths to maintain their public profile. Madonna [see MTV Legends pp. 20–21] put out the mildly diverting **Erotica** album, but aroused far more interest with *Sex*, a book of full frontal photographs of the singer hitching a lift, hanging over a wall or seemingly being molested by a group of dancers in a gym. *Sex* was an extraordinary and provocative project, but ultimately meant little.

That other '80s heavyweight Prince [see MTV Legends pp. 12–13] signed a mega-deal worth over $100 million with his record label **Warner Brothers**, but delivered an album that bore as its title only a squiggle that united the male and female gender symbols - ♀.

Sinead outrage

Morrissey would have sympathized with Sinead O'Connor, who had a troubled year that ended with her antagonizing millions. Sinead became involved with the pro-abortion movement in her native Ireland, and when she appeared on MTV's US show *Saturday Night Live* she ripped up a photograph of the Pope in protest against what she saw as the hypocrisy of the Catholic Church.

Shortly afterward Sinead appeared on the bill of a 30th anniversary tribute to Bob Dylan in New York, together with Stevie Wonder, Lou Reed and Tom Petty. The other artists were received well, but Sinead was booed from the stage and left in tears. Soon afterward she announced her retirement from the music industry, but then changed her mind.

Day at the zoo

Sinead's compatriots U2 [see MTV Legends pp. 28-29] had a far happier year. They took their extraordinary Zoo TV tour out on the road, bombarding their audiences with massed banks of TV sets that flashed subliminal and opaque messages. Bono surfed the TV channels, telephoned royalty and world leaders and ordered **pizzas** from the stage every night. The whole extravagant, imaginative, defiantly mischievous show put every other tour of the last ten years in the shade.

George wants out

One of the great rock business litigations of recent years began in 1992, a story that was to run and run. George Michael [see MTV Legends pp. 22-23] decided that he wanted out of his deal with **Sony** Music, despite a contract that tied him to the label until 2003. Michael claimed that Sony neither understood him nor treated him fairly. He also complained that the company, unlike their predecessors, CBS, showed no sensitivity toward their artists and treated them only as "promotional tools for software". Sony said they didn't agree with George and didn't intend to back down an inch, and so the battle lines were drawn.

Kriss kross over

Pop rappers Kriss Kross were on top of the world with their *Totally Krossed Out* album. **Right Said Fred** were also looking skyward with their album *Up* and a string of hits, the biggest of which had been the wonderfully daft 'I'm Too Sexy'. Lionel Richie and country star Billie Ray Cyrus also enjoyed great years, as did Annie Lennox, with her album *Diva*.

 IN 1992

MTV passed the **10 million** household mark in Germany alone, and in April reached 35 million subscribers throughout Europe. In January, Eric Clapton recorded an *Unplugged* show and later in the year, Annie Lennox, Joe Cocker and Was (Not Was) joined the series. Over four million people entered the Dinner With Michael Jackson competition in March (see MTV Legends pp. 18-19) and the Belgian winner was flown to Palm Springs to chill with Michael on a video set. In June a British viewer who won the MTV/Zoo TV competition was linked up by satellite from his home to U2, who were live on stage in Stockholm! In December MTV supported **World Aids Day** with a day of programming dedicated to raising awareness.

Right Said Fred: Keeping their shirts on for 'Deeply Dippy'

93

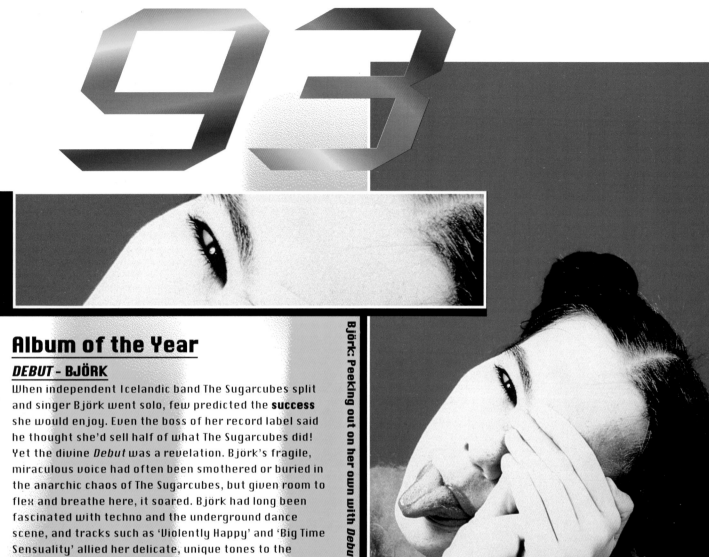

Album of the Year

DEBUT - BJÖRK

When independent Icelandic band The Sugarcubes split and singer Björk went solo, few predicted the **success** she would enjoy. Even the boss of her record label said he thought she'd sell half of what The Sugarcubes did! Yet the divine *Debut* was a revelation. Björk's fragile, miraculous voice had often been smothered or buried in the anarchic chaos of The Sugarcubes, but given room to flex and breathe here, it soared. Björk had long been fascinated with techno and the underground dance scene, and tracks such as 'Violently Happy' and 'Big Time Sensuality' allied her delicate, unique tones to the energy of club music with **scintillating** results. Björk's alien, otherworldly beauty and charm landed her on magazine covers across the globe and the wonderful *Debut* ensured that Iceland had contributed its very first superstar to the world of pop.

Jackson shock

A stunned music world watched in astonishment as the most famous pop star on the planet was accused of one of the most heinous **crimes** of all - child abuse. Michael Jackson [see MTV Legends pp. 18-19] was out on tour in August when the story broke. Jackson was accused of molesting a 13-year-old boy, Jordy Chandler, at his Neverland ranch in Hollywood. The world's media instantly pursued the star, who reacted by breaking off his Far East tour dates (claiming illness) and fleeing to London, where he secretly checked into a clinic in order to get "treatment for painkiller addiction".

A major legal trial appeared imminent - and yet the case never came to court. At the end of the year, Jackson paid Jordy, his parents and their lawyer a total of **$20 million** in an out-of-court settlement.

Growing pains

Pearl Jam and Nirvana [see MTV Legends pp. 24-25], the two new superpowers in American rock, had decidedly different years. **Pearl Jam** released the heavyweight *Vs* as their follow-up to *Ten*, enjoying huge sales and - on the whole - critical acclaim. Life was good in Camp Vedder. Nirvana put out *In Utero*, but it was clear that Kurt Cobain was having major problems with adjusting to his new role as public property. In June he was arrested in Seattle after police were called when he and Courtney Love argued over whether Cobain should keep **guns** in their house. Yet the year ended on a high note. Nirvana, with mentor US band Meat Puppets, recorded an *Unplugged* session for MTV, which came to be recognized as one of the best in the entire series.

The "second wave of grunge" also hit home with

Smashing Pumpkins, Spin Doctors, Stone Temple Pilots and 4 Non Blondes all enjoying great success, although critics were far less enamoured of these bands than they were of the originators of the genre.

Rap follies

Hip-hop experienced an extraordinarily turbulent 1993, with a large number of its stars spending more time in **court** than on stage or in a recording studio. Snoop Doggy Dogg was the main casualty. The laidback rapper saw sales of his debut album *Doggystyle* go through the roof but was then sensationally arrested at the MTV USA Awards and charged with first-degree murder. Snoop was driving the car from which his bodyguard allegedly shot dead a youth on the street. He was bailed for $1 million, and the trial was to hang over his head for the next two years.

Snoop's producer, ex-NWA man Dr. Dre, faced a variety of charges including **assaulting** a TV rap presenter and a police officer, while Tupac Shakur was arrested for sexual assault. Flavor Flav of Public Enemy was charged with attempted murder then went into detox to try to break his drug addiction. Ice T left Warner Brothers, accusing them of refusing to release his latest album, and the label later quietly dropped Geto Boys and cartoon rockers GWAR as the **censorship** debate continued to rage. The FBI also discovered - and foiled - a plot among fascist groups to assassinate Ice Cube and Ice T. On a more positive note, Dr. Dre's *The Chronic* became one of the biggest-selling hip-hop albums of all time.

Blow by blow

It wasn't only rap rebels fighting the law. Other pop stars arrested during the year for offences varying from assault to disturbing the peace included Eddie Vedder, Billy Idol, Dave Gahan of Depeche Mode, Ugly Kid Joe's Whitfield Crane, B-52's singer Kate Pierson and Brad and Tim of Rage Against The Machine. Rage Against The Machine also achieved notoriety on the Lollapalooza tour, where they stripped totally **naked** on stage in an anti-censorship protest!

4 Non-Blondes: What's going on?

Crazed and confused

Some pop stars continued to push sanity to its limits. The ever-eccentric Prince [see MTV Legends pp. 12-13] excelled himself. He began by unexpectedly announcing his **retirement** from the music business - at the age of 34 - reportedly because his label refused to release a mini-album on June 7 to celebrate his birthday! He then changed his mind but declared that he was no longer to be known as Prince but as ☥, the strange hieroglyphic squiggle he'd used to title his last album.

Sinead O'Connor dropped out of headlining a peace festival in Ireland at short notice and apologized by writing a strange and anguished poem as an advert in an Irish newspaper. She then went on to sell her mansion in Los Angeles and give the proceeds to the **Somalian** relief fund!

Janet joy

While Michael Jackson [see MTV Legends pp. 18-19] was enduring a turbulent and difficult 1993, his sister Janet [see MTV Legends pp. 16-17] was having a very much better time. She released her warmly-welcomed *Janet*

album and also nixed her reputation as the squeaky-clean member of the Jackson clan by appearing on the cover of *Rolling Stone* magazine, topless but for the hands of her boyfriend. Madonna also made use of breasts - but not, for once, her own - as she included topless dancers in her Girlie Show tour revue.

Meanwhile, Whitney Houston made her Hollywood debut and was genuinely impressive starring opposite Kevin Costner in *The Bodyguard*.

Meat back on menu!

One of the more unlikely triumphs of '93 was the global success of Meat Loaf's mighty *Bat Out Of Hell II* - 15 years after he recorded the original! Mariah Carey's *Music Box* was huge and *The Sign* by Ace Of Bass hit not just in their native Scandinavia but right across Europe.

Enter macphisto

U2 [see MTV Legends pp. 28-29] released the *Zooropa* album and continued to tour the globe with Zoo TV. Bono once again phoned all and sundry from the stage, including a deeply moving call to war-torn **Sarajevo,** and

IN 1993

In January MTV went **Dutch** with a weekend of special programming from the Netherlands. The Pet Shop Boys flew to Russia in March to help launch a syndication agreement providing 43 hours of MTV programming per week to over 88 million homes in the former Soviet Union.

April saw the arrival on MTV of *Beavis & Butt-Head*. In the same month, George Michael (see MTV Legends pp. 22-23) chose MTV for his first television interview in three years.

July saw MTV link up with U2 again, and a lucky competition winner was able to film the band live on stage.

In October, as part of the Free Your Mind campaign, MTV presented the One Europe? weekend, which featured a series of reports and debates on the complex issues involved in European unity and how they affect the youth of Europe.

Unplugged sessions this year included k.d. lang, Rod Stewart, Duran Duran and the classic December performance by Nirvana.

Frank zapped

On a rather different note, the year witnessed the sad death of one of the true **innovators** of rock. Frank Zappa, who rose to fame with the Mothers Of Invention and in later years became an outspoken critic of the creeping censorship affecting the music business in the USA, passed away from cancer of the prostate in December.

2 Unlimited: Techno! Techno! Techno!

introduced his new surreal alter ego, **MacPhisto** - an ageing cabaret/game show host character sporting devil's horns.

Depeche Mode enjoyed a triumphant 1993. The band had been heavily supported by MTV for years and *Songs Of Faith & Devotion*, their third major US album, topped the charts and elevated them to the rarefied air enjoyed by only a handful of bands.

Gone camping

A flurry of fun, disposable pop hits from European bands brightened up 1993, which the bores who drone on about "real music" absolutely hated and everybody else utterly adored. Holland's 2 Unlimited had a huge hit with 'No Limits' and its brazen chorus of **"Techno! Techno! Techno!"**. Culture Beat, Ace Of Base, Haddaway and Dr Alban enjoyed similar discofied smashes: this was the year that techno penetrated not just the mainstream but the playground.

Take That and East 17 both rose to fame and began their legendary rivalry. Those who tried to follow them, but never quite made it, included Bad Boys Inc and Worlds Apart.

94

and 'Doll Parts' howled at the Moon about male sexual exploitation of women, and Courtney sounded fuelled by a hard, bitter ire. A month after this album was released, Hole bassist Kristen Pfaff died of a heroin overdose - yet still the volatile Love, in the midst of a personal hell, took the album out on tour. It was an act of remarkable courage.

Final Kurt-ain

The death of Nirvana's Kurt Cobain cast a huge **shadow** over 1994. The singer blew his face off with a shotgun at the home he shared with Courtney and their daughter, Frances Bean, on April 8. (At this point, Nirvana were one of the biggest, and certainly hippest, bands in the world.) The news was hardly a shock - Kurt had survived an overdose in Rome just one month earlier - yet the sense of loss and waste was, for all music fans, overwhelming. The brilliant MTV *Unplugged* album that Nirvana recorded in late 1993 became something it was never meant to be - an epitaph to their **genius**.

Jackson fear

Michael Jackson [see MTV Legends pp. 18-19] spent 1994 trying to put behind him the child abuse allegations of the previous year, but was **thwarted** in his attempts. Shortly after the singer paid $20 million in an out-of-court settlement to Jordy Chandler, there were more tribulations for the superstar. Another youngster made similar allegations, as did various former members of Michael's staff at the Neverland ranch. After a peculiarly short

Album of the Year

LIVE THROUGH THIS - HOLE

No album can ever have been released in more tragic circumstances than the ironically-titled *Live Through This*. The record appeared a mere three weeks after **Courtney Love**'s husband, Nirvana's Kurt Cobain [see MTV Legends pp. 24-25], had committed suicide, and the media feeding frenzy around Courtney was at its height. She appeared to be a sitting duck for certain critics, who regarded her as a parasite on Cobain's huge talent - yet this album blew any such unfair ideas away. *Live Through This* was brilliant, inspired rock'n'roll, a scathing and often vicious study of sex and spite and a woman's lot in the modern world, which Courtney draped over gleaming guitar riffs and then delivered in her trademark mix of l'il girl lost lisp and ferocious scream. Songs such as the twisted, almost unbearably **painful** 'Violet' courtship, Jackson showed that his power to amaze was undiminished when he married Elvis Presley's daughter, **Lisa Marie**, on May 26 in the Dominican Republic. The marriage was not to last, and few commentators saw it as anything more than good PR and damage limitation on behalf of Jackson.

Court in the act

If 1994 was noted for one trend, it was the extraordinarily large amount of **litigation** involving top music stars. George Michael's [see MTV Legends pp. 22-23] lengthy battle to free himself from Sony Music saw the singer lose his case, yet he vowed to continue the battle. U2 [see MTV Legends pp. 28-29], Metallica, The Cure and Pearl Jam were also involved in court actions against various arms of the music industry.

Yet the most surreal story, naturally, concerned ♆. ♆ declared that he was now to be known as The Artist Formerly Known As Prince [see MTV Legends pp. 12-13] and began a campaign to free himself from Warner Brothers, despite having joined the company's board in 1993. He also appeared in public with the word "SLAVE" written on his cheek.

Taking the rap

Tupac Shakur was now widely regarded as the baddest of all the gangsta rappers, and this year saw him charged with sexual abuse and assault and, in a separate incident, lose a testicle when he was shot during an **armed** burglary. Yet, musically, 1994 saw great G-Funk records from the Californian triumvirate of Warren G, Nate Dogg and Snoop Doggy Dogg, and the emergence of the visceral thrill and baffling brilliance of the Wu-Tang Clan.

On the road

The Rolling Stones' **Voodoo Lounge** outing was officially confirmed as the largest grossing tour in rock history. Meanwhile, Pink Floyd played live for the first time in five years, but their date at London's Earls Court almost ended in tragedy when a temporary stand erected for the show collapsed. Luckily, nobody was hurt. The same couldn't be said for The Cranberries' singer **Dolores O'Riordan**: she broke her leg skiing and was forced to play some shows from a wheelchair.

The Rolling Stones: The biggest and the loudest

Mudstock

An attempt to recreate the idyllic, peace-and-love **Woodstock Festival** of the '60s was regarded as a fiasco. The organizers gathered Bob Dylan, Red Hot Chili Peppers, Salt'N'Pepper, Nine Inch Nails, Orbital, and Henry Rollins together in August, but torrential rain and inadequate security meant that the event was a disappointment.

Europe calling

This year saw the music world shift its gaze somewhat from America to **Europe**, despite high-profile and successful US releases such as R.E.M.'s *Monster* [see MTV Legends pp. 26-27], Pearl Jam's *Vitalogy*, Counting Crows' *August and Everything After* and Soundgarden's *Superunknown*. There was no doubt that the tragic death of Kurt Cobain had marked the end of the US-dominated grunge era of music. There was a vacuum to be filled and Europe was ready and willing to fill it.

The British are coming!

From the United Kingdom came a new wave of homegrown guitar rock, which soon became known as Britpop. **Blur** released the quirky *Parklife* and Pulp emerged with the laconic *His'N'Hers* album. Suede, Elastica, Echobelly, Sleeper and Radiohead also consolidated their new-found fame. The moody, atmospheric "trip-hop" scene also emerged, spearheaded by Portishead, Tricky and Massive Attack.

Maybe? Definitely!

Yet one band was to dwarf them all. **Oasis**, from Manchester, had spent the previous year gaining a reputation for incendiary live shows and also for surreal and belligerent interviews, which would often see the band's singer Liam Gallagher and his songwriter/guitarist brother Noel come to blows. Everybody knew Oasis were the ones to watch - but the

band were about to up the ante.

The success of their debut album *Definitely Maybe* turned Oasis from a mere success story into a phenomenon. The band's classic **Beatles-style** harmonies and ragged glory swept all before them, and singles such as 'Live Forever' and 'Cigarettes And Alcohol' won them thousands of converts. Three weeks after its release, *Definitely Maybe* became the fastest-selling debut album of all time by a British band and Oasis were well on their way to going supernova.

Disco delights

The **Eurodisco** contingent of 2 Unlimited, Culture Beat and Cappella continued to make ace bubblegum hits almost at will, and Haddaway's 'What Is Love?' was the anthem of the summer for many people. Take That reaped the benefit of two years of hard work by breaking through and earning Europe-wide teen adulation, while Wet Wet Wet enjoyed a huge hit with 'Love Is All Around'. On the dance scene, The Prodigy recorded *Music For The Jilted Generation* and served notice of their intentions, and the dark yet fascinating rhythms of drum'n'bass were dominating the clubs. In the States, **Boyz II Men** swept all before them.

Death metal?

One of the most disturbing and peculiar music stories of the year concerned the emergent death metal scene in Norway. Bard Eithum of the band Emperor and Varg Vikernes of Burzum were both **jailed** for murder - the latter after boasting of his crime to a rock journalist who interviewed him! There were various instances of death metallers burning Norwegian churches to the ground.

Equally surreal were the actions of veteran Slovenian band Laibach - of the Neue Slowenische Kunst (New Slovanian Art) movement - who, with a teutonic twinkle in their eyes, declared the formation of their own national state and issued **passports** to all who wished to become citizens. For the

purposes of their European tour, every venue they played became a "colony" for the night.

Up in smoke

Yet the weirdest publicity stunt of the year was conducted by **KLF**. The cult dance band and art terrorists withdrew £1million from their bank account, flew to the remote Scottish island of Jura and burned the money to a crisp - "in order to see what it felt like".

 # IN 1994

In March MTV burned rubber and announced sponsorship of the **Formula One** MTV Simtek Ford team.

In June, MTV's Vote Europe campaign encouraged young people to vote in the European Parliamentary elections. The campaign featured interviews with national heads of state plus EC president Jacques Delors and former Soviet leader Mikhail Gorbachev, and culminated in a **live** studio debate with MEPs from all the major parties. In the same month, German superstar Herbert Grönemeyer became the first non-English speaking artist to be featured in the *Unplugged* series. Other stars performing acoustic sets included Lenny Kravitz, Bob Dylan and Björk, as well as a reunion of Robert Plant and Jimmy Page under the title *Unledded*!

Miles Hunt, former singer of UK band the Wonder Stuff, joined MTV Europe to present the alternative show *120 Minutes*.

The Artist Formerly Known as Prince turned on MTV Network Europe's new UK channel VH-1 in London in September, and the first **MTV Europe Music Awards** - which were held in Berlin - featured George Michael, Björk, Eros Ramazotti, Take That, The Artist Formerly Known As Prince and Aerosmith (see MTV Legends pp. 12-13 and 10-11).

95

Album of the Year

JAGGED LITTLE PILL - ALANIS MORISSETTE

At the start of 1995, nobody outside of Canada had heard of Alanis Morissette. By the end of the year everybody had. This supremely **accomplished** debut album was not so much a collection of love songs, rather it was a collection of life songs, a series of inventive musings on men and relationships and the play of the sexes, and it touched raw nerves in fans right across the world. With a rare passion and prodigious honesty, Alanis covered the full range of emotions from the sunny celebration of 'Hand In My Pocket' to the sheer falling-in-love bliss of 'Head Over Feet' to the bitter, jilted rage of the ferocious 'You Oughta Know'. Alanis's frankness and easy charm won over just about everybody and she set off on a seemingly never-ending **tour** around the world, stopping only to pick up awards at every ceremony along the way. For Alanis Morissette, 1995 was quite a year.

Here's the story

Alanis Morissette may have been the success story of 1995, but Oasis ran a mighty close second. The UK rockers followed up 1994's debut *Definitely Maybe* with *(What's The Story?) Morning Glory*, and their fame skyrocketed. So addictive was Oasis's mix of anthemic rock, cocky lyrical sloganeering and respectful nods to The Beatles that the record remains well on target to be the best selling album made by a British artist *ever*.

Pop wars

Intense rivalry between Oasis and their prime Britpop rivals Blur blew up this same year. The **competition** between the two was hyped up by the media and encouraged by both bands, but Blur's album *The Great Escape* sold far fewer copies than the Oasis album, and the latter continued to steamroller all before them. The rivalry took an unsavoury turn when Noel Gallagher told an interviewer that he hoped Damon and Alex of Blur would "catch AIDS and die", but the Oasis man later withdrew the remark and made a full **apology**.

Alanis Morissette: First Canada, then the world

Foo Fighters: A brave return for Dave Grohl

Love is all around

Hole singer Courtney Love careered around the globe this year, clearly still traumatized by the suicide of her husband, Kurt Cobain. Courtney posted rambling messages on the **internet** insulting other stars, was twice in court for attacking fans (she was acquitted both times) and was arrested for insulting an attendant on a flight to Australia. Courtney also punched Bikini Kill-singer Kathleen Hanna at Lollapalooza and threatened to leave the tour in protest at the presence of Snoop Doggy Dogg and his "misogynist" lyrics. She eventually stayed, unlike the pregnant Sinead O'Connor, who quit Lollapalooza on health grounds and was replaced by Elastica. A more positive aspect of the fall-out from the end of Nirvana [see MTV Legends pp. 24-25] was that drummer Dave Grohl returned with his new band, **Foo Fighters**.

Robbie goes

Pop fans across Europe had their hearts broken on July 18 when it was announced that **Robbie Williams** had left Take That. Nobody was quite sure if he'd resigned or been sacked, but the reaction was staggering. Groups of zealous girl fans tried to track down Robbie to persuade him to change his mind, and one teenager in Germany even attempted suicide. Gary, Mark, Howard and Jason announced that they would be continuing as a four-piece and went out on tour, while Robbie set about the trendy pop star pastime of **suing** his record label in an effort to get them to release him.

Jackson ill

Michael Jackson [see MTV Legends pp. 18-19] spent 1995 still doggedly trying to keep his position as "King Of Pop" and rehabilitate his reputation, which had been so badly harmed by the unproved allegations of child abuse levelled against him. He seemed to be succeeding when the single 'Earth Song' was a massive worldwide hit, but in December he **collapsed** in New York and was rushed to intensive care with a mysterious illness.

Gangsta grief

Snoop Doggy Dogg's trial for accessory to first-degree murder finally opened in October. **Tupac Shakur** was sentenced to at least 18 months in jail for sexual assault. Flavor Flav of Public Enemy had a year to forget. He was jailed for three months for firing a gun at his neighbour, faced further charges for allegedly possessing crack cocaine and firearms, and broke both of his arms in a motorbike crash. One of the original gangsta rappers, Eazy E of NWA, died of AIDS in March.

The year also saw the demise of one of the greatest and most adored cult stars of all – Grateful Dead front man and founder **Jerry Garcia**.

Doctor! Doctor!

R.E.M. [see MTV Legends pp. 26–27] set out on a world tour to promote *Monster*, but their outing turned into the most jinxed tour in history. Drummer Bill Berry was lucky to survive after suffering an aneurysm on stage in Lausanne. When R.E.M. restarted their tour, bassist Mike Mills had to receive surgery to remove an intestinal tumour, and then singer Michael Stipe was forced to undergo a hernia operation.

Depeche Mode-singer **Dave Gahan** also fetched up in hospital, in deeply unhappy circumstances. Gahan slashed his wrists during August in an apparent suicide attempt, then went missing for a few days on his release before turning up safe and well. Pearl Jam singer **Eddie Vedder** was also lucky to escape serious injury – or worse – when he was rescued by coastguards after being swept out to sea when swimming off the coast of New Zealand with Tim Finn of Crowded House.

Scanner tracks Björk

Björk released *Post*, the follow-up to her universally acclaimed 1993 *Debut* album, but was forced to recall the record on the day of its release because her label had failed to clear a sample by underground artist **Scanner**. The two artists reached an amicable agreement and *Post* went back into the shops.

Missing manic

Mystery surrounded the disappearance of the Manic Street Preachers' guitar player, **Richey Edwards** (full name Richey James Edwards). He was due to fly with the rest of the band to America, but instead checked out of their London hotel and drove to his home in Wales. His car was later found abandoned by the Severn Bridge – a local beauty spot and a famous location for suicides. The 28-year-old star had a history of depression, self-mutilation and drinking, but no body was found, and fans continue to **hope** against hope that Richey is alive, well and happy somewhere.

Weller and Sir Paul: *Help!*

U2 take a ride

There was no U2 [see MTV Legends pp. 28-29] album in 1995, but the band did get together once again with groundbreaking producer **Brian Eno** to release the ambient *Passengers* project, which featured a duet between Bono and Pavorotti on the track 'Miss Sarajevo'.

Suggs, Edwyn Collins and the Human League all mounted comebacks this year, and from the ashes of Happy Mondays rose Shaun Ryder and Black Grape with their debut album *It's Great When You're Straight...Yeah!*

 [see MTV Legends pp. 12-13]. continued his **dispute** with Warner Brothers, and informed audiences at his live shows that "Prince is dead!"

Help! for Bosnia

September saw some of the biggest names on the **European** music scene come together for one hectic day in London to record an album to raise funds for War Child, the charity set up in an attempt to relieve the suffering in war-torn Bosnia. Sir Paul McCartney, Noel Gallagher, Paul Weller, Suede, Sinead O'Connor, Manic Street Preachers, Blur, Neneh Cherry and even Johnny Depp contributed to *Help!*, and the record was in the shops just one week later - a logistical near-impossibility and a thoroughly admirable achievement.

Two by two

Bono and Pavarotti were not the only **unlikely** pairing of the year. Neil Young sang with Pearl Jam, Nick Cave got together with Kylie Minogue, David Bowie and Morrissey went on tour together, and the most surreal collaboration of all saw Mariah Carey singing with the Wu-Tung Clan's Ol' Dirty Bastard. It was virtually impossible to imagine a more unlikely union.

MTV IN 1995

MTV Networks Europe launched a new version of VH-1 for **German** viewers in March and within one month the service had over one million subscribers. In May an influential research study revealed that MTV Europe is the most watched channel among 15-34 year olds in Europe. June saw MTV sign a new distribution agreement with Italian channel Telepiu 3 to broadcast to over 11 million homes throughout Italy - MTV celebrated with a star-studded party in Milan.
In November the second MTV Europe Music Awards were held at Le Zenith club in Paris. Hosted by Jean Paul Gaultier, the evening featured David Bowie, Bon Jovi (See MTV Legends pp. 14-15), The Cranberries, Simply Red, East 17, Björk, Robbie Williams, Kylie Minogue, Michael Hutchence, Jean-Claude Van Damme and a cast of thousands! (See MTV Database for full details of winners.) Artists who recorded ***Unplugged*** sessions this year included Phil Collins, Kiss, The Cranberries, Sheryl Crow and Hole.

96

Michael Jackson: Live, but interrupted, at the Brit Awards

Album of the Year

EVERYTHING MUST GO –
MANIC STREET PREACHERS

Everything Must Go may not have been Europe's biggest-selling album of 1996, but it was without doubt the most moving and poignant. After the **disappearance** of their guitarist Richey, the previous year, Manic Street Preachers could easily have retreated into mawkish sentimentality or simply jacked the whole rock'n'roll game in. Instead, they retreated to the studio and emerged with a passionately resilient and eloquent record which honed their trademark keen, questioning intelligence into a series of classic rock tunes. James Dean Bradfield transformed from a good singer to a great one, and the album not only topped a plethora of critical polls but yielded a string of **hit** singles ('A Design For Life', 'Everything Must Go' and 'Australia'). Manic Street Preachers, who enjoyed constant MTV support, came of age and crossed over from cult status to mainstream adulation of a strength and fervour enjoyed by very few groups. Not bad for a band who were being written off just twelve months previously.

Fight! Fight!

The year opened with some extraordinary examples of pop stars behaving badly. Pulp-singer Jarvis Cocker set the ball rolling at the **Brit Awards** in London in February when he ran on stage while Michael Jackson [MTV Legends pp. 18–19] performed a lavish production of 'Earth Song'. Jarvis pranced and looned around the stage before being removed by security men. Jarvis was arrested, but later released without charge.

Björk on the wild side

There were even more spectacular scenes when Björk arrived in Bangkok on the Asian leg of her world tour. The Icelandic singer was greeted at the airport by a local female news reporter who had continually **harassed** Björk for an interview since her arrival in South East Asia. Björk took exception to this request, knocked the journalist over and banged her head repeatedly on the ground before being dragged away. Björk later apologized, and no charges were brought.

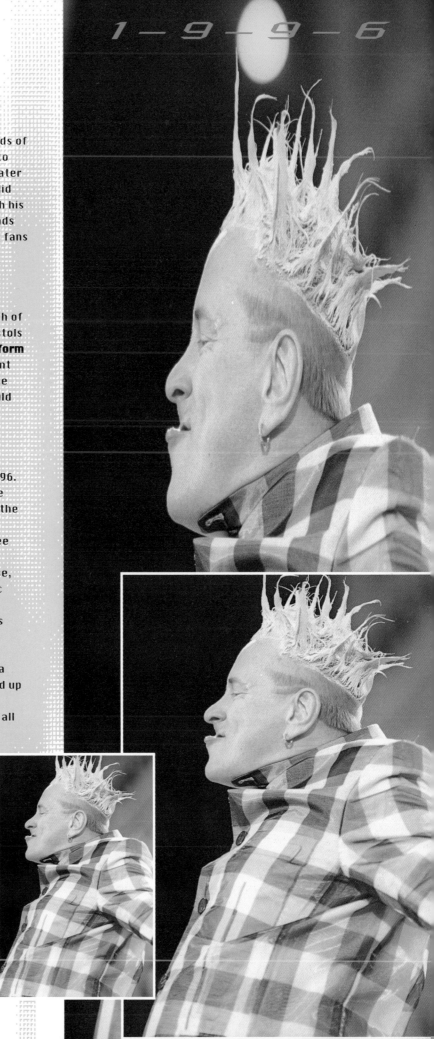

Take That split

The following month brought heartache for thousands of young girls as Take That announced that they were to **split**. Gary Barlow went on to enjoy major success later in the year with his debut single 'Forever Love', as did Robbie Williams (who had quit the band in 1995) with his cover of George Michael's 'Freedom' [see MTV Legends pp. 22-23], but MTV Europe's cameras filmed tearful fans right across the continent.

Punk's not dead!

As one major band ended their career, another bunch of music icons started theirs all over again. The Sex Pistols announced on MTV in January that they were to **re-form** for the Filthy Lucre tour in the summer. The tour went ahead, and most critics grudgingly conceded that the Pistols could play far better now than they ever could back in the halcyon days of punk!

Major albums

Many major artists returned with **new** albums in 1996. The Cranberries' *To The Faithful Departed* had a more polished, rockier sheen than their earlier work, but the band had to pull US tour dates when singer Dolores O'Riordan fell ill. *R.E.M's New Adventures In Hi-Fi* [see MTV Legends pp. 26-27] was a typically low key and oblique outing yet delighted their enormous fan base, and Beck's *Odelay* proved him to be one of the music world's most inventive singer-songwriters.

Celine Dion enjoyed incredible worldwide success with 'Falling Into You' and George Michael finally returned after his epic battles with the soft-tinged *Older*. Tricky's *Pre-Millenium Tension* was hailed as a dark, visionary masterpiece, and the Fugees cleaned up with *The Score*, from which the singles 'Killing Me Softly', 'Ready Or Not' and 'No Woman, No Cry' were all massive Europe-wide hits.

Taking the rap

Yet 1996 was not so bright for other rap stars. Snoop Doggy Dogg finally faced his first-degree murder charge in January for his alleged part in a drive-by shooting, before being acquitted of all charges. And in September, Tupac Shakur was shot dead in Los Angeles, the last act in a troubled and controversial existence. His album *All Eyez On Me*, meanwhile, went **double-platinum** worldwide.

The Sex Pistols: John Lydon is still Rotten

Oasis: The band on everyone's lips

Gallagher, who had a sore throat.

On other fronts, Oasis had a mixed year. *(What's The Story?) Morning Glory* continued to go from strength to strength, yet the band's autumn American tour was jinxed from the start. Liam Gallagher **missed** the band's first two US shows after refusing to fly to the States because he wanted to go "house-hunting" in England. He eventually flew out to the States, but the tour was aborted scarcely a week later after Noel Gallagher flew home alone after a major **bust-up** with his brother. Liam was also arrested in London as the year closed and charged with the possession of a Class A drug.

The needle and the damage done

Liam wasn't alone in facing drug problems in '96. Depeche Mode mainman Dave Gahan was rushed to hospital in Los Angeles after overdosing and escaped death only because of the prompt actions of paramedics. Smashing Pumpkins keyboardist **Jonathan Melvoin** was less fortunate, dying of a heroin overdose in July, and Stone Temple Pilots singer Scott Weiland was in and out of rehab during the year as he battled against addiction.

Faded Roses

Stone Roses, who were widely recognized as the band who ushered in a whole new dance movement at the turn of the decade, finally decided to call it a day after their headline performance at the UK's **Reading Festival** in August. The news was greeted with a horrified response in the music press. Ian Brown issued a statement declaring himself glad to be out of "the dirtiest business in the world". Drummer Mani went off to join Primal Scream and guitarist John Squire, who had left the Roses the previous year, formed a new band. He initially called it The Seahorses, then changed the name to Seahorses after being told the fuller title was an anagram of "He hates roses"!

Oasis reign on

The gigs of 1996? No contest. Oasis continued to rule the rock world, despite not actually releasing any new music, and at the height of summer their British shows at Loch Lomond in Scotland and **Knebworth** in the English Midlands broke all records. Oasis played to over 300,000 people inside two weeks, and an amazing 5% of the UK population applied for tickets! The shows were generally considered to be a huge success, and Oasis recorded for MTV *Unplugged* shortly afterward - without Liam

Spice of life

Perhaps the most astonishing success story of 1996 came right at the end of the year. When Take That split in February, there was much fevered speculation over who would snatch their teen idol crown. Fellow boy band Boyzone consolidated their previous triumphs and Backstreet Boys enjoyed success across Europe - but nobody had allowed for the arrival of the **Spice Girls**.

Mel B, Mel C, Geri, Victoria and Emma arrived with a vengeance in the Autumn and simply refused to go away. Their smart, **sassy** debut single 'Wannabe' raced to the top of the charts right across Europe and stayed there for weeks as the cheerily in-your-face Spices preached their happy gospel of Girl Power and female empowerment, and teenage girl pop fans knew they'd found some stars they could really believe in.

A few snobby rock fans sneered that the Spice Girls were **one-hit** wonders, but they were soon proved wrong. Their follow-up, 'Say You'll Be There', was an equal success, and the December triumph of the ballad '2 Become 1' ensured that a copy of their debut album *Spice* was the present that *every* self-respecting pop fan wanted for Christmas. As an eventful and fascinating 1996 came to an end, everything was looking very, very Spicey.

The Prodigy: At Knebworth, August '96

 IN 1996

April saw the launch of a brand new fashion and lifestyle show on MTV – *Stylissimo!* - and New York Drag superstar Miss 'Lady' Bunny joined the channel in June for special week of gay themed shows. In August the special Turned On Europe vehicle, equipped with film and edit facilities, set off for a major tour of Europe to compile one of the most comprehensive youth surveys ever.

As the year neared its close, MTV viewers voted for their favourite artists at the **MTV Europe Music Awards** in November (See Database section for full details).

97

Liam and Patsy: Will they? Won't they? They will!

As MTV Europe enters its second decade, 1997 looks like being a particularly busy year in music. January saw MTV in the States offer an exclusive preview of new U2 single [see MTV Legends pp. 28-29] 'Discotheque' and the accompanying bizarre video, which saw Bono and co dressed up as camp '70s icons the **Village People**. The Prodigy signed a huge American deal with Madonna's label Maverick, even though Mads herself had once stated that she found all techno boring and repetitive! Also on a dance tip, French stars Daft Punk released their acclaimed *Homework* album.

Oasis began the year as they ended the previous one - in the headlines. Singer Liam Gallagher was let off with a caution after having been **arrested** in December '96 and charged with possession of cocaine. Various UK Members of Parliament and tabloid papers called for Liam to be prosecuted and made an example of, but a police spokesman merely commenting that "a caution is normal for a first offence".

A sad loss to the music world was Scottish singer Billy MacKenzie, singer in cult '80s band **The Associates**, who committed suicide while suffering from depression.

YMCA-U2

February brought U2 back on to the musical agenda. The Irish band released *Pop* to mixed reviews. They also chose the unlikely setting of a **K-Mart** store in New York to launch, on MTV, their PopMart world tour, which is scheduled to visit just about every point on the globe over the next two years.

Spice Girls continue to enjoy staggering success worldwide. The Girls topped the British charts with 'Mama' - the first ever band to achieve this with their first four singles, and sat proud on top of the US chart with 'Wannabe'. The band also picked up awards for Best Single and Best Video at the prestigious Brit Awards, where other prizes went to Manic Street Preachers, Fugees, Kula Shaker, Beck and The Prodigy, and The Bee Gees received a prize for Outstanding Contribution To Music.

Former East 17 singer Brian Harvey was having a hard time of it - Harvey, sacked from the band for endorsing **Ecstasy** use, was arrested in London for assaulting a photographer.

Definitely married

In March the East vs West Coast wars that riddle American rap music claimed another victim. The Notorious B.I.G. aka **Biggie Smalls** was shot dead as he left an awards ceremony in Los Angeles where he had presented a prize to Toni Braxton. He was 24 and had just finished recording his new album *Life After Death...Til Death Do Us Part*. In a further twist, Death Row records president Marion "Suge" Knight, who was himself serving a nine-year jail sentence, claimed from his cell that he knew the identity of the man who had killed Tupac Shakur in 1996.

Industry rumours which suggested that Oasis' Liam Gallagher was to marry actress **Patsy Kensit** were confirmed in April when the pair finally got hitched.

Beetle-Blur

UK popsters **Blur** released an eponymous album which was distinctly stripped-down and lo-fi, compared to the band's usual jollified and jovial output. Legendary electronic pioneers Kraftwerk announced that they were to play their first festival, headlining the UK summer techno all-nighter Tribal Gathering.

Grunge lost another one of its mainstays, **Soundgarden**, who went their separate ways in April.

With a staggering album from the Prodigy kicking off the summer in style and another to come from Oasis, the second half of 1997 looks set to keep up the frenetic pace. And another MTV decade has only just begun...

Blur: Back in force for 1997

U2: Making the world go *Pop* again

THE WORLD OF MTV
MUSIC TELEVISION ®

As the 1996 **MTV Europe Music Awards** at London's Alexandra Palace reeled towards its last rounds of lager and champagne, the backstage guest area was awash with celebrities. To the left, **Jean Paul Gaultier** and the **Smashing Pumpkins**' **Billy Corgan** were comparing bald spots, to the right **Michael Hutchence** was crooning 'Imagine' to **Paula Yates**, and heading for the exit as fast as their little legs could carry them were **Tricky** and **Massive Attack**'s **3D**.

Throughout the night it had been a similar story; **Jarvis Cocker** and **Helena Christensen** sharing the pinball machine; host **Robbie Williams** hiding behind a rubber plant; **Mick Hucknall** and **Chelsea FC**'s **Gianluca Vialli** chatting in Italian about whatever it is that rock stars and football stars have in common; **Björk** and **Kylie** exchanging fashion tips; and MTV co-host and comedian **Julian Clary** merrily deflating egos. (Remark of the night, to Jarvis Cocker: "Look at the state of you. Can I say the words **'Wash'** and **'Go'**?")

MTV, where it all happens

Lost For Words

If anyone is still under the misapprehension that all MTV does is play pop videos, then they have never seen the **MTV Europe Music Awards**. Although only in their fourth year, they are already renowned for attracting the world's greatest acts to **party**, perform and get lost for words when they come to pick up their **gongs**.

In their inaugural year, when the ceremony was held in **Berlin**, words escaped **U2**'s lead singer **Bono** while he was accepting the **Free Your Mind Award** on behalf of **Amnesty International**, although not before he summed up the importance of the organization:

"If you're a leader of some apparently respectable, seemingly democratic regime and your secret police have been up all night pulling the fingernails out of your political opponents, the last thing you want is **20,000 postcards** from Amnesty International members around the world who know what you've been up to.

"Free your mind and your ass will follow," he concluded.

Meanwhile, host **Tom Jones** didn't even attempt to pronounce the name of the artist whose live performance closed the awards. Instead, he just held up the internationally recognised sexually ambivalent symbol, which stands for **Victor**... or **TAFKAP**. That was before he was simply The Artist. Other stars who played on the night included **Björk** (and her unfeasibly large paper-yes, paper-dress), **Take That** (who picked up the award for **Best Group**), perennial rockers **Aerosmith** and **George Michael** (performing **'Like Jesus to a Child'**, a couple of years before it was released).

The whole show was staged in a purpose-built auditorium in front of Berlin's **Brandenburg gate**. The great flood-lit monument - international symbol of freedom since the Berlin wall came down - provided a unique backdrop to the world-class performances. The creative theme of the **1994 MTV Europe Music Awards** revolved around a caravan design (the idea of video director/

photographer **Anton Corbijn**), reinforcing the themes of freedom and mobility for young Europe.

The **1995 MTV Europe Music Awards** ceremony in **Paris** saw the **Zenith** venue transformed into a fantastic circus show. Ironically, the event coincided with a national transport strike in France - but the show had to go on. By hook (of Holland) or by crook, by helicopter and Lear jet, a veritable B to Z (**Blur to Zucchero**) of stars made their way to a ceremony that boasted live performances from **David Bowie**, **The Cranberries**, **Bon Jovi** and **Simply Red**. (Scientists later calculated that if you put all the CDs they have sold end to end, it would reach **Uranus**.)

Plugged In And Unplugged

The **MTV Europe Music Awards** are by no means the only special programming which MTV produces. Tireless research and thousands of viewers' calls and letters every day ensure that MTV is plugged in to the youth of Europe, producing programmes and playing music accordingly. By its very nature, it's a channel which has to respond to the ebb and flow of its viewers' tastes and interests: where MTV leads, others follow, and all the while MTV takes its lead from what's happening out there, **on the streets** and in the clubs and concert halls of Europe.

Translating this into on-screen action has resulted in some real innovation. While tracking the trends, MTV has learned to create a few of its own. After resident cartoon couch critics **Beavis and Butt-Head**, the most renowned show on MTV is **Unplugged**, in which guest stars feature in live, acoustic performances. The idea was conceived after **Jon Bon Jovi** performed with an acoustic guitar at

BLOCK L
M 1

EUROPE MUSIC AWARDS 1996

ALEXANDRA PALACE
ALEXANDRA PALACE WAY
WOOD GREEN LONDON N22 4AY
THURSDAY 14TH NOVEMBER
DOORS CLOSE 18.30 HRS

Lee

BLOCK L
M 1

"If you've not got a pass, you ain't gettin' in"

friday, 23 august 1996
doors open at 6:45pm
taping begins promptly at 8:00pm

Ticket admits one and is non-transferable.

America's **1989 MTV Video Music Awards** in Los Angeles and the first **Unplugged** featured **Syd Straw** and **Squeeze**. Seemingly the antithesis of what MTV is all about - playing increasingly sophisticated pop promos - *Unplugged* not only drastically altered what MTV's programming parameters were, but also threw down a challenge to some of the world's most popular artists. Here was an opportunity for bands who had shown consummate taste in their choice of video director and recording technicians to **test their mettle** in the starkest of spotlights. Hundreds have risen to the challenge and, consequently, MTV has gone on to film unique performances by the world's greatest bands. **Paul McCartney** liked his recording so much that he took the then unprecedented decision to release it as an album. Thereafter, an *Unplugged* album became an additional option for bands who were between studio albums, greatest-hits packages and traditional live recordings.

Over the years there have been some remarkable *Unplugged* performances, from **Nirvana**'s emotive swansong to **The Cure**'s literally laidback performance on scatter cushions. Then there's been the plain cheating versions, such as **Bruce Springsteen**'s rewired *Plugged*, and Unledded, the reunion performance of **Led Zeppelin**'s **Jimmy Page** and **Robert Plant**. Filmed at London Weekend Television, the best kept "secret gig" in recent rock history saw Page, Plant, The Cure's **Porl Thompson** (on banjo!), Egyptian singer **Nashma Atta** and a Moroccan orchestra introduce Page and Plant's new album, reinvent Led Zeppelin's back catalogue and pay homage to **Blind Willie Johnson** ('Nobody's Fault But Mine').

Drummer **John Bonham**'s omission from the line-up was probably less of a surprise than the absence of **Liam Gallagher** from **Oasis**'s performance two years later and 200 yards up the road at The Royal Festival Hall. (Bonham had been dead for 13 years, Liam had a sore throat.) Probably the most controversial *Unplugged* yet, the bearded young Gallagher even bounded on stage after the set but no songs were forthcoming from his lips. Still, at least he made an appearance. The next week he claimed he was too busy looking for a new house to join the band on tour in America and Oasis's future seemed in jeopardy. Fortunately, it didn't take too long for him and Patsy to find a new home and within a week Liam was back on board, in time for Oasis to play at the **1996 MTV Video Music Awards** in New York.

The success of *Unplugged* has seen MTV expand upon its exclusive live performance programming. Many of the shows which had previously existed as a showcase for promo videos now feature guests performing a live set and the relatively new shows **Live 'n' Loud** and **Live'n'Direct** capitalize on the channel's expertise, capturing live shows-out and about in Europe or in the MTV studios themselves-with a uniquely intimate and imaginative treatment.

MTV VJ Simone Angel

Dance Commandos

While *Unplugged* excels in providing a rare insight into the world's most famous artists, MTV also caters to more leftfield tastes with its specialist music programmes. According to MTV's resident dance commando **James Hyman**, club music coverage has been "a subtle snowball" since 1988, as people began to realize that dance music "wasn't just faceless bedroom DJs having one hit and then vanishing", and record companies started investing time and money in dance acts. Hyman also thinks that dance fans have done more to break down European boundaries than their peers in rock 'n' roll.

"Go to the **Tresor** hard techno club in Germany and they'll drop **Goldie** tunes. **Faithless** are huge in Germany. **'Born Slippy'** was the song of **The Love Parade**. If you go to **Tribal Gathering** the balance of Europeans has evened out. It's not like going to see **Placebo** at **The Forum**."

MTV currently boasts a whole range of dance programmes - **Partyzone**, **Dance Floor** and the **Dance Floor Chart** - as well as the brand new show, **Base**, which focuses on the oft-ignored black music genres of rap, hip-hop and jungle.

Originally a purely video-intensive treat, *Partyzone* widened its parameters with an interview and video history of **808 State** in 1993. Later, the show added live performances to its programming after a spontaneous, acoustic performance of **'Go'** by **Moby**. "Moby came in and swapped clothes with **DJ Simone Angel** and it all got very mad," says the producer, who started as an enthusiastic temp in the MTV press office while finishing his degree in 1988 - and never left the company.

"*Partyzone* has really changed the face of dance music on TV - we've done video remixes (everything from **Dave Morales** to the **Dust Brothers**) and over 200 interviews. We interviewed Goldie the day he signed to **London Records**, we've been championing **The Prodigy** since '91 and we went to one of the first jungle raves ever, **X-By Any Means Necessary**, in '93."

For Hyman, Partyzone's piece de résistance was a two-hour "scratch video" session with **EBN** (Emergency Broadcast Network), who later contributed to the visuals of U2's **Zoo TV** tour.

Headbangers

If *Partyzone* is a mirrorball reflecting one Euronation under a groove, the near-legendary and now sadly defunct *Headbangers Ball* was a big, hard-rocking biker boot stomping across the continent. Bizarrely, the two musically incompatible programmes in fact coexisted just a few yards apart from one another, amid the chaos of the open-plan, canal-side offices in **Camden**.

Headbangers Ball began life under the monicker **MTV's Metal Hammer** - the magazine sponsored the programme for two-and-a-half years-before adopting its new title. Most of heavy rock's household names started off in the *Headbangers Ball* slot, from **Smashing Pumpkins** to **Nirvana**, **Soundgarden**, **Metallica**, **Hole** and **Sepultura**.

"We were playing **Marilyn Manson** 18 months ago," enthuses producer and presenter **Vanessa Warwick**. "Now it's all over the channel."

British rock gets its share of airplay too. At the start of the '90s the programme championed **The Wildhearts**, **The Almighty** and **Thunder**. If some of the names seem unfamiliar it's because *Headbangers Ball* prided itself on being an authority for the discerning rock fan.

"It was a serious music programme-people who watched the show knew a lot about the music and didn't really care where the bands had their hair done or bought their clothes."

However, not all the bands treated it that way.

When Nirvana played the Roskilde festival, Vanessa Warwick found **Kurt Cobain** would not play the game.

"I got quite upset because I was asking proper questions and he really gave me a hard time. And I had just been stung on the face three times by a wasp. I asked, 'Do you think you're suffering from the **Guns N'Roses** syndrome, and that people are more interested in your antics than listening to your music?', and he answered, 'I'm a **red rooster** pecking at the ground.'"

Ironically, Warwick would provide **Eddie Vedder** with a shoulder to cry on four days after Kurt Cobain's suicide, when the **Pearl Jam** singer unburdened his feelings about the Nirvana singer's death, probably as serious and emotional an interview as you're ever likely to see.

But *Headbangers Ball* was not without its humour. Warwick recalls recording a link whilst sitting in a jacuzzi in LA.

"The crew were jeering and making comments about **Pamela Anderson** while I was trying to introduce the show. Then, rather like **Barbara Windsor** in *Carry on Camping*, my bikini went ping! and flew across the room!"

The Indie Kids

Toby Amies, self-confessed "token indie kid" and presenter of *Alternative Nation*, doesn't have a swimwear story to match Warwick's but admits, "Whenever things get particularly unpleasant, chances are that's the bit they'll broadcast."

It's the sort of inverse logic with which Amies has to contend each day-when he presented the gossip round-up Hot (with his tongue firmly in his cheek), he was expected to play devil's advocate, and was therefore more likely to alarm corporate MTV with loose talk about **Michael Jackson** and **Boyzone** than any-one else.

"There's been a couple of things I've said which they've had to cut, but there's no smoke without fire, is there?

Here you have this large corporation pushing you as this vaguely anti-establishment figure. You end up thinking, 'Maybe I should fuck this up as much as possible'."

So far, Amies' biggest spanner-in-the-works triumph has been to get Captain Beefheart's **'Ice Cream For Crow'** on two-monthly rotation.

"The last major achievement was getting them to play a **Can** video for **'Oh Yeah'**, which is six minutes long. It's great - it's like six geography students on stage...and a guy juggling umbrellas."

Boy Band Flesh

Even when catering for an audience with more mainstream tastes, MTV is always experimenting with programme formats which break new ground. At any one time you might find a top band rummaging through their favourite vids on *Startrax*, discover the soft, sexy, soulful world of **VJ Camila**'s *Amour*, be tempted to vote for your favourite hits by *Select MTV*, witness the exotic women of America practise their pelvic floor exercises on *The Grind*, or catch **East 17** hanging out with **VJ Davina** and chums. The ratings might shoot through the roof when U2 are on air, but it's hormonally-charged, topless lads who most often make viewers turn off their sets and turn up at the MTV studios.

The biggest event was just before Take That split. The band were going to perform on the balcony outside but it all went **Gary Barlow**-shaped when thousands of fans turned up, blocking the surrounding roads and causing a near riot in showing their devotion. It was nearly as big a commotion as when **Robbie Williams** pulled his trousers down and showed his bum on air.

MTV VJ Toby Aimes

MTV's *Turned On Europe*

But Seriously...

MTV has never been backward in providing a pound of popstar flesh, but over the last decade the station has expanded its brief with film, fashion, sports and news services. Perhaps the most significant change at MTV Europe came in 1993 when the news team decided that they wanted to report on more than just what Bon Jovi was up to on his tour and began a series of non-music "socially responsible" reports on such issues as **HIV** and **AIDS** awareness and anorexia. In April, MTV dedicated a weekend to the subject of racism and fascist networking in Europe and in July organized **Planet Earth**, a celebrity-led series on environmental issues.

Although it was enlightening seeing Björk show how to turn recycled cardboard into furniture, the news team realized it would be far less restrictive to dispense with the pop stars and concentrate on the viewers themselves. The following year, MTV focused on the European parliamentary elections, and political superstars such as **Mikhail Gorbachev** and **Jacques Delors** found themselves vying for airspace that would otherwise be occupied by **MC Solaar** et al.

Since then MTV has produced documentaries on belief systems (everything from **New Age Jews** to **Norwegian Devil Worshippers**) and new political activism. MTV supports **World AIDS Day** and has Year End Editions of MTV News which, in successive years, focused on the Palestine peace agreement, Ireland and the **Dayton Accord** in Sarajevo.

"Sometimes it is weird to go from lightweight pop news to hard news," admits **Fiona Friel**, VP of Factual

Programming, "but I think the Year End Edition in Sarajevo was a real whirlwind of information. One minute Toby's standing talking to a girl in the snow who shows you the house she used to live in before it was bombed, the next it's into Hits Of '95, but you don't go, 'That's awful'. Youth culture is a mix of those experiences."

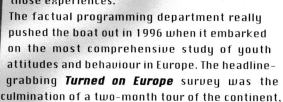

The factual programming department really pushed the boat out in 1996 when it embarked on the most comprehensive study of youth attitudes and behaviour in Europe. The headline-grabbing **Turned on Europe** survey was the culmination of a two-month tour of the continent, collecting data and video diaries which were filmed by viewers themselves. If you wanna know where the hotbeds of intolerance or liberalism are, or which nations drink the most beer and have the most **pervy sex**, the *Turned on Europe* survey has the answers.

Extreme Antics

Up to 1995, most MTV sport was imported from America and mainly comprised extreme antics, trademark fast editing and funky music. In the last two years, however, MTV Europe has developed its own stable of programmes that reflect the sporting lifestyle as much as they do the action. Thus, when MTV's snowboarding extravaganza took place in Madonna in 1996, the snowboarding daze was augmented by nights spent off piste with **Whale** and groove-riding with **The Chemical Brothers**. Since then, Goldie has become the guest presenter of *Snowball*, while *MTV Wheels* -which covers anything from skateboards to disabled basketball-is steered by *Jamiroquai*'s **Jason Kay**.

At The Movies

Movie coverage was first added to the schedule in 1988. Subsequently, the idea has been adopted and dropped by MTV Europe's American sister channel, but the daily bulletins and weekly round-ups of *Cinematic* and *The Big Picture* remain a staple part of the European viewer's diet.

At its inception, MTV's snappy **'infotainment'** was in stark contrast to the grey, chin-stroking approaches that dominated the medium of movie review shows. Producer **John Dunton Downer** soon became a regular at the **Cannes Festival**.

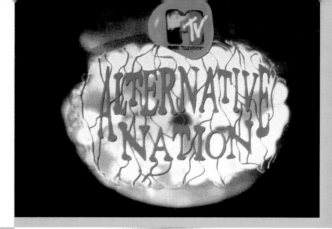

Nude And Rude

What with Robbie Williams's bum and Japanese skin flicks you'd think that MTV wouldn't want to risk any more cheek on the channel, but ***Singled Out*** -the ultimate relationship show-risked a beach-blanket ban when it went to Hedonism, an **XXX-rated** nude-and-rude 18-30 holiday resort. It may have had nothing to do with Swedish presenter **Lily Myrhed** (although she once confessed "Whenever I get excited, the most natural thing to do is show my butt"), but every time a camera rolled somebody in the audience decided to bare all.

"Basically, it's a naturist resort and it's **nude and rude**," recalls **Tamsin Summers**, Vice President of production. "We had to keep shooting and reshooting to make sure we ended up with a show for MTV and not a blue movie."

MUSIC TELEVISION®

"Television is a trashy medium-you have to admit that and make the best of it, as opposed to trying to make it into some boring monolithic literary thing. I think there was an old guard that we played a part in dispelling. MTV's version was still respectful, still informed and quite with it. Our take on the movie world is: 'It's fun, it's glamorous, it's absurd, it's outrageous the way the film companies spend this money on promotional stuff etc, but we love it.'"

Like MTV's music programming, the film programmes offer as much diversity as possible for a populist channel.

"The mainstream reigns supreme but we refuse to ignore the outer edges. As long as you have your **Mel Gibson** and your **Sharon Stone** and your **Sylvester Stallone** movies in the mix you can stop for a minute to check out some weird **Herzog** rerelease or the weird cult of pink porn from Japan."

MTV w Lily Myrhed

STYLISSIMO!

Street Chic

The only place where you're likely to see more flesh is on the world's catwalks. And chances are you'll find MTV's *Stylissimo* team there, filming the fashion, meeting the models and gossiping with the gurus. Stylissimo is more than a riot of colour to fill out a funky soundtrack-it's a magazine show that features new talent, designer profiles and the latest street chic. If you don't know your **Alexander McQueen** bumsters from your **John Galliano** elbow patches, then it's time you got with *Stylissimo*, honey.

A Unique Identity

It's clear that MTV Europe is committed to decon-structing the myth that all it does is rotate a few videos, 24 hours a day. But the small details matter too, especially when your logo has to compete with some of the most imagin-ative and technically advanced promos in the world.

When MTV was launched, the idea of getting design students to create hand-made, one-off channel idents was anathema. Terrestrial TV was in the dark ages, where corporate logos were static, staid and rigidly two-dimensional, while MTV's

logo would appear up-side down, fart, and jump off the screen. Ten years, hundreds of idents and a sackful of international awards later, earthbound television has caught up.

For creative director **Peter Dougherty**, the difficulty is how MTV can be different when everyone's copied it.

"The only choices are to go for either less disrespectful or much more disrespectful. The limits are being pushed. I just got two idents from Japan: one features the logo on a little girl's knickers, which we know is big in Japan but could cause a stir in Europe, and the other one has these kids running into the bedroom going 'daddy, daddy, daddy'. They pull back the sheet and there's this **horrible oozing reptile** that morphs into a bloody MTV logo and then becomes an executive with wings and flies out the window, joining all these other businessmen flying off to work. And I showed it to the person here who deals with broadcast regulations and he said, 'You'd better not show it when children could be watching.'"

But the antics of animated anti-heroes *Beavis and Butt-Head* seem to have rendered the world unshock-able, or at least unmoved by the more salacious or scandalous on-screen images. And that's great news for the channel: as it continues to push back the boundaries there's even more scope for continued evol-ution within the **wonderful world of MTV.**

One of MTV's tonsil-vibratingly good ident sequences – what would Munch have said?

MTV database

UNPLUGGED PERFORMERS

	FIRST TX
Crowded House/Tim Finn	13 May 1989
Squeeze/Syd Straw	26 November 1989
Smithereens/Graham Parker	29 January 1990
The Alarm/Nuclear Valdez	11 February 1990
Joe Walsh/Dr. John	18 February 1990
Neil Young	25 February 1990
Stevie Ray Vaughn/Joe Satriani	4 March 1990
Michelle Shocked/Indigo Girls	11 March 1990
Sinead O'Connor/The Church	18 March 1990
Don Henley	22 April 1990
Great White/Damn Yankees	6 May 1990
Hall and Oates	5 June 1990
Elton John	12 June 1990
Aerosmith	20 September 1990
Crosby, Stills & Nash	30 September 1990
Ratt/Vixen	7 October 1990
Black Crowes/Tesla	2 December 1990
The Allman Brothers Band	9 December 1990
Poison	13 December 1990
The Cure	26 February 1991
Winger/Slaughter	24 March 1991
Sting	10 April 1991
Paul McCartney	13 April 1991
R.E.M.	24 April 1991

YO! UNPLUGGED RAP

A Tribe Called Quest	1 May 1991
MC Lyte	
De La Soul	
LL Cool J	3 July 1991
	13 May 1992
Elvis Costello	
Pearl Jam	20 May 1992

R&B UNPLUGGED

Boyz II Men	20 May 1992
Shanice	3 June 1992
Joe Public	14 June 1992
	22 July 1992
Mariah Carey	21 August 1992
Paul Simon	21 September 1992
Eric Clapton	28 September 1992
Queensryche	28 November 1992
John Mellencamp	6 January 1993
Annie Lennox	22 February 1993
Was (Not Was)	13 March 1993
Bruce Springsteen	28 March 1993
Arrested Development	
Roxette	
Denis Leary	
k.d. lang	

MTV-EUROPE MUSIC AWARDS

LOCATION: ....Berlin
DATE: ....24 November 1994

MTV's first European Music Awards were broadcast **live** via MTV's global network to a potential audience of over **250 million** homes from the largest temporary structure ever built in Berlin's Pariser Platz. The super-structure took **17,500 man hours** to create and housed an audience of some **2,500 people**.

MTV raises awareness of key **social issues** with the special Free Your Mind award. The award is based upon the ideals of MTV's global **Free Your Mind Campaign** which aims to encourage **freedom** from all kinds of intolerance and prejudice.

And the winners are...

BEST GROUP	**Take That**
BEST MALE	**Bryan Adams**
BEST FEMALE	**Mariah Carey**
BREAKTHROUGH ARTIST	**Crash Test Dummies**
BEST ROCK ACT	**Aerosmith**
BEST DANCE ACT	**The Prodigy**
BEST SONG	**Youssou N'Dour featuring Neneh Cherry for '7 Seconds'**
BEST DIRECTOR	**Mark Pellington for Whale's 'Hobo Humpin' Slobo Babe'**
BEST COVER	**Gun for 'Word Up'**
FREE YOUR MIND	**Accepted by U2's Bono on behalf of Amnesty International**

■ MTV Europe is available to over **130 million** cable and satellite subscribers across the continent.

■ Approximately **100 different videos** are played every day on MTV.

■ The **first video** played on MTV Europe was 'Money For Nothing' by Dire Straits, aired on 1 August 1987. ("I want my MTV...")

■ MTV Europe employs over **500 people** from 18 different countries.

■ MTV Europe's London library has **18,000 video clips**. The stock grows by 55 videos every week.

■ For the stars at the 1996 Awards in London's Alexandra Palace, MTV provided **50** dressing rooms, **50** sofas, **150** armchairs, **60** coffee tables, **75** rubbish bins, **150** mirrors, **90** make-up lamps, **75** clothes rails, **17,000** square metres of red carpet and **1,000** metres of partitioning for privacy. It took five days and a crew of **100** construction workers just to unload the equipment.

MTV-EUROPE MUSIC AWARDS

LOCATION: ....**Paris**
DATE: ....**23 November 1995**

Held at Le Zenith in Paris, the ceremony was hosted by internationally renowned **fashion** designer Jean Paul Gaultier. There were **live** performances by David Bowie, Bon Jovi, The Cranberries, Simply Red, Blur, East 17, MC Solaar with Diana King and H-Blockx.

Star presenters included Catherine Deneuve, Michael Hutchence, Jean-Claude Van Damme, Björk, U2's The Edge, ex-Take That'er Robbie Williams, Patsy Kensit, Kylie Minogue, Pulp's Jarvis Cocker, Carla Bruni, Eva Herzegova, Jovanotti, Nina Hagen, Sven Väth, Zucchero and Ray Cokes.

The five nominations in each category were compiled by MTV Europe's "Academy" of **700 key figures** from the European Music Industry, including record label heads, music marketers, agents, promoters and members of the press. MTV Europe's young adult audience chose the winners, voting via 'phone, fax, post and e-mail.

The Free Your Mind award went to environmental group **Greenpeace** in recognition of almost 25 years of environmental campaigning, and for Greenpeace's swift action in raising international awareness of the French Government's nuclear testing in the South Pacific.

And the winners are...

BEST GROUP **U2**
BEST MALE ....**Michael Jackson**
BEST FEMALE ....**Björk**
BREAKTHROUGH ARTIST..................**Dog Eat Dog**
BEST ROCK ACT ....**Bon Jovi**
BEST DANCE ACT ....**East 17**
BEST SONG ....**The Cranberries for 'Zombie'**
BEST LIVE ACT................................**Take That**
BEST DIRECTOR ....**Michel Gondry for Massive Attack's 'Protection'**
FREE YOUR MIND........**Accepted by Agnes B on behalf of Greenpeace**

UPTOWN 31 May 1993
Mary J Blige
Christopher Williams
Heavy D & The Boyz with The Swing Mob
Jodeci
Soul Asylum
10,000 Maniacs/Michael Penn
Midnight Oil

SPOKEN WORD I
99
Maggie Estep — 2 June 1993
Barry Yourgrau — 13 June 1993
Reg E Gaines — 4 July 1993
Bob Holman
Edwin Torres — 28 July 1993
Henry Rollins
Anita Liberty
Dana Bryant
Pete Spiros
Tracie Morris

Rod Stewart
Duran Duran
Nirvana
Stone Temple Pilots
Tony Bennett — 23 September 1993
Herbert Gronemeyer — 13 December 1993

SPOKEN WORD II
MC Lyte — 14 December 1993
Toby Huss — 2 February 1994
Bahiyyih Maroon — 1 June 1994
Eric Bogosian — 13 June 1994
Matthew Courtney
Hal Sirowitz — 21 June 1994
Gil Scott-Heron with Brother Larry
McDonald
Wanda Phipps

SPOKEN WORD III
Max Blagg
Danny Hoch
Maggie Estep
Jim Carroll
John S Hall
Paul Beatty — 21 June 1994

Lenny Kravitz
Jimmy Page/Robert Plant
Björk
Bob Dylan
Sheryl Crow
Melissa Etheridge
Hole — 12 July 1994
The Cranberries — 12 October 1994
Inside Unplugged — 16 November 1994
Live — 14 December 1994
Phil Collins — 7 March 1995
Kiss — 21 March 1995
Chris Isaak — 17 April 1995
Hootie And The Blowfish — 18 April 1995
Alice in Chains — 18 April 1995
Seal — 19 April 1995
Tori Amos — 9 October 1995
Oasis — 31 October 1995
George Michael 2 December 1996 — 23 November 1995
9 October 1996
25 June 1996
4 June 1996
4 June 1996
22 April 1996

MTV-EUROPE MUSIC AWARDS

LOCATION: ....**London**
DATE: ....**14 November 1996**

More than 500,000 MTV viewers from all over Europe voted for their favourites. The ceremony came live from one of the first BBC broadcasting sites, Alexandra Palace in London, where 800 production staff, stage-hands, riggers, lighting and sound technicians, backing singers and dancers put together the entertainment.

The MTV **Amour** Award was selected by viewers of MTV's late night soul and swingbeat show, while the Select MTV Award was the **ultimate** viewers' choice award. *Select* is MTV's daily interactive jukebox show. Over 4,000 viewers call in every day, requesting their favourite music videos. The nominations in this category were selected by viewers during a special Select MTV Weekend (3 and 4 November 1996). This was a staggering **nine-hour** marathon of on-air requests during which Europe's favourite 100 videos were compiled and then reduced, by viewer votes, to the five nominations in this category.

Jarvis Cocker from Pulp accepted the Free Your Mind award on behalf of those largely unsung heroes all over Europe who care for those with fatal or debilitating illnesses.

And the winners are...

BEST GROUP ....**Oasis**
BEST MALE ARTIST ....**George Michael**
BEST FEMALE ARTIST .....**Alanis Morissette**
BREAKTHROUGH ARTIST..................**Garbage**
BEST ROCK ACT ....**Smashing Pumpkins**
BEST DANCE ACT ....**The Prodigy**
BEST SONG ....**Oasis for 'Wonderwall'**
MTV AMOUR.............................**The Fugees**
SELECT MTV..............**Backstreet Boys for 'Get Down'**
FREE YOUR MIND.........**Accepted by Pulp's Jarvis Cocker on behalf of "The Buddies and Carers of Europe"**

MTV EUROPE BIG TOP TENS

The BIGGEST and the BEST and the GREATEST of all. Here they all are in the most splendid of musical lists, the world-beating artists and their finest works.

MOST PLAYED VIDEO OF ALL TIME ON MTV EUROPE

Nirvana ......Smells Like Teen Spirit

TOP 10 OF THE TOP 100 SINGLES OF ALL TIME

1 **Nirvana**.... Smells Like Teen Spirit
2 **R.E.M.** ....Losing My Religion
3 **Queen** ....Bohemian Rhapsody
4 **Genesis** ....I Can't Dance
5 **Pearl Jam**.........................Jeremy
6 **Madness** ....Our House
7 **The Fugees** ....Killing Me Softly
8 **George Michael** ....Freedom
9 **Bon Jovi** ....These Days
10 **Michael Jackson** .. Black Or White

TOP 10 ARTISTS OF ALL TIME

1 ....**U2**
2 ....**Madonna**
3 ....**Aerosmith**
4 ....**Michael Jackson**
5 ....**George Michael**
6 ....**Prince**
7 .........**R.E.M.**
8 ....**Nirvana**
9 ....**Oasis**
10 ....**David Bowie**

TOP 10 OF THE TOP 100 SINGLES OF THE '90s

1 **Nirvana** ....Smells Like Teen Spirit
2 **Neneh Cherry** featuring **Youssou N'Dour** ....
   ....7 Seconds
3 **George Michael** ....Too Funky
4 **R.E.M.** ....Everybody Hurts
5 **Coolio featuring LV**.........Gangsta's Paradise
6 **The Cranberries** .... Zombie
7 **U2**....................................Mysterious Ways
8 **Michael Jackson** ....Earth Song
9 **Bruce Springsteen** ..... Streets Of Philadelphia
10 **The Artist (TAFKAP)** ♀ .....The Most Beautiful Girl In The World

index

⚥ 12-13, 91, 138, 143, 148, 151, 159, 164, 167
2 Unlimited 165
501 Special Service 85

a

A-Ha 32
Abdul, Paula 33, 141
AC/DC 33
Ace of Base 34
Adams, Bryan 34, 157
Adamski 109
Aerosmith 10-11, 107, 144
Aimes, Toby 184
Alice in Chains 35
Amos, Tori 35
Anthrax 101
Armstrong, Billie Joe 70
Arrested Development 36, 59
Artist, the see ⚥

b

B-52's 26, 36
Babylon Zoo 37
Backstreet Boys 37
Bangles 38
Barlow, Gary 184
Beastie Boys 38, 139
Beat 66
Beatles 141
Beautiful South 39
Beck 39
Bell, Andy 62
Beloved 40
Bettencourt, Nuno 64
B.I.G. 178
Big Audio Dynamite 40
Björk 40, 69, 145, 162, 172, 174
Black 41
Black Crowes 42
Black Grape 71
Black Sabbath 46
Blind Melon 42
Blur 43, 92, 168, 170, 179
Bon Jovi, Jon 14-15, 109, 181-2
Bono 28, 29, 72, 173
Bowie, David 43, 98, 114, 140, 148, 159
Boyz II Men 47
Boyzone 44
Braxton, Toni 44, 102
Breeders 45, 96

Bros 45, 145
Brown, Bobby 46, 73
Brown, James 46
Bush 84
Bush, Kate 35, 148
Byrne, David 122

c

Cardigans 46
Carey, Mariah 47, 152
Carlisle, Belinda 47
Cave, Nick 97, 106
Nick Cave and the Bad Seeds 48
Chapman, Tracy 48, 88, 143
Charlatans 31, 49
Cher 49, 50
Cherone, Gary 64
Cherry, Neneh 50, 76, 88, 146
Christians 141
Child, Desmond 11, 15
Clapton, Eric 50, 53
Clarke, Vince 62
Clash 40
Cobain, Frances Bean 24
Cobain, Kurt 24-5, 66, 70, 72, 134, 136, 154, 158, 162, 166
Cocker, Jarvis 101, 174
Collins, Phil 51, 69
Collins, Rob 49
Coolio 51
Cranberries 52, 167, 175
Crash Test Dummies 52
Crosby, Stills, Nash & Young 134
Crow, Sheryl 50, 53
Crowded House 53
Cult 140
Cure 54, 140, 148, 182
Curiosity Killed The Cat 54
Curtis, Ian 89
Cypress Hill 55

d

Dando, Evan 82
D'Arby, Terence Trent 126, 141
Day, Morris 12
De La Soul 55, 148
De Mann, Freddie 20
Deee-Lite 56, 150
Deep Forest 56
Depeche Mode 57, 152, 165

dEUS 58
Dire Straits 58, 141
Disposable Heroes of Hiphoprisy 59
Dougherty, Peter 187
Dr. Dre 59, 91, 114, 130, 163
Duran Duran 60
Dylan, Bob 91

e

East 17 60
Edge, The 28
Edwards, Richey 84
Elastica 120
Eldritch, Andrew 112
EMF 61
En Vogue 61
Enigma 62
Eno, Brian 29, 43, 173
Erasure 62
Estafan, Gloria 153
Eternal 63
Eurythmics 63
Everything But the Girl 64
Extreme 64, 65

f

Fahey, Siobhan 63, 110, 141
Fairport Convention 27
Faith No More 65, 125
Die Fantastichen Vier 65
Farrell, Perry 77, 155
Ferry Aid 139
Fine Young Cannibals 66, 149
Flack, Roberta 67
Flint, Keith 100
Foley, Zac 61
Foo Fighters 66
Frankie Goes To Hollywood 67, 141
Franklin, Aretha 63
Franti, Michael 59
Fugees 67

g

Gabriel, Peter 51, 68, 69, 88
Gahan, Dave 57, 172, 176
Gallagher, Liam 92, 168, 176, 178
Gallagher, Noel 131, 168, 170, 176
Garbage 68
Garratt, Siedah 19
Gehman, Don 27

Generation X 75
Genesis 51, 68, 69
Gibbons, Beth 99
Gift, Roland 66
Glastonbury 101
Glitter, Gary 79
Go-Go's 47
Green, Al 63
Green Day 70
Grohl, Dave 66
G.u.n. 70
Guns N' Roses 71, 140, 144, 146, 147, 157

h

Hall, Arsenio 21
Happy Mondays 71, 119, 159
Harket, Morton 32
Harvey, Brian 60
Harvey, P J 48, 97
Heaton, Paul 39
Henley, Don 53
Hole 25, 72, 158, 166
Horn, Trevor 67
Hothouse Flowers 72
House of Pain 73
Housemartins 39
Houston, Whitney 46, 73, 140, 164
Howie B 29
Hucknall, Mick 111
Hutchence, Michael 75
Hynde, Chrissie 50

i

Ice Cube 59, 74, 91, 130, 155
Ice T 74, 130, 158, 163
Idol, Billy 75, 153
Inspiral Carpets 92
INXS 75
Isaak, Chris 76
Isley Brothers 102

j

Jackson Five 16, 18
Jackson, Janet 16-17, 32, 102, 127, 141, 148, 164
Jackson, Michael, 16, 17, 18-19, 32, 53, 101, 102, 140, 156, 162, 166-7, 171, 174
Jagger, Mick 125

Jam 131
Jam, Jimmy 12
James, Richey 172
Jamiroquai 76
Jane's Addiction 77, 152, 154
Jarre, Jean-Michel 93
Jovanotti 78
Jesus & Mary Chain 77, 100
John, Elton 22, 78, 121, 136, 141
Johnson, Holly 67
Jones, Mick 40
Jones, Quincy 18, 102

k

Kay, Jason 76
Kelly, R 102
KLF 79, 169
Knebworth 92
Knight, Gladys 102
Knopfler, Mark 58
Kool & the Gang 51
Kraftwerk 93
Kramer, Billy J
Kravitz, Lenny 80, 149
Kriss Kross 161
Kula Shaker 80

l

Laibach 169
lang, k d 81
Lauper, Cyndi 81
Le Bon, Simon 60
Led Zeppelin 182
Lemonheads 82
Lennon, John 151
Lennox, Annie 63
Lewis, Terry 12
Lillywhite, Steve 28
Live Aid 138-9
LL Cool J 82
Loder, Kurt 20
Los Del Rio 83
Love, Courtney 25, 72, 158, 162, 166, 171

m

M C Hammer, 130, 152
M C Solaar 85
McCartney, Paul 18, 182
MacGowan, Shane 98
Madness 83
Madonna 20-1, 80, 81, 85,

88, 93, 140, 147, 151, 157, 159
Manic Street Preachers 84, 172
Manson, Shirley 68
Marley, Bob 67
M.A.R.R.S. 84
Massive Attack 85, 126
Mayfield, Curtis 153
Meat Loaf 49, 86
Mercury, Freddie 157
Metallica 86, 87
Meyer, Russ 17
Michael, George 22-3, 36, 78, 152, 161, 167
Midnight Oil 87
Mike & the Mechanics 69
Miles, Robert 87
Milli Vanilli 149
Minogue, Kylie 48, 145
Mishra, Jyoti 133
Mitchell, Willie 132s
Monsters of Rock 15, 86, 109
Morrissette, Alanis 21, 34, 88, 104, 137, 170
Morrissey 159
Myrhed, Lily 186

n

Nate Dogg 130
N'Dour, Youssou 50, 88
New Kids on the Block 88, 89
New Order 89
Nine Inch Nails 90
Nirvana 24-5, 66, 136, 154, 158, 162, 166, 182
No Doubt 90
NWA 59, 74, 91, 137, 144, 155

o

Oasis 92, 121, 168-9, 170, 176, 178

Ocean Colour Scene 131
O'Connor, Sinead 13, 53, 91, 151, 160, 164, 171
Offspring 92
Orb 93, 153
Orbital 93

p

Palmer, Robert 94
Paradis, Vanessa 80
Parker, Alan 21
Patton, Mike 65
Pearl Jam 55, 94, 134, 158, 162
Penn, Sean 21, 147
Perry, Joe 10-11
Pet Shop Boys 95, 156, 157, 165
Petty, Tom 95
Phoenix Festival 133
Pierson, Kate 36
Pink Floyd 96, 167
Pirner, Dave 115
Pixies 96, 142
PM Dawn 97
Pogues 98
Pointer Sisters
Police 26, 119
Pop, Iggy 98
Portishead 99
Presidents of the United States of America 99
Presley, Lisa Marie 19
Pretenders 141
Primal Scream 77, 100
Prince see ♀
Prodigy 100, 177
Public Enemy 101, 136-7, 141, 144, 155
Pulp 101, 168

q

Queen 22, 102, 130, 157

r

Radcliffe, Mark 133
Radiohead 103
Rage Against the Machine 103
Ramazzotti, Eros 104
Red Hot Chili Peppers 77, 104
Reed, Lou 105
R.E.M 26-7, 137, 156, 158, 172, 175
Rice, Tim, 23
Right Said Fred 161
Robinson, Smokey 34
Robinson, Tom
Rolling Stones 70, 106, 125, 167
Rollins, Henry 106
Rose, Axl 71, 140, 157
Ross, Diana 18
Rowe, Debbie 19
Roxette 107
Rubin, Rick 11
Run DMC 11, 107, 139
Rutherford, Mike 69
Ryder, Mitch 71

s

Sade 108
Salt-n-Pepa 108, 141
Scorpions 109
Seal 109, 156
Sex Pistols 175
Shaggy 110
Shakespears Sister 63, 110
Simone, Nina 141
Simple Minds 70, 111
Simply Red 111, 141
Sisters of Mercy 112
Skunk Anansie 112
Slash 71
Smashing Pumpkins 113
Smith, Robert 54
Smiths 110, 141, 159
Snap 113

Snoop Doggy Dog 59, 91, 114, 130, 137, 163, 171, 172, 175
Sonic Youth 55, 114
Soul Asylum 115
Soul II Soul 115, 149, 152
Spearhead 59
Spice Girls 116, 177, 178
Spin Doctors 117
Spiteri, Sharleen 123
Springsteen, Bruce 14, 34, 88, 117, 182
Stakka Bo 118
Stereo MCs 118
Stewart, Dave 63, 141
Sting 88, 119, 147
Stipe, Michael 26, 27, 103
Stone Roses 71, 119, 147, 148, 152, 176
Stone Temple Pilots 120
Streisand, Barbara 34
Strummer, Joe 98
Style Council 131
Suede 120
Sugarcubes 41, 144, 144-5, 162
Swing Out Sister 121

t

Take That 78, 121, 171, 175, 184
Talk Talk 122
Talking Heads 122
Tears for Fears 123
Texas 123
The The 124
Therapy? 124
Thorn, Tracey 64
3T 32
Tikaram, Tanita 125
Time 12, 13
Tin Machine 43, 148
Die Toten Hosen 125
Traveling Wilburys 145
Tricky 126, 175
Tupac Shakur 59, 127, 163, 167, 172, 175

Turner, Tina 34, 127
Tyler, Steve 10-11

u

UB40 128
U2 28-9, 111, 125, 140, 144, 154, 160, 164-5, 173, 178, 179
Underworld 128

v

Van Halen 64, 129
Van Halen, Eddie 18
Vandross, Luther 129
Vanilla Ice 88, 130
Vearncombe, Colin 41
Velvet Underground 105
Vig, Butch 68

w

Warhol, Andy 54, 141
Warren G 130
Waters, Roger 96, 150
Watt, Ben 64
Weezer 131
Weller, Paul 131
Wet Wet Wet 132, 141
Weymouth, Tina 122
Whale 132
Wham! 23
White Town 133
Williams, Robbie 78, 121, 171, 184
Wonder, Stevie 51, 53, 76
Wynette, Tammy 79

y

Yello 134
Young, Neil 94, 134

z

Zappa, Frank 153, 165
ZZ Top 15, 135

acknowledgements

The publishers would like to thank the following sources for their kind permission to reproduce the pictures in this book:

All Action/Richard Beard, Eammon Clarke, Olly Hewitt, Dave Hogan, Simon Meaker, Sue Moore, Tim Paton, Duncan Raban, Paul Smith, Jim Steele, Justin Thomas;
London Features International/Ross Barnett, Kristin Callahan, Andy Catlin, Paul Cox, Katherine Davis, John Eder, Simon Fowler, Bruce Kramer, Lawrence Lawry, Phil Loftus, Kevin Mazur, Ilpo Musto, Phil Nicholls, Mark ?ior, Ken Regan, Derek Ridgers, Tom Sheehan, ?olfson;

MTV Europe; Pictorial Press/Jeffrey Mayer, William Rutten, Rob Verhorst;
Retna Pictures/Matt Anker, A J Barratt, Robin Barton, Jay Blakesberg, David Corio, Andrew Cornaga, Steve Double, Karl Grant, Adrian Green, Niels Van Iperen, Joseph King, Andy Liguz, Michael Malfer, Mark McNulty, Neal Preston, Steve Pyke, Bob Ramirez, Ronnie Randle, Paul Rider, Ed Sirrs, Chris Taylor, Midore Tsukagoshi, Howard Tyler, James Vita, Deverill G Weekes;
Rex Features/Action Press, J Sutton Hibbert, Dave Hogan, Tony Kyriacou, Hayley Madden, Brian Rasic, Crispin Rodwell, SIPA, Stephen Sweet, Richard Young;
SIN/Piers Allardyce, David Anderson, Colin

Bell, Andrew Catlin, Melanie Cox, Joe Dilworth, Steve Double, Martyn Goodacre, Pentti Hokkanen, Hayley Madden, Anna Meuer, Tony Mott, Phil Nicholls, Roy Tee, Ian T Tilton, Kim Tonelli.

Thanks are due to Clare Williams at MTV Europe and to Vincent Rubio Arlandis for the use of *Little MTV Show Just for Lonely Women* on page 1.

Every effort has been made to acknowledge correctly and contact the source and/or copyright holder of each picture, and Carlton Books Limited apologises for any unintentional errors or omissions which will be corrected in future editions of this book.